PRAISE FOR *INNOVATION BREAKDOWN*

"Finally, a behind-the-scenes look at the mysterious and often poorly executed approvals process of the FDA. An important book for consumers, physicians, investors, and scientists—anyone who is interested in medical advances that can save lives."

—JOSEPH PIERONI, retired CEO and President, Daiichi Sankyo Inc.

"By focusing on the fate of one small company, Joseph Gulfo has written a riveting tale of how the FDA slows down crucial medical innovations, just when we need them the most. Policymakers on both sides of the aisle should absorb his prescriptions for fixing the system."

—MICHAEL MANDEL, PhD, Progressive Policy Institute

"Dr. Gulfo has written an important book that deserves to be read by everyone interested in having access to new medical treatments. The enormous and all too often insurmountable challenges in bringing breakthrough medical products to doctors are not unique to small biotech and medtech companies, rather, even the industry-leading firms struggle against these forces. And, in the end, it's the patients who suffer."

—BRIAN LEYLAND-JONES, MD
Vice President, Molecular and Experimental Medicine
Avera Cancer Institute, Sioux Falls, SD

"Finally, an incisive look at the path that medical innovation takes through the FDA, the courts and the public advocacy groups and the crippling effect it has on advancing new treatments to treat and diagnose disease. Today's regulatory/legal/public advocacy complex is stifling progress and killing medical breakthroughs. Joseph Gulfo lays out why this has happened, how to fix it and how to make all our voices heard."

—NANCY LURKER, CEO, PDI Inc.

"A fascinating read of the relentless challenges a passionate entrepreneur faced and overcame to bring a medical breakthrough to patients."

—SUSAN SCHERREIK,
Founding Director, Seton Hall University Center
for Entrepreneurial Studies

Jon —

I hope you enjoy this book
reading it. I did
more fun
LIVING it!

A POST HILL PRESS BOOK
ISBN: 978-1-68261-391-7
ISBN (eBook): 978-1-61868-958-0

Innovation Breakdown:
How the FDA and Wall Street Cripple Medical Advances
© 2014 by Joseph V. Gulfo
All Rights Reserved
First Post Hill Hardcover Edition: June 2014

Cover Design by Ryan Truso

Post Hill Press
posthillpress.com

Published in the United States of America

To Adele

Contents

Contents

INNOVATION BREAKDOWN

HOW THE FDA AND WALL STREET CRIPPLE MEDICAL ADVANCES

JOSEPH V. GULFO

Introduction

You've heard of stand-up guys. Well, I'm a start-up guy. I've spent my entire twenty-five year career working for small company start-ups and "turnarounds" in the biopharmaceutical and medical technology communities. I've overseen the development and regulatory approval of three breakthrough medical products. I've also raised $160 million in the public markets. My passions are cancer and medical innovation.

Innovation Breakdown—How the FDA & Wall Street Cripple Medical Advances highlights lessons that I have learned over my 25+ years, focusing particularly on the incredible and unprecedented behavior by the U.S. Food and Drug Administration (FDA) as well as the utterly destructive influence of Wall Street's fast money hedge funds on a promising little company. The victim of that treachery and destruction? MELA Sciences, a small medical device manufacturer that has spent 17 years endeavoring to mitigate the debilitating effects of melanoma, the most aggressive form of skin cancer known to man. Over 150,000 Americans are diagnosed with melanoma *every single year*, and one American dies *every single hour* of the disease. That's a tragic statistic, and for two reasons. The first: it's always a tragedy when anyone dies. The second: *no one* should die of melanoma. Why? Because it's the only cancer you can see coming, and it can therefore be eradicated if it's caught in time. And that's what MelaFind, a revolutionary product made by MELA Sciences, can help us do. But only about a hundred and fifty of the machines are in use today, as opposed to the much greater number that ought to be. As a result, more people are dying from melanoma than should be. The real victims of the FDA and Wall Street, in other words, are the patients.

The book includes a collection of first-hand, personal, and tell-all stories about the long and arduous journey MELA took to get MelaFind to market and the innumerable moments along the way when it was nearly derailed. First, the FDA tried to destroy it. When they couldn't, Wall Street tried. Neither succeeded, but they left the company so wounded that it might not actually survive, alone, in the end. The stories are alternatingly tragic and humorous, fascinating and frustrating. But they all highlight the unnecessary challenges of bringing true medical innovation to the people who need it—the patients. Here's the bad news: the system is horribly broken and needs to be fixed. But here's the good news: I know how to fix it.

Innovation Breakdown is much bigger than one product or one person. The story of MelaFind, in other words, is simply the prism through which I hope to advance some broader truths and reveal the pervasive dysfunctions of a system that is supposed to help advance the cause of our collective heath but is actually hindering it.

I wrote this book for several reasons, the most important of which was to sound the alarm about an emergency situation that matters to everyone. And it is this: if a revolutionary device such as MelaFind has to endure what it did in getting to market, there's almost no hope for those things that are equally revolutionary but also a little more complicated—a list that includes pretty much *everything* under development. Why is that? Because MelaFind isn't some futuristic biotechnology technology that does something like analyzing your DNA in real-time in the hopes of telling you about your medical future. It doesn't require a visit to an operating room, nor, in fact, does it require that you endure even the slightest bit of pain. It simply takes a picture of a questionable mole and gives your dermatologist greater certainty in deciding whether that mole should be removed or not. That's it. And that's what makes this story so flabbergasting—if something that is both non-invasive *and* potentially life-saving had so much difficulty first getting through the FDA and then through the gauntlet that is small-company public market financing, what does that portend for other true scientific breakthroughs that have the potential to help tens of millions of Americans live happier, better, and longer lives? MelaFind is based on technology that's been deemed good enough to be used in the U.S. Star Wars missile defense program that protects us from enemies outside our borders. And yet a bunch of Washington bureaucrats and Wall Street shysters tried to stop us from using it to protect us from enemies inside our own bodies.

I hope this book can educate the public about the innovation, regulatory approval, and marketing challenges that every medical technology company faces at one time or another. I hope that it will inspire people with its tales of persistence and leadership and also entertain with real-life drama and humor, often in the face of pending doom and certain failure. I hope it will encourage others who have experienced similar treatment at the hands of regulatory agencies and other parts of this broken system to speak out in support of its reform, for that is the only way it can be fixed. But most importantly, I hope it will inform the collective consciousness of both the importance and opportunity of breakthrough medical innovation as well as the alarming threats that it faces. The implications are nothing short of profound: a failure to better foster innovation in this country will have disastrous effects not only on our health but on our economy too.

Part One lays out, quite clearly, the devastation caused by skin cancer, and makes clear the need for something that can better help us detect it when it is curable. It also describes how medical innovation occurs in small companies and details the challenges in moving those start-ups along a course that is anything but straightforward. It addresses issues such as the psychology of inventors and founders *versus* investors, the challenges of attracting and retaining talent, and the vagaries of early phase product development.

Part Two takes a deep dive into the unlawful actions and cover-ups by the U.S. FDA that had to be overcome in our effort to bring MelaFind to market. That is, to obtain approval of a non-invasive product that saves lives. It is a brutal blow-by-blow account of a public slugfest that forever damaged the company. While the right side won in the end, it was nevertheless a bitter—and important—enough fight that it ended up being chronicled by the country's major media—the *Wall Street Journal*, Bloomberg TV, and *Fortune* magazine.

Part Three explains how the unnecessary and very public battle with the FDA left an indelible mark on the company, a taint that was exploited by nefarious Wall Street actors who then preyed on the company for their own benefit. It details how with a Scarlet Letter on its back and an albatross around its neck, Wall Street's short sellers and dark pool traders made it impossible for the company to advance the product along the normal, yet time consuming and expensive, course toward widespread use and adoption. That's a path that *every* medical innovation must take en route to becoming a medical staple, but it's also a path along which Wall Street's bad actors lie in ambush.

Here's the silver lining, though: until this system *is* fixed, it does offer long-term investors extremely attractive opportunities to invest in oversold stocks like MELA. I was unable to secure such investment as CEO of the company, but had I been on the other side of the table, I surely would have invested myself. The opportunities are numerous.

Part Four offers a cure for the broken system that nearly ruined the company, and in doing so has arguably killed countless patients by delaying, if not ultimately preventing, widespread adoption of this product. Simply put, the FDA has stopped pursuing its mandate to promote the public's health. Instead, it has put up every road-block imaginable to stop true breakthrough medical innovation. If we don't cure what ails the system, it's going to succeed in stopping it entirely. The book concludes with a prescription for change, a Medical Innovation Manifesto.

I hope you enjoy reading it more than I did living it.

JOSEPH GULFO
June, 2014

I Don't Want to Fight Anymore

A Doctor Who Didn't Want to Practice Medicine

I WAS FEELING awfully good about myself on a bright and crisp early November morning in 2003. For starters, it was my favorite time of year. I could wear wool again after another New York summer of high heat and humidity. I like wearing suits, particularly wool suits. I have always thought of myself as an old soul, fancying myself born in the 20s, wearing wool suits, overcoats, and a fedora hat. I have a soft spot for November, too, because that's the month I started dating my girlfriend, Adele, thirty-one years ago. We've been married for the past twenty-six years.

I was feeling good about myself because I had just done what Allan Ferguson, a well known and very successful venture capitalist, had challenged me to do five years before. I'd originally intended to create a new type of venture capital fund, and I'd asked Allan to help me. We'd tried, but we ended up unable to do so. Allan then suggested I go prove my thesis about how to best manage medical innovation, and then take another run at raising the fund. And that November, step one was complete: I'd shown that the thesis was true.

I wasn't always an aspiring venture capitalist. Growing up, I wanted to be the world's greatest neurosurgeon. But then I met one, and I didn't want to be one anymore. At that point, I wanted to be the world's greatest diagnostician. Have you seen the television show *House?* I wanted to be him, minus the sex and Vicodin addictions. After a brief flirtation with the seminary—I went to Seton Hall as an undergrad, graduating in 1984—I attended medical school at the University of Medicine and Dentistry of New Jersey. I started my residency at New Jersey's Morristown Memorial Hospital when I graduated in 1988. I focused on oncology—the treatment of cancer. It's the most challenging practice in medicine, given all that we don't know and the perniciousness of cancer itself. I've always sought out the biggest challenges I can find, and if I was going to be a doctor, I wanted to take on the big C.

There was only problem with my career choice: I soon realized that I hated dealing with sick people. I didn't hate the people themselves; I hated the responsibility of having people's lives in my hands. When one of my patients who'd been undergoing chemotherapy suffered a perforated bowel, resulting in feces in her abdominal cavity and the threat of an E. coli infection, I had to make a decision between letting a surgeon handle her (with a 99% chance of death) or the medical intensive care unit (a 95% chance). I chose the latter and had to endure a mother accusing me of effectively ordering her daughter's death sentence. Four weeks later, I wheeled her out to her car. That was a wonderful feeling, but I realized that I couldn't deal with making that kind of choice every day. But I'd have to: every oncology patient faces such junctures in their treatment. And so I ended my career as a "real doctor" almost as soon as it had begun.

In 1989, I took a job at a contract research organization, or CRO, called Oxford Research International. At Oxford, I worked as a Regulatory Affairs Associate, a Medical Writer, a Clinical Research Associate, and the Medical Director. In two-plus years, I gained tremendous exposure to the pharmaceutical and medical device industries. I'd been ready to learn, and had the good fortune of reporting to a highly seasoned set of professionals who were willing to teach.

Aileen Ryan, my first boss, was a walking and talking Code of Federal Regulations—she knew the exact citation and page numbers within the CFR covering virtually every project that came in the door. After letting me struggle with a project for a while, Aileen would tell me exactly where in the CFR to find several other ways of skinning the cat, and then recommend the best course of action for that particular set of circumstances. Another smart, savvy, and creative person I worked with was Bob McCormack, an expert in Chemistry, Manufacturing, & Controls, or CMC. The two of them made a great team, and I eagerly soaked up all they had to impart. We were good at what we did: the things that I worked on at Oxford actually *worked*—we submitted successful applications to start human studies, successful dossiers for drug approvals, and had a track record of successful meetings of all sorts with the Food & Drug Administration on behalf of the firm's clients.

Jim Conklin, another MD, advised me that having learned how the industry worked, my next step was to go to a sponsor company to run my own projects. With Jim's help, I secured an interview with a biotech company called Cytogen. They offered me a job as Associate Director, Clinical Affairs, and I took it in November of 1990, excited to work with the largest and most impressive group of MDs and PhDs I'd ever seen under one roof. Cytogen was working on cutting edge monoclonal antibody technology for use in immuno-diagnostics and immunotherapy. I loved it. I spent four-plus years at Cytogen, where a successful clinical program the led to the approval of a monoclonal antibody for prostate cancer (ProstaScint).

I left Cytogen in July 1994 to join a little emerging biopharmaceutical company called Anthra Pharmaceuticals as the #2 executive as well as a director. Anthra's specialty was developing novel anthracyclines, the family of molecules to which doxorubicin, the most successful chemotherapeutic drug up to that time, belonged. The lead product, Valstar, was for the treatment of superficial (early stage) bladder cancer. My tenure at Anthra—from July 1994 to October 1998—was equally rewarding, although it came with a little drama and one large fight.

In a clinical study of patients who had failed prior first line treatment and were destined for cystectomy (bladder removal), Valstar had met the criteria (called primary endpoints) that the FDA had insisted upon before the start of the study—a greater than 20% complete response rate. We filed a New Drug Application and were planning an IPO (Initial Public Offering) to raise the funds to launch the product commercially and continue development of two additional drugs.

We went on the European IPO road show—visiting many investment funds to familiarize them with the company, the products, management, and the business opportunity. We returned to the U.S. for an already-scheduled FDA Advisory Committee Meeting (also known as a Panel Meeting), and, provided that went smoothly, the U.S. IPO road show. If the panel approved us, we'd then raise the money we needed, be wildly successful, and take a victory lap. Or at least that was the plan.

But the FDA meeting was a disaster. The whole purpose of Advisory Committees is to provide the FDA staff with the benefit of the review of top practicing physicians in the field of medicine for which a new product is intended. Remarkably, though, the FDA did not supplement our panel with doctors who'd actually treated the disease. Instead, they sent Valstar to the Oncology Drug Advisory Committee. Oncologists do not treat superficial bladder cancer—urologists do.

I'd already asked the FDA if they would add a few urologists to the panel. But they'd refused. What's more, they'd scheduled the Advisory Committee meeting during the American Urologic Association meeting, so I also had difficulty finding any urologists to come and present the data on our behalf. One did come—Dr. Bart Grossman from The University of Texas MD Anderson Cancer Center. But he was the only person in a room of 500 people, including the Advisory Committee members, who had actually treated patients with the disease.

If they'd found themselves in the same situation with one of their own drugs, a big pharmaceutical company like Pfizer or Merck would have withdrawn the NDA, re-filed it, and waited for FDA to reschedule the panel. In other words, they would have "forced" the FDA to include urologists on the panel. Their billion-dollar balance sheets and earnings from a huge portfolio of products already on the market make them largely immune to cash concerns. They can afford to wait another year for an Advisory Committee meeting, and do. And while shareholders might punish them for the delay, all will be forgiven if the drug ends up getting approved in the end.

But a little biopharma company that doesn't have very much money—and is also afraid that a favorable public financing window might soon close—simply cannot withdraw an NDA, re-file it, and take another run at it a year later. A little biopharma company has neither the money, the clout, nor the reservoir of goodwill with the FDA to force them to do anything. So we had to go for it; we had no choice. Innovation is a bitch.

I spent three months preparing for the presentation. I knew every piece of data backwards and forwards—every patient, every slide number, every analysis. On June 1, 1998, I remember waking up in the hotel at which the panel meeting was taking place and taking a look at my laptop. Side-by-side on my screen were two icons—one for the slides for the Advisory Committee meeting and the other for the IPO road show. I realized the enormity of the situation: If we didn't nail the former, the latter would be dead in the water. And so even though the FDA review division and I seemed in lock step and that I felt we were as close to a shoe-in as one gets in this game, I also knew from my experience at many other Panel meetings that surprises do happen. I was nervous.

As far as I was concerned, the Advisory Committee presentation came off without a hitch. Bart Grossman, in particular, made a brilliant case for the drug. But the panel nevertheless voted 11 to 0 against approving it, all because of a dramatic comment by a panel member who didn't even treat the disease! He was one of the best urologic oncologists in the country from a world-renowned premier cancer center. I know him well, and had even published with him on Cytogen's prostate cancer antibody. While I would send my father to him if he had late stage bladder or prostate cancer, this late stage cancer expert does not treat superficial bladder cancer. But the FDA had inexplicably invited him—and not a urologist, who treats the disease—to be a supplemental Panel member. Why? My best guess is because he'd published prolifically on late stage bladder cancer. But they shouldn't have invited him—he neither administered front line therapy for superficial bladder cancer, nor did he perform cystectomies (bladder removal) on those that had failed treatment. Valstar was intended for possible use when the former had failed but there was still hope of avoiding the latter. And this expert wasn't the kind of doctor who would be managing the patient at that point.

At the midday break, I was told two things by our lead FDA reviewer:

(1) My presentation was "fair" in that I had given equal weight to both the benefits and the risks of the product; and (2) we had the Panel recommendation and approval "in the bag." But then came the afternoon session, when the late stage disease expert slapped the table and said, "I don't care how good the data are—*complete response* is the *completely wrong* endpoint for this disease." It was the Johnnie Cochran moment of the Panel meeting—the veritable "if it doesn't fit, you must acquit" indictment of Valstar's case. And just like a group of impressionable weak-minded jurors that blindly follow a smart and forceful defense attorney who manages to raise a specter of "not-so-reasonable" doubt, the Panel members fell in line behind him. Indeed, ten of the smartest oncologists in America—the same ten that had been so impressed with my presentation and the data— voted unanimously against the product. The lead FDA reviewer did nothing to salvage the situation. I was shocked to my core, thinking I was in a parallel reality. And the company's bankers were pissed.

Adding to the drama, I had invited my parents to watch their son go up against the brightest oncologists in America. They had no idea what I did for a living, or how the MD that they paid for was being used since I'd left my residency. And they got to watch their son fail, and quite publicly so. I remember my father telling me he wanted to buy me a drink, but I had to decline because I had to race to the airport to get to San Diego for the American Urologic Association meeting at which we were planning a pre-launch product training for the sales force, which was standing by with great anticipation to hit the market with this great new product. I told him that I had to go be with the team even though we'd lost.

Before I left the meeting, I asked the expert, whose pithy but yet ill-informed comment doomed us, why he'd done what he'd done.

He told me that he was trying to dramatize a general point to the FDA that survival and progression-free interval are the most appropriate endpoints in cancer trials. In other words, he was using our Panel to provoke broader discussion for future drug studies of future drugs. I looked at him and said, "And you had to choose *our* Panel to do so?"

When I landed, I tried to give the sales team hope, despite the fact that something had gone terribly wrong. I also told every key opinion leader in bladder cancer what had happened at the meeting. They were not happy—surgeons get like that when internists encroach on their turf. They knew that cytologic (absence of cancer cells in urine) and cystoscopic (visual) evidence of complete response in topical drug therapy was very durable (long lasting), and so, complete response *was* the appropriate endpoint. The late stage disease expert's point was appropriate for systemic therapy of late stage cancers where the assessment of response is performed using radiology. But it wasn't appropriate here. I had allies and I would soon call in the cavalry.

Back in New York, the IPO was quashed, and our bankers—the high profile firm Allen & Co.—turned on me. One of them asked me, "What do you have to say for yourself?" I replied, "The FDA made a mistake!" I exercised our right to a Supervisory Review Meeting and met with Dr. Robert Temple at the FDA. I took 11 of the brightest urologists in America (including Richard D. Williams, University of Iowa Hospitals & Clinics; Mark Soloway, University of Miami; Gerry Chodak, University of Chicago; Paul Lange, University of Washington; Bart Grossman, MD Anderson Cancer Center; and others) with me to plead our case. Dr. Temple realized what had happened. I told the story to member of Congress and the Senate, and asked them to urge the FDA to have doctors who actually treated the disease included on the next Advisory Committee Panel. The FDA ended up acceding to our request, and when we went back to the Advisory Committee three months later—without performing any new clinical studies—the Panel voted 10-to-1 in favor of the product. One month later—on October 1, 1998—we received formal approval. Our banker sent me a case of wine.

The company failed anyway. The three-month delay caused by the "hiccup" in approval had killed any possibility of a financing, as the IPO window had slammed shut due to the bad economy in late 1998. And so even though we'd gotten the drug approved in the end, we were nevertheless unable to sell shares to the public. The company made another attempt at an IPO after I had already left, but that wasn't successful either. The drug then languished due to manufacturing concerns that were costly to address, and was even taken off the market at one point because of formulation impurities. But none of that changed the fact that it did what it was supposed to do, and that the delay at the FDA had almost destroyed it.

Anthra ended up being acquired by Indevus Pharmaceuticals, which was itself later acquired by Endo Pharmaceuticals. The product is currently on the market, and generated $27 million in sales in 2012. That's excellent for a specialty pharmaceutical product, especially fourteen years after its approval. I take great pride in knowing a significant number of patients are able to avoid cystectomy (total removal of the bladder) because of our work and forbearance. However, two other promising drugs in the company's portfolio developed by Dr. Mervyn Israel—the man who discovered doxorubicin while at the Dana Farber Cancer Center in Boston—never got the chance to be developed. And Anthra did not enjoy business success as an independent entity, despite the struggle and victory—all because of the FDA Panel debacle that never should have happened.

But it wasn't all for naught. The banker kept close ties with me, asking me to perform evaluations of certain companies on his behalf over the years. The epic battle actually set the course for the rest of my career. I'd become known as a guy who got things through the FDA, no matter what.

Do It Yourself

IN MID-OCTOBER 1998, a week or so after the Valstar approval, I was reading BioCentury, a trade journal that details significant happenings in the development of biologics and drugs, with special emphases on financings, corporate deals, and FDA actions. I was reflecting on my experiences in the wake of the Valstar approval and a thought occurred to me. And I immediately called Bob Maguire from Cytogen and Bob McCormack from Oxford, two of the most experienced clinical and regulatory scientists that I had ever met. I reminded each of them that the overwhelming majority of products in pharmaceuticals and biotechnology fail in late stage development—late Phase II and Phase III. And then I asked them both a question, "In the middle of Phase II, when you know the drug/biologic has activity and isn't noxious, why do development programs fail? Is it because of the people or the product?" Both had answered before I could even fully articulate the question: "The people."

That's when I had my idea for a profoundly different paradigm in emerging biopharma and biotech company investment. I'd concluded that the venture capital model of investing was wrong. Venture capitalists spread a little bit of money over a lot of different companies on the assumption that most development programs fail because the product itself doesn't end up working. Their theory is that the more shots on goal, the more chances they have that one will end up in the net. My experience was just the opposite—when the right people took the shot, the puck went in the goal; no luck needed. So all you needed to do was assemble the right team and then raise enough money that would not only allow you to develop your product but also keep you well-funded during your fight through the opposing team's defense—including surprises and inefficiencies in the system, such as those Anthra had encountered at the FDA. At that point, you'd pretty much be taking a shot on an empty net. Sure, people even miss those shots from time to time. But not that often.

My friend in venture capital, Allan Ferguson, liked my idea. We thought we might be able raise between $100 million and $150 million for a fund that would pick three or four companies that we would then run ourselves. With enough capital, and the right people running the companies, we thought we'd dramatically increase their odds of getting to a significant value-realization event such as an IPO or sale. Allan even liked the five companies that I had tentatively identified for investment, and so we tried to raise the money.

After a couple of months of meetings, we'd found no interested institutional investors. So Allan suggested that I pick one of the five companies in my mock portfolio and make it happen. If I could do that, he said, I'd have a track record to raise a fund.

I ended up going with a company called Antigen Express, a cutting edge breakthrough immunology outfit based in Massachusetts. I loved their technology platform, and I loved the founder, Bob Humphries, who discovered MHC Class II, which is the family of molecules on lymphocytes that are responsible for cell-based immunity. I joined the firm in August 1999 as chairman and CEO. The company was a laboratory with a few MDs, PhDs, a technologist, and me. It was focused on DNA vaccines and peptide vaccines for the treatment of cancer, HIV, asthma, allergy, and viral diseases.

The pre-clinical animal studies and laboratory results were very promising as predictors of activity for ultimate use in human patients. It turned out to be harder than I thought, however, even with great data. Even though we'd managed to raise $1 million, that wasn't enough to prevent the company from almost running out of money as we waited on further grant funding. We made good progress but the route was quite circuitous because the company did not have enough money to set a formal product development plan in place and execute against it. A real development effort takes several years, but the company was living off grants, which are very much influenced by the scientific and world issues *du jour*. Because of that, we were always changing our pitch: when the Anthrax scare occurred, we submitted grant applications for the development of an Anthrax vaccine, and put the hepatitis and dengue fever vaccines on the side. When Dan Rather dedicated a 48 hours segment to "gene therapy," our next several applications tilted our DNA vaccine approach in the direction of "gene therapy," and the peptide vaccines were left on the side.

Successful product development requires a clear plan and steady funding to see that plan through. Lurching from grant to grant does not allow for effective product development. Bob had great plans, but it was my job to get the money. Drug development isn't that different from the rest of life when it comes to that: if you want to raise money, you've got to effectively sell an idea. Unfortunately, most people—including investors—are followers, not leaders. This makes for a particularly difficult challenge when developing novel products, which by definition have no predecessor. Investors want something new and different, but they also want some comfort that it will work. And so they seek that comfort in "comparables"—other products similar to what you have proposed that have already proven successful. The only problem was that while the company's scientists were giving me fabulous data, they weren't giving me something that would both turn investors' heads with its potential *and* show them the comparables that would give them the confidence to invest. Specifically, they were giving me data about pigeon cytochrome C, a protein found in pigeons that serves as an excellent predictor of human immune responses. But the comps that would get investors' attention just weren't there—the product was *too novel*.

In the spring of 2001, I told Bob Humphries that I couldn't raise money using the pigeon cytochrome C data. I asked him to give me data about something more popular instead, such as "her-2 neu"—a molecule on breast cancer cells that is targeted by Herceptin, a massively successful monoclonal antibody for breast cancer developed by Genentech. If Antigen Express could develop a peptide vaccine against her-2-neu, it would be a grand slam—much cheaper, easier to administer, and easier to ship and store. Bob replied that I was stupid—that pigeon cytochrome C was the most critically studied laboratory model of immunological activity in man and that anyone who knew anything about immunology knew that. I told him that the people with the money couldn't care less—that they were followers and we therefore needed to first point them to an already-successful product in a disease that affected many people—the comfort of the comparable—and then show them that we could develop a superior drug to treat that same disease. Then, and only then, would they "follow"—that is, invest in the firm.

So Bob partnered with Constantin Ioannides at MD Anderson, an expert in pre-clinical models of her-2-neu, and developed her-2-neu peptide vaccines that attracted significant grant money, and ultimately made it into human studies at the National Institutes of Health. It also caught the attention of a company called Generex that was developing drug delivery technologies for asthma and cancer, and Generex approached us about a merger. As a condition of the deal, I insisted that the Antigen development programs be funded for three years. They agreed. And so it was that in December 2003, I merged myself out of a job in order to secure a steady and reliable funding stream for a great technology platform! But I actually considered *that* my job, so I did what I had to do.

I hadn't taken a salary at Antigen, but I had been a significant investor. The merger resulted in a modest financial return for both the investors and myself. But the company would have ended up worth much, much more than we'd sold it for, if we'd only had the money to keep it independent for longer, adding more value over time. So it was a very frustrating experience—a fight of a different sort, but a fight nonetheless. And it was the biggest disappointment of my career to that point. I felt that I'd let Bob Humphries down, and truly believed that the Antigen Express technology could have spawned many successful products and adjuvants—products that make other immune-based therapies more safe and efficacious.

But the simple fact was that we'd almost run out of money. The her-2-neu peptide vaccine did reach Phase II at the National Institutes for Health for breast cancer. My mother had breast cancer, so that made me happy. And even if we hadn't gone as far as we'd wanted to, I'd still managed to pick a promising opportunity and guide it through to a value-realizing conclusion. But man, I was tired.

The Phone Call

LATER THAT DECEMBER, I received a call from a familiar number—it was John Simon, the banker who'd been involved with Anthra. He was calling to ask me what I was thinking of doing next. I assumed he was interested because of my track record: I had helped get several drugs and a monoclonal antibody approved, and then identified a very promising technology, overseen its development it and then orchestrated its acquisition. But I really didn't know what I wanted to do next. All I could say was that I didn't want to fight anymore.

"Great," he replied, "because I've got something for you." He reminded me of a startup that I had helped him perform some preliminary diligence on three years previously. The company was called Electro-Optical Sciences, and it was developing an objective, automatic, non-invasive, computer vision-based, point-of-care diagnostic device for the detection of melanoma when it is most curable. The name of the device was MelaFind.

He told me that he and others had invested a combined $3 million after my first exposure to the company and that they had the option to invest $9 million more if certain development milestones were achieved. But the milestones had not been achieved to that point, and the investors wanted me to take a look at what had been done and then advise them whether they should invest the remaining $9 million. He asked if I would consider doing another diligence exercise for him.

Diligence is the term for the process by which an outside group interested in doing business with a company takes a deep, critical look at that company, often with the help of experts. It's not only a "check" on what the management of the company has represented to be the case, it's also an effort to identify those critical items essential to the success of the business so that the investors understand their risks and are better equipped to structure an investment. The investors had previously performed so-called legal diligence, confirming equity ownership through the prior financings and verifying that the intellectual property was being properly protected.

(They hadn't considered engineering diligence to be necessary given the pedigree of the founding team, which I will return to in a moment.) The diligence they wanted me to perform was regulatory and clinical.

The First Impression

DAN LUFKIN, THE lead investor in the Series C round of financings, called me a few days after I'd spoken to John Simon. As one of the co-founders of Donaldson, Lufkin & Jenrette in 1959, and a legendary supporter of small, high-growth companies, Lufkin had made all the money he'd ever need long ago, so the fact that he was an investor in Electro-Optical spoke volumes. And when he led off the call by saying, "I hear that you're the best guy to get products through the FDA," that spoke volumes too. How could I resist? He arranged for me to visit the company the following week.

From my home in Wilmington, Delaware, the trip entailed a drive to the train station, an Amtrak train ride to Penn Station, one stop on the 1,2,3 line to 42nd Street to connect to the shuttle to Grand Central Station, and finally a MetroNorth train to Irvington, New York. (The train that I would ultimately take in the morning left Wilmington at 5:20 AM, so I would lay out my clothes the night before, wake up at 4:45 AM, shower, shave, leave the house at 5:00 AM, park the car, get a cup of coffee, and run to the first of four trains I would ride over the next three-and-a-half hours-plus.)

Electro-Optical's offices were in an old high two-story brick structure—one of many built on the Hudson River in Irvington, NY over a hundred years ago. Originally a foundry that made a variety of products that were then transported by boat, the building had once made greenhouses for public facilities and private homes but had been converted to office space at some point in the previous decade. In 2013, they call the area "SoHo on the Hudson" because of the downtown New York feel of the place. But it didn't feel anything like SoHo in 2003.

The conversion wasn't impressive. I guess some might say that the building had charm. But I wasn't charmed. The signage was terrible. The staircase to the second floor was rickety, narrow, and covered with ripped green indoor/outdoor carpeting. Every door squeaked. The halls were narrow and maze-like. Ever the optimist, though, I arrived at the door and put on a smile.

The office was bare bones, no frills, drafty, and open. The hardwood floor was buckled and creaky—no doubt the result of roof leaks over the years. Most of the lighting came courtesy of 15-foot high windows that rattled in the wind. The floor was so pitched, in fact, that the copy machine had to be anchored down so it didn't roll across the room. A few light fixtures hung from very high ceilings but didn't come close to providing uniform coverage.

There were numerous chairs, desks, tables, cabinets, and book-shelves. But there was no "furniture." My mother taught me that "furniture" is part of a set, or complements other pieces. But nothing matched at all. There were metal desks and chairs, wood desks and chairs, chairs on rollers, chairs on glides, glided chairs with no glides. There were square-edged tables, round-edged tables, and square-edged tables that were rounded! There were some sound-proof modular walls, but they weren't properly assembled, merely leaning on or squeezed in between other pieces of furniture.

There was a narrow walkway to more rooms off the main room. In the middle of this walkway was the kitchen—with a small refrig-erator and a cramped, small sink with dirty dishes piling out of it. There was a small room on the other side of the kitchen, and a door off that to the "clean room"—which wasn't so clean. Beyond this was an area that was slated for "manufacturing." The benches looked like they'd been put to the curb after being in someone's garage for 50 years, and tools were strewn everywhere, along with white lab coats that were not so white.

There was yet another room off the mechanical area. But that one was pitch black, and the fifteen-foot windows were painted-over. I later learned that the software maven who worked in there didn't want sunlight on his screen or for his body to sense the time, lest his diurnal rhythms compel him to sleep when he was in the midst of reducing a great breakthrough to code.

My overall impression was that everything was an afterthought. Nothing seemed to be there by design or accomplished with volition and purpose. It occurred to me that I could never, ever work effec-tively in these circumstances—it was so utterly foreign to me. What was I going to find out when I started looking beneath the surface? I was about to find out.

Meeting the Team

I HAVE BEEN part of numerous diligence processes. They are intrusive and disruptive to a business, and the resulting tone of the interaction can be combative. Because of that, I have always tried to perform diligence in a non-threatening manner. When I met with the founding team and a couple of key individuals who had joined shortly after the company got started, I tried to be as cordial as I could.

The discussions actually started off more two-way than I'd expected. While I was trying to obtain the information that I needed to do the task requested of me, the team also asked a lot of questions of me. But it still didn't go very well in the end. While they focused on my background and experiences, they also bent over backwards to point out the extent to which neither was directly applicable to their situation. I did not sense a scintilla of respect for my real world "in the trenches" experience. I felt that they were close-minded and very guarded.

It wasn't a warm, friendly, or open-minded exchange. But it was also obvious why that was the case. In their minds, I was representing "the money." I was the enemy. I was not to be trusted. So I tried to play Atticus Finch and put on their shoes and walk around in them for a while to truly understand them. When I did that, I realized that they were trying to invalidate me. Instead of getting to know me for its own sake, they were trying to learn as much about me as possible so that no matter what I reported back to the investors, they would be able to dismiss the feedback *a priori* simply because it was coming from me.

In a series of meetings in the weeks just before Thanksgiving 2003, I did what I could to allay their concerns. Slowly, they started answering questions and providing me with information. I realized fairly quickly that these were tremendously intelligent and gifted people. Their depth, critical thinking, precise expression, and raw intellect were all palpable. At the same time, however, I remembered what Steve Dow, a well-known venture capitalist at Sevin Rosen, once said to me: "Remember that tremendously gifted people have equally tremendous blind spots." So I started looking for those blind spots, the gaps between what they had done and what they'd been trying to do in order to move the enterprise forward. Those were as easy to see as the extreme gifts. While they were undoubtedly "off the charts" scientists, they also had no experience in dealing with tough, no nonsense investors or working with the FDA—things that they'd never had to do working in academia and later consulting on defense projects. And I already knew that apart from performing due diligence, I might be in a position to help them do what they needed to do.

But they didn't want my brand of help at first, so it was a struggle to get the information I needed. I realized over the course of repeated visits that they would only answer direct questions—and minimally at that. But they were very clear about one thing: They stated many times, and in many ways—including as I was leaving their offices on what they no doubt hoped was my last trip to see them—that they would be starting the pivotal trial for FDA approval of MelaFind imminently. It was a bad idea, and I told them so.

Reporting My Findings

OVER THANKSGIVING WEEKEND in 2003, I finalized my report and recommendations. The following Monday, I called Dan Lufkin and gave him the verbal versions, the bottom lines of which were: (1) YES, I think you should proceed with the second tranche of the Series C investment because the clinical data are real and I definitely see an approvable claim and a significant medical need; and (2) NO, do not start the pivotal study that the team had showed me in my diligence exercise.

He bristled and told me the same thing that the company's management had—that they would be starting the study imminently. I told him that was a big mistake, because the protocol that had been prepared was an absolute joke—it was too short, not specific enough, and missing essential elements that all protocols for clinical studies must possess, especially those for pivotal registration studies. I also told him that they didn't have a true relationship with the FDA, and that might prove a problem.

He replied that the scientists had just returned from a meeting with the FDA. I knew about that meeting, but pointed out that it had been with the Science and Technology Division of the FDA, not the crucial Review Division. He told me that I was playing with semantics, and that the team had assured him that they'd had a meaningful discussion with the FDA, and that was all that mattered. Had they agreed on an approach to the trial, I asked? I didn't think so. Significantly agitated at this point, he asked how could I be so sure since I hadn't even been there. I said, "That's simple. I know because there is no 'Oh Shit Close the Company' letter in the FDA Correspondence file!"

At this point, he must have thought I was crazy. I told him that in every innovative program that I'd ever been involved with, there was an 'Oh Shit Close the Company' letter in the file. What this means is that there is a letter from the FDA basically saying that what you propose makes no sense, what you seek to do is not necessary, and that you have utterly wasted their time and yours. Of course, it doesn't say that specifically, but rather implies it by the questions that are asked, the objections raised, the items demanded, and the general tone. You're supposed to conclude that they are not on board with your product and not eager to be persuaded to the contrary.

I told him that it was at *that* point that you knew you had started communicating with the FDA—because they are almost never comfortable doing new things or setting new precedents, so there is always a reflexive "no." That's when you can begin to engage them, educate them, discuss, negotiate, bring them around, and poof, you arrive at an understanding and a mutually-acceptable way forward. So to start a pivotal study—an expensive and long trial that you think will satisfy the basis of approval—when you haven't yet established a relationship or gotten them past the "go away" stage is simply naïve and foolish. Lufkin seemed to be hearing me, but also didn't seem to want to listen to any more of it at the moment. So our call came to an end.

A couple of days later, he called again. He told me that one of the milestones that hadn't been achieved with the first tranche of investment was the hiring of a CEO. The investors had told the lead founder, who was also the first CEO of the company, to find an experienced executive as his replacement. And he still hadn't done so to that point. That's when Lufkin asked me, "How would you like to run the company?"

Why Did I Do It?

WHY DID I even think about doing it? For starters, the job would require seven-and-a-half hours on trains each day, leaving at a ridiculous hour, and leaving no time for anything else in my life. I also had no chemistry with the team whatsoever. They were physical scientists and I was a biological scientist. I was a "spirit of the law" guy and they were "letter of the law" ultra-precise individuals. They were high-minded and genius intellectuals from the best schools in Eastern Europe and America. I was born in Brooklyn and liked to rely on my street smarts. I was a former seminarian, attending daily Mass when I could, while they had Jewish heritage from persecuted parts of Europe. (One was a Talmudist Rabbi.) I loved sports; they loved Rubik's cubes and 3D chess. Last but not least: I liked neatness, and dirty dishes didn't bother them.

So again, why did I do it? I have come up with three reasons. One, John Simon was extremely smart, an engineer by training, and he and his fellow investors were very, very successful. If they smelled an opportunity, I'd be an idiot not to follow their lead. Two, I knew I could help them and that if the product delivered everything that the founders told me it was doing in the studies up to that point, I thought that I could get it approved—and without much of a fight. Who, after all, would argue against a non-invasive product that could save lives? And three, I am addicted to science and medical innovation and I love being around smart people.

Over the Christmas holidays, I called Lufkin and said yes, but on one condition—that we would not start the pivotal trial until I was satisfied that a proper relationship with the FDA had been established. He asked me how long I'd need to do that. I told him three-to six months. He told me that the company was running out of money. I replied that I wouldn't ask the investors for the $9 million second tranche until we'd established the relationship, and I wouldn't even take a salary until then. At that point, we started negotiating in earnest. I agreed to be President & CEO and a Director. The plan was to run the study, obtain the approval, and then sell the company for $100 million-plus. They offered me a 5% stake, which might therefore be worth $5 million in just 12 to 18 months. This was going to be a lay up! I'd take that $5 million and start my venture capital fund, with yet another success to prove my thesis.

I started working the first week of December 2003 while an employment agreement was being drafted according to the terms that we'd discussed. But after reviewing the contract, which was negotiated by the lead founder and Lufkin, I thanked them for the opportunity, wished them well, and told them that I'd had second thoughts. I explained that the contract had me "carved-out" of FDA interactions and the clinical study, and that I couldn't accept that for two reasons.

First, no CEO is carved-out of *anything*. (Lufkin is nothing if not loyal, and in this case he was being loyal to the company's founders. His belief in the team was so strong that he'd let it trump this basic management tenet. While I later grew to admire this about him, I could not accept the ramifications of it in this instance.)

And second, I reminded Lufkin of what he'd told me the first time we'd spoken, which was that I was an expert at running clinical trials and shepherding products through the FDA. If they were going to "carve" me out of anything, that would be the last area that would make sense.

He sent a new contract.

I signed it on January 5, 2004. It was supposed to be an 18-month gig. It turned into a decade.

It was a struggle to get the diligence done, a struggle to deliver the report, and a struggle to accept the offer to join.

So much for not fighting anymore.

2

From Star Wars to Skin Cancer

Outta This World

THE FOUNDERS OF Electro-Optical Sciences had previously worked as researchers at the prestigious Riverside Research Institute, a former Columbia University think tank established in the 1950s that was focused on advanced engineering technologies, including lasers, coherent optics, radar systems, and space-based sensors. Backed primarily by the government and defense organizations, many RRI discoveries were intended for national defense. But some also changed the face of medicine. One such example was ultrasound technology, which was originally developed for and used by the military. The biomedical research group of RRI adapted ultrasound imaging for detection and monitoring of disease, as well as for therapeutic purposes. They also developed magnetic guided catheters and pioneered both the pacemaker and balloon catheterization technologies.

Between 1989 and 1991, several RRI scientists from the Research Optics Division left to form Electro-Optical Sciences (EOS), an independent company exclusively focused on the research and development of advanced novel computer vision technologies. EOS started as a government contractor for several agencies of the Department of Defense (including the Defense Advanced Research Project Agency, or DARPA), the Office of Naval Research, and the Air Force. Their specialty was electro-optical processing technology, including hyperspectral imaging, with applications ranging from space object identification to missile defense.

The government worked with a number of these independent groups to develop a wide range of advanced technologies, several of which, including ground-based and airborne laser systems, were coordinated under the umbrella of the Ballistic Missile Defense Organization, also known as the "Star Wars" program. Electro-Optical Sciences was tasked with devising automated computer vision capabilities for those systems.

The founders were experts in mathematics, physics, optics, and engineering. They were in a class by themselves, educated in elite Eastern European and American academic programs during the Cold War. I have often heard the phrase "scary smart" used to describe the very rare individual one meets whose intellect astounds. I cannot imagine ever using this phrase again because I have had the privilege of working elbow to elbow for the past ten years with absolute genius. Of course, that's another overused word. But every one of these folks *was* a genius—correction, they were all *off-the-charts* geniuses.

The IQ of one of the founders, Dina Gutkowicz-Krusin, is actually immeasurable, which means there is no test capable of determining the limits of her intelligence. Dina's clarity of thinking is amazing—it's totally objective and she's able to cut to the essentials of any issue in an instant. Give her three days and a hypothesis she floated off-the-cuff comes back as a theory, an axiom you can bet on every time. They say that science is truth; what she says is irrefutable and absolute. I was utterly amazed every time we interacted. I was also exasperated because of the classic rigidity that comes with these gifts. Nevertheless, she was, in my opinion, the "secret sauce" of the company.

Another founder—Michael Greenebaum—not only had tremendous intellect, but a photographic memory as well. Big deal, right? A lot of people have "photographic memories." Well, Michael doesn't see a forest. He doesn't see trees. He doesn't see the leaves on the trees. Nope, he sees the veins of the leaves of the trees, and he doesn't forget a single one. And he's a nice guy, to boot. He's the company's intellectual property expert and documentation czar, and regularly finds things that expert teams of counsel from the country's best intellectual property and regulatory law firms have somehow managed to miss.

The Savvy Misfit

THIS WAS A group of the intellectual elite, having risen to the highest levels of all academic and intellectual pursuits. And the U.S. government sought them out for their unique gifts. They knew they were special. It naturally followed that several of them were quite preoccupied with the topic of intelligence. The founders were always measuring me, judging and testing the limits of my understanding of their world. I would often disappoint. (So much for being Valedictorian of my high school and college!)

My wife thought I was just being paranoid about being judged until one day when one of the founders admitted to me that they actually did discuss my intelligence level. Another member of the founding team later told me that he had asked Dina what she thought of me, intellectually speaking. Her response? "He's a very good student."

But I was self-aware and savvy enough to know when to ask a question and when not to ask a question. The team was rightfully guarded about their prior work, and I never pressed. Over the years, though, in comments they made about their past experiences, and in seeing some old documents and grants, it was obvious that they were in a class by themselves and the world was a safer place because of their great work. Now, they were going to make the world a healthier place, and I was going to help them.

From the Sky to the Skin

EOS WAS A successful company. But the team wanted to branch out from defense projects and started speaking to doctors and pharmaceutical companies about possible applications for computer vision-based systems in medical practice, product development, and clinical studies. At the request of a pharmaceutical company, for example, they developed a computer vision system for counting hair follicles for clinical trials of a drug for alopecia. To that point, pre-and post-treatment counting of follicles had been "subjectively" assessed. In other words, pictures would be sent to about 100 people who would actually count the strands of hair in before and after photos, and an average was taken of those counts. EOS trained a computer to do the counting—objectively and quickly.

I was shocked when Dina explained to me that the projects for national defense were much more straightforward than the melanoma effort. In her characteristic manner, she explained to me that the defense targets (both airborne and on-ground) were known, defined, and measurable with current optical methods and equipment. Moreover, the background and environment within which these objects moved and resided was known (e.g., sky, ground, clouds, climate, star formations) and finite. With melanoma, the "target of interest"—the features of its shape and growth that could be appreciated by the new multi-spectral imaging system they were developing—had yet to be scientifically codified. What's more, the background, a hyper-variable biologic system—that is, skin—with no absolute uniformity of depth or blood flow, was basically infinite. Dina had eloquently articulated the difference between physics and biology. And physics geniuses though they were, they were now entering the world of biology.

Another project EOS worked on was the profile measurement of wrinkles for the development of topical skin treatments. Prior to the development of an optical device to do so, the state of the art involved creating rubber molds cast on the skin surface and, using a mechanical device to count the wrinkles, and measuring their depth by hand. With the company's technology, everything could be done by a computer vision system—again, objectively and quickly.

EOS also developed a light-based system for the detection of dental cavities earlier than X-rays could, and without the ionizing radiation. They called it DIFOTI, for Digital Fiber-Optic Trans-Illumination. EOS later licensed the product to KaVo, a Danaher company. Danaher redesigned the device and launched it in Europe in 2012.

The EOS team also started working with dermatologists at New York University on a computer vision system that could select the difficult-to-heal wounds that would respond to treatment. Wound healing is a very difficult clinical discipline, and increasing the certainty about which wounds would or would not respond to state of the art treatment promised to be clinically useful. It was while working on this project in 1995 that they met Dr. Alfred Kopf—the Godfather of Melanoma.

The Melanoma Project

ALONG WITH HIS colleagues Drs. Robert Friedman and Darrell Rigel, Dr. Kopf developed the ABCDE criteria for melanoma detection. In a nutshell, a pigmented mole that exhibits Asymmetry (mirror images not super-imposable), Border irregularity (versus smooth and contoured), two or more Colors, a Diameter greater than 6 millimeters, or is Evolving (changing over time), is clinically atypical and should be considered for biopsy to rule out melanoma.

While the criteria captured a majority of melanomas, Dr. Kopf told the EOS team that he could nevertheless use more help in distinguishing those clinically atypical lesions that needed to be biopsied from those that didn't. Drs. Rigel and Friedman told me years later that when they developed the ABCDEs, they would each see the same patients individually and compare notes—only to find that the three experts often disagreed over which lesions needed to be biopsied. That, in a nutshell, dramatized the high degree of subjectivity (and need for objectivity) that showed the need for, and opportunity of, MelaFind.

It was a perfect application of EOS computer vision systems—that is, bringing objectivity to an area of medicine where it was sorely needed. And the downstream benefits of doing so could mean saving lives. The scientists dove in. Dr. Kopf provided glass-mounted 35-millimeter color slide photos of pigmented skin lesions that had been biopsied so that the final histopathology (microscopic) diagnosis was already known. The founders developed a digital scanning and image processing method and trained a computer brain (also known as a classification algorithm) to distinguish between known melanomas and non-melanomas. Then they tested the system on a set of images that hadn't been used in the development of the classifier. It worked! Quite well, in fact.

Dr. Kopf also taught the EOS scientists about the pathophysiology of melanoma. It starts between the epidermis (outermost layer of skin) and dermis (the layer of skin with blood vessels, glands, hair follicles, and lymphatics) and typically grows radially (horizontally) first before it grows vertically and invades and kills. The team realized that they needed to see below the surface, and for this they needed light with longer wavelengths and more energy, so they needed to develop a camera system that included infrared, and a lens system that could provide excellent resolution across a wide range of visible and infrared wavelengths. They did it, but the resulting device was the size of a refrigerator. Dermatologists don't want refrigerators in their offices, so it had to be miniaturized. It took five years, but the miniaturization worked as well—they developed a handheld device that ran off a laptop, and prototype systems were shown to be working in clinical trials in late 2003. That's when I came on board.

The Melanoma Opportunity

SKIN CANCER IS very common, affecting well over a million people per year. Ultraviolet radiation from the sun and tanning bed use are unequivocally associated with skin cancer, but it also shows up in areas of the body that do not get significant sun exposure. The overwhelming majority of skin cancers are basal cell carcinoma, followed by squamous cell carcinoma. Basal cell carcinoma can grow to significant size and result in cosmetically unappealing outcomes if ignored, but it rarely kills. Squamous cell carcinoma can be lethal if ignored for too long. But this is also quite uncommon.

Melanoma is different. If it grows just one millimeter into the dermis, it can be lethal. The fifteen-year survival rate for melanoma that is confined to the epidermis or less than one millimeter deep into the skin is 93%. But the fifteen-year survival for melanoma that invades deeper than one millimeter is only 68%, and it declines precipitously from there. One American dies every hour of melanoma. Very often, these are young patients in the prime of their lives. It is the most common form of cancer in women aged 25 to 29, and the number one cancer killer of women aged 30 to 35. The incidence is roughly split among men and women, but peak incidence in men occurs at an older age. But it does not discriminate: people of either sex, of any race, and of all ages can develop and die from melanoma.

One of the investigators in the MelaFind program, Dr. Armand Cognetta from Tallahassee, Florida, told me some interesting things about melanoma when I met him shortly after joining the company. At the time, I was trying to determine whether his center would be appropriate for participation in the pivotal trial. Ideally, one wants to select centers that report a high incidence of the disease in question so that the study can be expedited—efficiency goes a long way to keeping costs down when running clinical studies. I asked him how many melanomas he saw per year. He looked at me and said, "It isn't important how many melanomas I see per year. What's important is how many see me."

Dr. Cognetta was trying to teach me something about the disease. Basically, his point was that curable melanomas can be very difficult to detect, and all too often they are simply missed. He told me that he drives home after work thinking about whether he missed a melanoma that day. Other dermatologists have said the same thing—they wake up at night wondering whether they've missed one themselves. His number one concern, in other words, wasn't how many he was detecting, but how many he might be missing.

Dr. Cognetta told me something else that has stuck with me, namely, "Melanoma gives cancer a bad name!" He asked me whether I'd ever seen anyone die of melanoma—the black ascites (abdominal fluid), the black cerebrospinal (brain) fluid, the amputations, and the pain. He was adamant that no one should ever die of melanoma, period! Why? Because melanoma is on the skin, and is therefore visible—both to the patient and to the doctor. It's not like ovarian cancer, for example, which isn't visible, and by the time a woman has symptoms it can be the size of a grapefruit and of an advanced stage.

No, melanoma is there for all to see. And it can be detected if patients and doctors know what to look for, and also take the time and effort to really look. He told me that he'd once conducted a survey of university residency programs and found that on average, graduating dermatology residents have only seen a dozen early stage (curable) melanomas in their training. While a cure would obviously be a wonderful thing, the bigger opportunity in melanoma is training patients and doctors to spot melanoma when it is still in the epidermis (*in situ*) or minimally invasive (less than one millimeter deep). But Dr. Kopf and his colleagues had shown that you can only do so much with the naked eye. The obvious next step was to develop technologies to better help doctors detect melanoma when it is curable. That's why Dr. Cognetta was in the MelaFind program. He ended up providing the highest number of melanomas in our pivotal trial.

Almost a decade later, just a week after the FDA had approved MelaFind in November of 2011, I was on the Jim Bohannon radio show talking about melanoma. A woman from Pittsburgh named Irene—a breast cancer and melanoma survivor—had called to tell her story. She'd had a mole that multiple doctors told her not to worry about, but subsequently, it had suddenly started to grow and she had insisted that they take another look. A biopsy revealed an advanced melanoma with a positive sentinel lymph node. She had just completed interferon therapy when she called the show.

As I was speaking to her, Dr. Cognetta's words came back to me. What if the doctors whom this patient had asked about her mole had used MelaFind when they'd first seen her? Add to that our disease awareness, patient mobilization, and education efforts as a company, and we would undoubtedly have many opportunities to prevent what had happened to Irene from happening to anyone else. That was and is the hope; it was and is the goal; and it was and is the reason that the challenge everyone at the company was working on was so worthwhile.

Gene Rodenberry Would Have Been Proud

WE TOOK THE company public in an initial public offering in October 2005. I'll return to the reasons why in the next chapter, but the simple point is that we needed money. After that, the company gradually transitioned to a more operational and tactical focus as opposed to a merely theoretical one. I increasingly started taking "ownership" (in management-speak) as the tasks at hand turned toward execution of plans and strategies far more straightforward than the esoteric high-minded theoretical physics of pattern recognition, fundamental digital data analysis, and wavelet and non-wavelet signal processing that made the project possible. We were hiring more and more people, particularly younger people, who knew only one EOS—the current company, not the company of old. (EOS eventually changed its name to MELA Sciences in February 2010. For the purposes of this story, though, I will call it MELA Sciences—or simply MELA—from this point forth because starting in 2004, EOS had only one principal focus—the early detection of melanoma to save lives.)

Trying to explain to new people the history of the company, the science behind the device, and the behaviors of a number of the absolutely critical individuals wasn't easy. I was comfortable with the unknown. I liked learning new things, and human behavior fascinated me. But working with this group utterly compelled me to finish the process of becoming an open-minded and "diversity-embracing" person.

I remember trying to explain to a new employee why as CEO I didn't put my foot down over certain things, or why I had a double standard when it came to certain situations, or people. I told the employee about a Star Trek episode where the crew had to deal with the most intelligent and advanced life form ever, The Scalosians. Their water accelerated the speed of human thought and movement, and Spock had purposefully drunk the water in order to undo the damage that The Scalosians had done to the USS Enterprise. Having had the opportunity to immerse himself into their culture and thinking, Spock looked back in awe as the Enterprise was leaving the planet and marveled at their superiority to humans. When Kirk would have none of it—they'd tried to kill his ship and his crew—Spock simply said, "They are to us as we are to the amoeba."

I explained to the new employee that Dina was like Deela, the Queen of the Scalosians, and we were mere amoebas—her intellect was such that we weren't even on the level of Captain Kirk when compared to her! Unlike Deela, however, Dina wasn't trying to destroy a ship. Rather, she was trying to change the course of a disease. And our jobs were to contribute to that effort as best we could.

The United Nations

GIVEN THE NATURE of our work—engineering, algorithm development, software development, and medicine—we needed a highly intelligent workforce. We hired the best we could find, and nothing else mattered. We hired seasoned professionals who had just left big companies, and we provided first time jobs for newly minted, smart college graduates. There were few absolute experience requirements because we were doing something that was truly novel. And what emerged was a highly eclectic group of individuals bound together by a very noble goal—to see to it that no one died of melanoma by helping to catch it early. This goal bridged many a geographical, social, age, gender, religious, and scientific gulf. And it was all that mattered.

Nevertheless, getting things done day to day meant setting objectives, communicating, controlling, optimizing, and doing it again. That is Management 101. For this breakthrough effort, though, we needed to think out of the box, be creative, not be impeded by

roadblocks, and look past petty differences. This required leadership, of course, but how do you lead a very eclectic group like
the one at MELA Sciences? I quickly learned that "giving a piece
of myself" was not the way—my life experiences meant absolutely
nothing to a young hire who was of Indian descent, born in Japan,
lived in multiple countries, attended Wesleyan and Barnard, wrote
and performed music, and had an alternative lifestyle. She did not
know who Rocky was. She was a toddler when Apollo 13 was in the
theaters. She knew nothing of Walt Frazier. The same held true, to
some degree, for virtually all of my employees.

One day, I looked around and realized that we had at least one
person from every continent and every major religion on staff.
We were our own little United Nations. The "Ugly American" that
I am, I decided to have a company baseball game and cookout. It
was an utter debacle. Three quarters of the employees had never
held a baseball bat in their hands. The Indian guys thought we were
playing cricket and ran to first base holding the bat. The European
contingent wanted five strikes, not three. Baseball mitts were on the
wrong hands. Some people threw the ball at the runners, not the
base to which they were running. It was like a scene out of The Little
Rascals. Little did I know that it made an everlasting impact on all
of them. They still talk about it to this day.

The Melanoma Battle Cry

WE WERE AIDED by constant reminders in the media and in trade
journals and in our personal lives of the terrible disease that melanoma is—and quite unnecessarily so. Many famous people developed melanoma while we were plowing ahead, including Sandra
Schilling, wife of the Boston Red Sox Cy Young Award winning
pitcher Curt Schilling. She created the Shade Foundation, which
was dedicated to raising money to build canopied parks for children. John McCain also had several melanomas and melanoma was
in the news a lot during his bid for the White House in the 2008
presidential campaign.

Other notables who've had melanoma: Bob Marley, Journey's Steve Perry, Burgess Meredith, Danny Federici (the keyboardist from Bruce Springsteen's E Street Band), and Maureen Reagan (daughter of President Ronald Reagan). Meanwhile, the American Academy of Dermatology launched a number of campaigns designed to promote full body skin checks. One of these featured the actress Marcia Cross (of *Desperate Housewives* fame), who donned a blue patient gown to emphasize the need for and ease of whole body skin checks. Cynthia Nixon from *Sex and The City* also lent her support and celebrity to get the word out. We often received emails and letters from patients with melanoma, asking to participate in our clinical trials. We also got letters from family members of patients who had died from melanoma encouraging us in our efforts.

The media was also replete with reports of many drugs and biologics products that failed to show clinical benefit in late stage (metastases) clinical trials, and were therefore halted in development. One of the most high profile failures was a product called Genasense, from a company called Genta. But every failed trial further emphasized the importance of early detection when the disease is curable. A couple of new drugs were eventually approved for the treatment of melanoma, including Yervoy (from Bristol Myers Squibb) and Zelboraf (Roche). But they weren't very effective, and the battle cry for early detection got louder. The import of what we were doing became more obvious to anyone paying attention.

I have found that one job of a leader is to show each employee how what they are doing *that very second* contributes to the final collective goal. That way, they see the importance of even the most menial tasks, approach their jobs with passion, and feel pride in being part of the team. It was easy to do this for the MelaFind project. It was easiest, of course, for those directly involved in product development—in our engineering, software and algorithms, clinical studies, and regulatory efforts—because the product had the potential to change the disease. But what about those in marketing, medical affairs, investor relations, and PR? I told each of them that that the simple act of talking about the product and the disease was having an impact. And that spreading the message about the ravages of melanoma, its predilection for young women, the need for skin checks and use of sunscreen, was saving lives. Everyone was indispensible to the effort. And they knew it.

When melanoma is on your mind every day, it's easy to get caught up in it and think everything you see on the skin (yours and other peoples') is the cancer itself. I remember being on the beach, under an umbrella, lathered with 50 SPF sunscreen, when a 38 year-old friend of my sister-in-law approached. As he toweled off, I noticed something peculiar on his back. And I saw it from five feet away, without my glasses, and fighting sun glare. I told him that while I didn't want to alarm him, he probably should have it checked by a dermatologist. He told me that he'd had a melanoma a few years before and he'd missed a few follow-up appointments, so he'd go back immediately. I received a call a short time later thanking me—a biopsy had revealed a Stage II melanoma. The sad part is that if he'd kept his regular appointment schedule, it would have likely been identified and excised much earlier, when it was totally curable.

Several employees shared stories just like that one—from their personal lives or from the news—and it served to further dramatize the importance of what we were doing and inspire everyone. Once, when I was speaking to Dr. Gary Peck, a top melanoma expert from Washington DC, I told him that I didn't want to overemphasize the message about the disease, lest we make people paranoid about it. Dr. Peck stared at me and said, "When it comes to melanoma, it is the paranoid who survive!" I've repeated his line more than once.

Another day, I received a call from a melanoma specialist who runs the pigmented skin lesion clinic at one of the most prestigious medical institutions in the world. He told me that he had just gotten the biopsy results back on a lesion that he'd excised a few days ago—it was a Stage I melanoma. He was upset with himself because he'd seen the patient six months before, examined the lesion closely at that point, and had elected not to biopsy it. He couldn't understand how he had missed it, and he told me that he couldn't wait for MelaFind to hit the market. I relayed his story at the next company meeting.

The most eye-opening story that we heard came from a story in *Self Magazine* about several women with melanoma, one of whom was a dermatologist named Liz Tanzi. She was pictured with a scar on the inside of her calf, visible from the front. Dr. Tanzi had noticed a lesion there about a year before, considered it herself, and then asked two dermatologists what they'd thought about it. All three—Dr. Tanzi, and the two others—had felt that the mole wasn't suspicious enough to merit a biopsy. A year passed and Dr. Tanzi realized that she just didn't like the look of it. What's more, she felt it might have changed. So she biopsied it herself, and it came back as a Stage I melanoma. Dr. Tanzi felt that it was probably *in situ* (100% curable) when she'd first noticed it.

If a well-trained dermatologist can miss a melanoma on a very visible part of her own body—a part of her body that she sees multiple times a day—what does this portend for the rest of us? In other words, just how difficult is it to detect melanoma at the most curable stage?

When we were preparing for the FDA Advisory Panel Meeting of MelaFind, I invited several noted experts to review our data and help us prepare our presentation. One of them, a former President of the American Academy of Dermatology, couldn't make it to our mock panel meeting, so he came on a separate trip. As we were reviewing the data and I asked his opinion of the best ways to address points raised by the FDA in a pre-panel dossier that had been sent to panel members, I suddenly came close to a complete breakdown. Why? Because after all our work, the FDA was reneging on its agreement with us (more on this later), and I was having to prepare for a meeting that should have been a "walk in the park" but was instead shaping up to be a walk on the plank! This doctor reached out his hand, grabbed my arm, and said, "Look at me! You can't give up now—patients need this!"

In a video montage we made of the history of MelaFind, Dina explains how difficult early melanoma detection was compared to the work that the company had done with the national defense projects. She goes on to say that had she known at the start how difficult the challenge would prove to be, she might not have taken it on in the first place. After a momentary reflection, though, she pauses and says, "But it was nice to start doing something that actually advanced life." We all felt that way.

3

Innovation Is Hard Enough

From Innovation to Successful Business

IN THE WORLD of healthcare product development, the time from which an inventor has a breakthrough idea to when an actual product is widely available can run from ten to fifteen years. Although the mile markers along the road are well known, the specific path to success is different every time. And they are all fraught with risk: over 95% of new products fail before making it to market. Whatever the reason—the product/technology fails to receive FDA approval (i.e., it doesn't work or regulatory difficulties stifle it), sufficient funding is unavailable, or a superior competitive product emerges—the most common result is failure.

As I've said before, innovation is a bitch.

If the product actually works—and can be proven to do so, with the right amount of investment, time, and rigorous clinical trials—the most critical element of ultimate success is a steady and reliable source of financing. Because not only is innovation a bitch—she also costs a lot of money. MelaFind itself consumed about $120 million before it finally made it to market. But it's not just about the simple amount of money required to get from here to there. The source of that money (the type of investors, in other words) and the demands of that money (the hoped-for return and time horizon of those investors) matter as much, if not more, when all is said and done.

The names change every time, but the roles played by different types of investors in a small healthcare company's early days don't vary too much. So-called "angel" investors provide a limited amount of capital to take a discovery from proof of concept to the "start-up" stage, when a company normally has just a handful of employees. If all proceeds according to plan, venture capital investors soon show up, bringing with them an expertise at turning start-ups into emerging companies with dozens of employees or more. Assuming continued success, companies are usually able to tap the public equity markets via an initial public offering at some point, using that capital to fund the final stages of development and the early stages of commercialization. While ultimate success is never assured, any company that makes it to the point of having a product it is allowed to sell (i.e., it has been approved by the FDA) is considered "mature" by innovation standards. Most never make it anywhere near that far. There's also the consolation prize, in which an established industry leader acquires the technology, product, or entire company at some point along the way. But that's a rare outcome as well.

The following figure graphically depicts the pre-commercialization stages of a breakthrough product's life.

The medical innovation field is one of the most highly regulated areas of business. And that is as it should be. The Food and Drug Administration *should* be uncompromising when it comes to our collective health. At every stage of the approval process, significant regulations dictate not only *what* needs to be accomplished, but also *how* it must be accomplished. This might come as a surprise, but regulatory approval of a truly breakthrough product invariably takes more time and costs more money than the actual discovery of the product itself. You might save a lot of rats' lives in the lab, in other words, but if you're going to start using something on humans, you need to be able to prove not only that it works unequivocally,

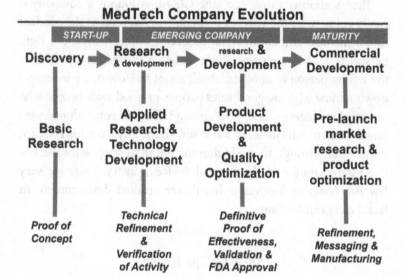

MedTech Company Evolution

START-UP	EMERGING COMPANY		MATURITY
Discovery ➡	Research & development ➡	research & Development ➡	Commercial Development
Basic Research	Applied Research & Technology Development	Product Development & Quality Optimization	Pre-launch market research & product optimization
Proof of Concept	Technical Refinement & Verification of Activity	Definitive Proof of Effectiveness, Validation & FDA Approval	Refinement, Messaging & Manufacturing

but also exactly how it works, the conditions under which it works best, the risks of using it, and how to mitigate those risks. And that's expensive. In some cases, the costs of the formal regulatory approval path exceed 90% of the total!

To be successful, too, it is absolutely imperative that a company attracts and retains some very specific people with very different skill sets. First, it needs its inventors or innovators. But second, and of equal importance, it needs people with the talent and experience necessary to move a technology or product through the FDA approval process. Finally, if and when a truly breakthrough product has finally been approved, it needs those with the sales, marketing, and management expertise required to make any product a commercial success. That last stage—from the moment of product approval to that time when healthcare practitioners are actually using it as a routine practice—can take *another* 10 years or more on top of the time spent developing it. (On the outside edge, then, it can sometimes take 20 years before a novel product makes it from an idea to a business success. If you're looking to make a fast buck, you best apply elsewhere.)

There's another thing, too. The CEO that founds a company is rarely going to be the CEO of that company as it turns the product into a medical and commercial success. In other words, the right person to lead a company at one point in this process is usually the wrong person at another. Think about it: How many inventors do you know who are good sales people, or good sales people who are good managers of a huge company? They do come along every now and then. Bill Gates led Microsoft all the way from his Harvard dorm room through to world domination in desktop software. But that rarely happens in the medical device industry. There are very few Bill Gates in innovative healthcare product development. In fact, I can't think of any.

Show Me The Money

INVESTING IN MEDICAL innovation is always a high risk/high reward proposition until the mature commercialization phase, whereupon it can suddenly become a very "safe" bet, one that is virtually immune to seasonal or economic cycles. Because of that fact, the motivations of investors tend to be much different at various points of a company's development. The earliest funding typically comes from the founders themselves or their friends (colloquially known as "friends and family"), as well as research grants. Next come angel investors, affluent individuals who focus on funding start-up projects. They are *investors*, so angels do have financial objectives, but they frequently bring an emotional connection to the situation as well—they or someone they love may be afflicted with the disease at which the product is aimed, for example. Sure, they want their money to bring a decent return, but many angels are also wealthy retired individuals who tend to be more interested in seeing "good things" done with it in the process.

It's when the venture capitalists arrive that things start to get complicated. On the one hand, they bring a lot that is truly crucial—an appetite for risk, a long view, the ability to deal with the idiosyncrasies of company founders, connections to talented individuals and reputable institutions, legal and regulatory assistance, and an understanding of corporate structure. On the other, they're not nicknamed "Vulture Capitalists" for nothing. But, from the point of view of a founder, you could also call them Vulture Egotists, because they tend to ascribe far more value to the non-cash contributions that they bring than they are ultimately worth, and, as such, invariably insist upon severely discounting the valuation of a company prior to their investment. Companies with many suitors can resist the most aggressive attempts at such; those without find themselves at their venture capitalists' mercy.

Public market investors don't have the same risk appetite as venture capitalists. Why? Because they lack the ability to force such a discount on a company, and the result is that their potential return is always more modest than a VC's, even if it can still be huge. Indeed, each successive "round" of investors is typically offered less potential return (i.e., they invest at higher valuations) in exchange for taking on less of the overall risk (i.e., the product is farther along in the approval process.)

While many investors lump biotechnology and biopharmaceutical companies together with medical device makers, there are significant differences not just between the two types of entities but also in how they are funded over time. Because the markets for drug and biologic therapies are well established, if a company can show a significant therapeutic improvement without a significant increase in cost, the product will be adopted. Because of that, biotech and biopharma companies are usually able to tap the public markets when there is evidence of clinical activity and a reasonable assurance of safety during Phase 2 of the FDA process. In other words, they can "go public" long before ultimate FDA approval has been granted. (The FDA review process toward that final approval doesn't start until after Phase 3 pivotal studies are complete.)

In medical devices, on the other hand, it is rare for a company to sell shares to the public prior to FDA approval. That's because in the medical device realm, 95% of new products are only subtly different than currently available alternatives, which means that the primary challenge is more marketing than technological. A new drug that is either much cheaper or works much better *will* make a biotechnology company a success; a new medical device that works only gives a company a *chance* at success, because then they have to figure out how to sell it. And what of the other 5% of medical technology products? They tend to be so novel that there is no established market for them. They are "disruptive" in that they seek to change existing treatment and diagnostic paradigms. Again, unlike cheaper or more efficacious drugs, the risk with these products is not just how long it might be before adoption takes hold, but whether it even takes hold at all.

That doesn't mean that nothing is predictable. Indeed, as a medical device company reaches progressive research and development milestones and then the various stages of FDA approval, the value of that company should increase accordingly. While still private, that increase can be seen as successive financings are consummated at higher valuations than the preceding ones. Once public, and after factoring in business cycles, political risk, and other external influences, the value of a company hitting its goals also tends to increase in predictable fashion. Early on, the upward adjustments can still be choppy, but when companies are mature and increasingly profitable, changes in their market value are usually quite reliably upward sloping.

That's not to say there aren't hiccups—there always are, particularly in the early stages—and if a hiccup happens to coincide with a need for funding, it usually results in a "down round." That's when the venture capitalists can turn from friend to (arguably) foe—putting on their "vulture" hats, they invariably try to make the case that there has been *significant* disappointment relative to development expectations and that a down round is warranted. If the company has no other alternatives, the vultures win.

True to form, and as I would expect from any investors, when I arrived at MELA Sciences in January 2004, the investors were not only discussing whether to proceed with the second $9 million tranche, they were also considering that *even if* they did hand over the money, it would likely have to be a down round, given that some things hadn't proceeded as planned to that point. This is part of negotiating. After pointing out that some *other* things had gone better than expected, I also explained, quite simply, that no company could be worth less the day after a new CEO walked in the door than it had been the day before. (Whether it were me, or someone else, the point is that MELA had hired a seasoned executive to take charge of the next stage in the company's journey.) I then added, unequivocally, that I would not countenance a down round. They gave in. The move endeared me to the other founders as they'd actually been convinced I was nothing but an agent of the investors. I wasn't.

Even when companies are publicly traded, investor reaction to disappointing product development news can be out of proportion to reality. So it behooves a company, especially a medtech company, to stay private, in the arms of the venture capitalists, for as long as possible so that the principal risk being transferred to the public is execution risk. If and when it does go public, it's also crucial that a company have several years of cash on hand so that it isn't forced to raise money when its value is artificially low—whether that's because of the natural vicissitudes on the product and commercial development processes or something external, such as the credit crisis of 2007-2010.

I'd like to make one final point about valuation. And it's this: it always takes time for the market value of a company to catch up to its true, or inherent, value. This is usually due to the time it takes for news that the company is performing well to permeate through the public investor base. Professional "fundamental" investors differentiate themselves by exploiting this very gap—by finding such "undervalued" opportunities and buying low. But it's also where predators operate. Hedge fund gamblers—I refuse to call them investors—and their affiliated manipulators also use the gap to their advantage, and in ways that aren't always above board. (I will explain much more about this later).

Here's the bad news: A troubling development has occurred in early-stage medtech investing over the past 15 years or so. Due to "regulatory uncertainty"—a euphemism for the complete and utter capriciousness and unpredictability in the FDA review process of new medical products—venture capitalists are becoming less inclined to fund very early stage companies. In the third quarter of 2012, for example, there were 65 venture deals for medical device companies, for a total of $434 million. Not only was that a 37% decrease in dollar amount from the second quarter, it was the lowest level of investment since 2004. A January 2013 article in Medtech Investing pointed out that numerous venture firms are losing medtech team members and one venture fund—OVP Venture Partners—was contemplating shutting down entirely. First and foremost among the reasons cited for reduced investment and focus: the lack of regulatory certainty with respect to FDA approvals.

The VC void has been filled with "angel networks," or quasi-organized groups of angel investors. While these networks can help companies advance to the point of an "exit" via acquisition by a larger company, or for traditional venture capital investment to step in, it's hardly optimal, as the capital available from angels is a paltry substitute for that which exists in the venture realm. What's more, angels rarely arrive with the value-add of venture capitalists, especially when it comes to the know-how of building a company the right way.

While the best-intentioned investors are behind a company all the way, navigating the above challenges of keeping a young company well funded is no small task. There is always a natural tension between management and investors, borne either out of a lack of knowledge about the process, communication issues, or "gaming" and positioning for more attractive valuations. And it's not always easy to know what phenomenon is operative. One of the reasons that I took the job with MELA Sciences was because I thought that being hired by "the money" meant that I would not have to worry about "fighting" in that particular ring. I thought I could focus instead on other challenges, such as the FDA approval process, without having to worry about our investors seeking an advantage at every turn.

I was wrong about that. It quickly became apparent that I was fighting in three distinct rings, simultaneously—with the investors, the company's founders, and the FDA. (Dan Lufkin has repeatedly told me over the years that he can always depend on one thing—that I will always be fighting. "You occasionally punch the wrong guy," he's added, "but you're always fighting." I've even launched a few in Dan's direction over the years, but he always took them in stride.)

Founderitis

THERE IS A disease state that infects start-up companies as they begin to operate outside the realm of the expertise of the people who formed them. It's called Founderitis. It usually starts on day one, because many new company founders have never done so before, let alone managed an ongoing business. While they will know some things that must be accomplished if a company is ever going to be successful, the typical shoe-string budget of newly-formed companies only compounds the challenges of founder inexperience, as they try to do most of those things as inexpensively as possible, which usually results in one setback or another. Then there are the things that they have no idea about at all. Put the two together, and most startups find themselves in septic shock before long. If by some stroke of luck, they still manage to show some value from the effort, venture capitalists will arrive with antibiotics, life support systems, transplant teams, and rehabilitation. But it's always a miracle when a start-up survives to fight another day.

When I arrived at MELA, the disease had actually become a full-blown epidemic. By that I mean that the condition of Founderitis affected not only the company, but also the vendors and suppliers with whom it dealt. Why? Because everyone was in awe of the résumés of the founding team. Interestingly, one of the biggest benefits of venture capitalist investors is not the money that they bring or their expertise at growing companies, but rather their lack of susceptibility to this disease. They are usually so awestruck by their own faces in the mirror that they do not impress so easily, and are therefore particularly effective at stamping out Founderitis. Unfortunately, there were no traditional venture investors in the company when I arrived, so I had to try and eradicate the disease myself.

Of course, I'd gotten a glimpse of the possible challenges I faced when I first met the team. But the list grew longer with each passing day. For starters, there were many relationships about which I was unaware. Two of the founders were related through marriage. Two employees were mentees of one of the founders. The top finance executive was a friend of one of the founders, and the legal/administrative head was the friend of another. The company also employed the son of a founder, the niece of a founder, and the son of the finance chief. One employee was married to another that reported to him. If I ever even consider doing this type of thing again, I will remember to ask for everyone's family tree before I do so—with maiden names!

The obvious problem with this set-up was that there were too many emotional—not business—ties between employees. (The upside was the passion they displayed and the lack of gossip—try trashing someone to one of their relatives!) And then there was me, with no ties to anyone whatsoever. I was the outsider, the interloper, and the thief in the night. It soon became clear that I was to be impeded wherever possible—for the good of the family! I could handle the relationships—I'd arrived too late to stamp out Founderitis, so I had no choice but to deal with it—but it wasn't the best of signs. It said to me that the founders hadn't tried to get the best people they could. They were geniuses, sure, but simply hiring people that they already knew told me that they did not respect the importance of that which they did not know.

Honey versus Vinegar

MANAGEMENT BOOKS SPEAK about two types of leadership—the personal (honey) and the positional (vinegar). The former derives from respect and admiration, and comes in time; the latter comes from fear. I needed to lead this group, but it was apparent that personal leadership was going to take a long time, and positional leadership wasn't going to be very effective. Dina, for example, nearly quit almost every week for the first several months, usually after a conversation with me. I was more scared of her quitting than she would ever be of being fired.

I also realized that I wouldn't be able to penetrate the circle of trust immediately. So I decided to stay out of their way. While I was in the office every day, I kept out of their business and focused instead on two things—developing a relationship with the FDA and navigating the government's byzantine reimbursement process. I stayed firmly at periphery as the rest of the team finalized the systems and manufactured a few dozen of them for the start of the pivotal trial. I also chose not to take a salary as a gesture of good faith—it was also a way for me to put skin in the game as well. I later learned that the decision earned the team's respect because they had reduced their own salaries a year earlier to conserve cash.

Still, I knew that ultimate success required that I get inside the circle eventually, so I carefully observed the group's dynamics. I attended working group meetings during which the esoteric details of optics and algorithm development were discussed in great depth. Because I was unable to judge the scientific merits of the discussions themselves, I chose to spend much of my time observing the team's behavior and interaction. That's when I realized that Dina was a force of nature. At the same time, I decided to bet on the person that Dina herself seemed to hold in highest regard, a young Latvian algorithm developer and programmer named Nikolai Kabelev. Nyq only opened his mouth when he had something intelligent to say, and when he did speak there was little substantive rebuttal to any points he had made.

I began going to Nyq to get the straight scoop on most things. He was excellent with deadlines, and was the kind of person who would work 72 hours straight to deliver on time. I bought Nyq a couch for his office so that he could get at least a couple hours of sleep when he went into non-stop work mode. Did he like me? I'm not sure, but he did develop a tolerance for me. Nyq measured people by what they delivered—he used the word often—and when he saw that I delivered too, he seemed to realize that I probably wasn't as bad as their worst fears had made me out to be. We developed a good chemistry. Though I was not involved in inventing MelaFind, I joined Nyq and Dina to form the core of the team that took it to the finish line.

But even those relationships weren't easy. With Nyq, for whom I developed "older brother" if not paternal instincts, emotional ties were a no-no. One day he said to me, "Joseph, I am from an Eastern European country, so, I am inherently distrustful of authority." Another day, he said, "You know, it was the nice military officers who you had to worry about." So be it. We would be cordial, but not too much more.

A few years into my tenure, Nyq and Dina stopped seeing eye-to-eye. This happens in all small companies, and a manager needs to manage the situation. My first problem, though, was that I didn't completely understand the technical details of either of their jobs, so I had no basis upon which to make decisions about who was right and who was wrong. All I knew was that the "secret sauce" (Dina) and the "key ingredient" (Nyq) were not mixing well—for 18 long months they only communicated with each other through me. And I couldn't order them to work together in the way a manager can when employees are easily replaceable because my threat would have had no teeth. They both knew that I couldn't replace either of them at that critical juncture. So I just kept on reminding them that the three of us needed to get along and deliver the project.

Interestingly enough, I now know that I could have actually ordered Nyq to do whatever I wanted him to do. One day, when I once again brought up a slide presentation I'd been urging him to help me with, only to be continually rebuffed, he looked at me and said, "You realize that if you simply tell me to do something, I will give you what you want." I realized then that Nyq wanted to be treated like a soldier, and he wanted me to be a strong and confident General. So I began doing just that. The results were golden.

A Roach in The Salad

THERE WAS ONE other employee who made an impression on me in those early days. She wasn't an engineer or a physics genius, but all of *those* people nevertheless seemed to like her a lot. Which was odd: It was her first job out of college, and she'd been born and raised in the United States, which hardly made her a natural pal for the middle-aged Eastern European geniuses. I'll call her Kathy, and she managed the clinical study sites and organized the interpretation of the pathology slides by our external panel of expert histopathologists around the country. Kathy was clearly very bright, but she also possessed an ability to see the big picture while still catching transcription errors like a transposed set of digits in the fourth and fifth places in a string of eight during auditing. I knew she'd do very well in the highly regulated industry we worked in.

I asked her to have lunch with me, and she agreed. I ordered a turkey burger and she ordered a salad. I asked her what her goals were, and told her that she had a unique set of skills—big picture and details—that were critical for success in medtech and biotech. And I proposed a deal. I would teach her the industry from a clinical and regulatory perspective if she would represent me with the founding group. All I really wanted, I said, was for them to realize that I wasn't so bad. If she could explain that to them—in her own way and in her own time—that would be extremely helpful to me.

While she was mulling it over, Kathy moved a few leaves of her salad, and a roach appeared! But instead of freaking out, she simply moved her plate to the side, looked at me, and said, "You've got a deal." She was completely unflappable! Kathy proved herself an extremely valuable member of our team over time, both in her actual job and in her ability to work well with everyone around her. The latter skill was instrumental in her helping me become accepted by the core team, which was critical.

Putting the Cart Before the Horse

DURING 2004, I concentrated on securing a relationship with the FDA while the technical team worked on finalizing various algorithms and software and making engineering tweaks to the hardware. When they were ready, we'd produce the systems that would be deployed to the clinical study sites around the country to conduct the pivotal study. In the next chapter, I will detail the process by which we not only established a dialogue with the FDA, but also how we cemented the path to approval by signing a rare binding protocol agreement. Suffice it to say that in late October 2004, we had that agreement in hand, and we were ready to start the study. At least from a regulatory point of view—meaning that the FDA had given us the green light to do so. The only question was whether we were ready.

We certainly had enough money to proceed. Or we were about to have it. Recall that I'd forfeited my salary until I delivered a "relationship" with the FDA. With the protocol agreement in hand, I contacted the investors and told them it was time to live up to their end of the bargain and hand over the next $9 million. Two of them took me out to dinner. At first, they congratulated me. They then asked me how I would feel about the investment coming to the company on a monthly basis, rather than all at once. I shouldn't have expected otherwise. Investors negotiate everything.

But I wasn't negotiating anymore. I'd done what I'd promised, and now I expected them to do the same. I told them that I'd understood our agreement to be for the whole $9 million at once. I also told them that while there might be some people out there that would be happy to come to them, hat in hand every month for more money, I wasn't one of those people. At the same time, I told them that I knew it was their money and my father had taught me never to tell people how to spend their own money. So, I said, I was happy to go away with no hard feelings—I had a good story to tell and could be satisfied with having delivered a great thing for a company as a favor to a friend. Their response? They committed to write the check for the whole $9 million.

When I arrived at work the next day, I told the founders that while I'd gotten the full $9 million, the investors would have preferred to meter it in slowly so that they could judge progress on a continual basis. And I asked them: were we *really* ready to take all of the money? If some things were still uncertain, if they wanted more time before starting the pivotal study, if there was any question that things would not proceed as planned, the best thing to do might actually be to take enough money—say $3 million—to get us to a value inflection point and then take the remaining $6 million at a higher valuation when we were definitely sure. I suggested this for two reasons. One, it would have been a nice gesture for me to go back to my dinner mates with a concession that addressed their concern. And two, I figured I would be able to negotiate a higher price per share for the remaining $6 million, which would be good for the founders. I gave them some time to think about it. A little later in the morning, the founder who headed the hardware effort looked at me, feigned pounding on an imaginary table, and stated emphatically, "We are ready!"

I was ready too. During the previous several months, I'd visited many of the dermatologists that would be participating in the pivotal study to assess their eligibility and also to establish a rapport with them. I developed close bonds with several of them in the course of those visits. In addition to visiting the clinical investigators and melanoma experts, I was also continually meeting with the FDA, and took five different melanoma experts to those meetings with me in the process of securing the protocol agreement.

In December 2004, we held an investigators meeting in New York City, bringing all of the dermatologists and study coordinators together for two days to review all the details of the study, Good Clinical Practices Guidelines, operation of the system itself, and the study's coordination logistics. There were about 50 of us at the New York Hilton on 54th Street and 6th Avenue. It was a fabulous meeting—professionally run, buttoned-up, and on the money. And it was a first for all of our employees. The young ones loved the experience and soaked it in. The meeting began early on a Saturday and ran until 6:00PM, when we had a closing dinner in a private dining room at the Redeye Grill on 56th Street and 7th Avenue. We spent about $100,000 on the meeting, but it was worth it. We'd worked a significant portion of the dermatology community into a froth over our device.

The founders finally saw the totality of what I brought to the table—the protocol agreement with the FDA, the second tranche of $9 million from the investors, and a very successful investigators meeting—and decided that I could be part of the team. All of the clinical sites were excited to start the study, too—they believed in the company, the scientists, and the product. They wanted to be a part of changing this terrible disease, and they believed that we could make it happen. Several of them told me that the company finally seemed "real" to them, that what had started as a cool research project was at that point a serious enterprise with direction and leadership. Everything was going just as it had been sold to me when I joined the company: the product worked, our investigators were excited, and we appeared ready to sail through the FDA approval process. At that point, I felt like the long reliever who is brought in when the team is up 10-3, and all I had to do was close out a few innings and that would be that.

We deployed the systems to the study sites and started the study.

Before I get to what happened next, allow me to step back for a moment and explain the product itself as well as the dynamics of a formal clinical trial. MelaFind is a camera with a brain. In the simplest sense, it takes a picture of a lesion and tells you whether it "thinks" that lesion should be biopsied due to the possibility of melanoma. It sounds simple, and it is. But clinical studies are not simple. Rather, a tremendous amount of data must be collected and, with any pre-FDA approval experimental product, there are rigorous procedures that must be followed.

In our pivotal study, for example, the dermatologist first needed to discuss the potential benefits of the system with the patient, who then had to sign an informed consent form. That was followed by a set of 30 or so questions that covered such things as biographical data and medical and sun exposure history. Once those had been entered into the MelaFind system, the dermatologist conducted a physical exam, indicated any clinically atypical lesions, and then documented those findings in the system as well. If they'd found possible targets, they then used a clinical camera (i.e., not MelaFind) to take two pictures of the lesion, from distances of 22 inches and 8 inches, respectively. (We used those pictures to compare the diagnostic performance of other dermatologists on the lesions that were included in the pivotal trial in later additional studies.) At that point, both the dermatologist and patient had invested 20 minutes or more in the process. And then it was finally time for the MelaFind handheld system to be applied to the lesion. MelaFind captured a multi-spectral image and analyzed it. Every lesion to which MelaFind was applied was then biopsied to determine whether it was a melanoma or benign. The only problem: the machine wasn't cooperating.

Six weeks into the study, I got a phone call. A dermatologist on the other end said, "I am not using this goddamned machine again until you fix it!" I asked him to calm down and tell me what was wrong. Here's what he said: About two-thirds of the time, MelaFind simply wouldn't operate as it had to within the constraints of a pivotal trial protocol. It had three chances to capture an image—none could take more than a minute—and when it failed to do so, the session was terminated. If that happened, all of the time spent up to that point would be for naught, and the patient was invariably disappointed and upset. (Patients are always in a heightened emotional state at the doctor's office, and they react accordingly.)

What's more, our doctors didn't get paid for incomplete cases. We were wasting everybody's time. Why? Because the machines weren't operating properly. The science of our melanoma detection was sound, but the hardware in which we'd packaged it wasn't up to scratch. It was as if we'd given you an iPhone with a touch-sensitive screen that only sensed every third or fourth or twelfth touch. Or one on which your iTunes store session would terminate if you didn't make your selection within a minute.

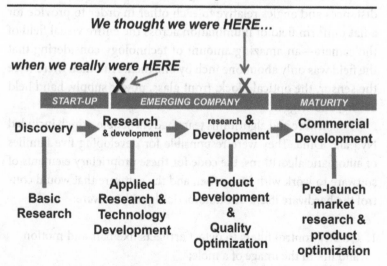

MedTech Company Evolution

We thought we were HERE...

when we really were HERE

X   X

START-UP	EMERGING COMPANY		MATURITY

Discovery → Research & development → research & Development → Commercial Development

Basic Research   Applied Research & Technology Development   Product Development & Quality Optimization   Pre-launch market research & product optimization

That was the first time it hit me—a possibility that I'd never even imagined—the product wasn't ready. Four months before, I'd sat at dinner with two of our investors, looked them in the eye, and told them we were ready. They'd wanted to monitor our progress by metering in the money, but I'd changed their minds with my show of confidence. I had fallen on the sword for the founders to get the $9 million. This was not good. It was not good at all.

We'll Fix It Later

MELA's TECHNICAL TEAM was comprised of two groups—hardware and software/algorithms. The hardware team had five members. They focused on things like the development of a very novel lens system—one for which no design previously existed. Our lens was comprised of nine pieces of glass arranged in a "barrel" that was 1.5 inches long and half an inch in diameter and could provide for 20-micron (one millionth of a meter) resolution in ten different wavelengths. It could see clusters comprised of just *three* skin cells. Another key piece of the hardware was the illuminator, a ring of 80 LEDs of ten different wavelengths that were arranged at precise distances and angles relative to each other in order to provide for a flat uniform field of illumination across the entire visual field of the camera—an amazing amount of technology considering that the field was only about one inch by one inch. And then there were the sensor, the optical block, front glass, power supply, hand held casing, and trigger.

The software and algorithms team had six people, which included Nyq and Dina. They were responsible for developing five families of automatic algorithms, the code for these proprietary elements of software to work with each other, and the software that would control the hardware itself. The automatic algorithms were:

1. Quality control filters to detect artifacts like hair and motion and ink in the image of a mole;

2. Segmentation, which allows the computer to automatically find the "brown spot" versus normal skin in the field of view and accurately identify the limits of the lesion. With melanoma, the important changes are often at the periphery of the mole, so the computer needed to be able to "see" these areas with great reliability and precision;

3. Calibration to ensure appropriate levels of image intensity depending upon the reflectance of the brown spot versus surrounding skin;

4. Feature identification, or the measuring of as many elements and characteristics of the "fingerprint" of a mole as possible to assess the way it was growing and the way it was arranged (also called "disorganization"); and

5. Classification, which designates a mole's disorganization as either "high" or "low" with respect to the architectural organization of the lesion. Melanomas are highly disorganized and benign lesions have a low level of disorganization.

So where were the problems? Remarkably none were associated with the most novel, esoteric, and breakthrough elements of either the hardware or the software. The damn thing actually did what it promised to do when the system itself was working. The problem was that the system didn't always work—the aborted patient sessions were caused by mundane things like power supply failures, USB failures, or a lack of repeatable alignment of the handheld or the glass-encased image of a mole for phantom calibration.

In short, it was the more perfunctory elements of the hardware and firmware that could not withstand the rigors of a specific, detailed protocol. It's not as if we'd done anything unusual. With non-invasive medical technology devices, most companies perform their early studies with prototypes. Not only that, ours was a "non-significant risk" study, which meant it didn't even have to be sterile. That's because it was "non-invasive"—nothing was going inside the patient's body.

We only had seven testing sites, and had only built 40 prototypes of MelaFind, so we weren't yet at the point where manufacturing at scale even made economic sense. That would all come later.

In our early studies, the clinical sites had been allowed as many attempts as they needed in processing a lesion. So these sorts of intermittent problems had not surfaced as *real* problems. But when we went back and looked at the failure codes, we saw that it had often taken as many as a dozen attempts to process a single lesion. During an actual pivotal study, there are "collars" placed on every procedure—in ours, for example, only three attempts were allowed per scan. But three attempts wasn't nearly enough for the current state of our systems. This was, in my view, a complete and utter disaster because the study would need to be stopped.

I asked a member of the hardware team about the issues. He told me that they had noticed them sporadically, but they'd been so focused on proof of concept that they'd simply said to each other, "We'll fix it later." But it was already too late to do so. When a company starts a pivotal trial—late stage development—the product should be ready for prime time, or at least nearly so.

I contacted the FDA and told them about the glitches. I promised that we would address all of them, verify and validate the changes, and then seek their permission to restart the pivotal trial when we were ready. The FDA agreed.

How did we end up in such a condition? On the one hand, it wasn't that surprising—cash-strapped start-ups are always trying to make great strides as quickly and efficiently as possible, and there's usually something that goes wrong as a result. Recall why I was brought in to the company in the first place—the investors did not feel enough progress had been made with the $3 million that they had invested, and before putting in an additional $9 million, they'd wanted assurances. Feeling the pressure to perform, the founders had focused on their head-turning breakthrough items with the limited money that they'd had.

But we had a company-specific problem as well, and, if I could go back in time, I would have addressed it immediately. And it was this: the people I was working with were prototyping experts, not manufacturing experts. The systems that they'd built for the military were one-of-a kind, and never mass-produced. As a result, there was no one on staff who was an expert at taking prototypes and making them robust. They'd always had some outside party—usually a government contractor—take care of that side of things. So they had no one on staff with experience working with an early development team to "design for manufacturing." This is obviously critical for a system intended to be mass-produced and made widely available. But it had also never occurred to me that the founders of MELA didn't have the best engineering minds in the country on speed-dial—it wasn't long ago that they'd been sitting around tables at the Pentagon, designing technologies that you and I wouldn't even be able to understand. And they'd have to call someone to make *those* things. So why hadn't they called them this time?

There's another point to be made here, too. If a company like GE Medical had developed MelaFind, financial resources would not have been an issue. There would have been an appropriate budget and a fair timeline upon which all parties had agreed. Not only that, there would have been a full complement of technical experts for all of the requisite development phases. But we weren't GE Medical. We were a scrappy little start-up with limited resources. If a venture capital firm had made the initial $3 million investment, we probably wouldn't have ended up where we had, either. They probably would have brought in someone experienced at the most immediate challenge—designing for manufacture—before they'd brought in someone like me. You don't need someone like me until you've got your design nailed down.

Unfortunately, the money hadn't come from traditional VCs. Rather, it had come from investors who had emotional connections to melanoma, none of whom had a principal focus or even a strong background in healthcare or the medtech development process. They, in turn, had brought me aboard to execute a pivotal study and get the product approved. And yet everybody had somehow missed the fact that the product wasn't ready. The angels were pissed. I was pissed. Stopping a pivotal study is simply anathema, an utter catastrophe. You should never start a pivotal trial until *everything* is in order. The team had told me that everything was in order with the product. The things that I had worked on were in order. I didn't even pick the date for the study itself; it had come from the team— up from the bottom, not down from the top. And yet there we were with the black eye of a stopped study. And it gave me great pause regarding whether I wanted to continue as CEO.

Bad Timing

WE HALTED THE study in February 2005 and immediately set about getting a handle on the bugs and glitches. The timing couldn't have been worse: the American Academy of Dermatology's annual meeting was scheduled for February 18 to 22 in New Orleans. We'd planned a huge presence at the meeting to keep our investigators en-ergized about the study, to perform market research with dermatol-ogists, and to get the whole dermatology community buzzing about the fact that our success was imminent. Instead, rather than being Richard Simmons, full of unbridled enthusiasm, we were more like Ricky Ricardo, with a lot of 'splaining to do.

My wife Adele joined me on the trip. After arriving, we had lunch at Mr. B's Bistro with one of our board members—he of the "crazy place" remark—and his wife, who I'll call Barbara. He knew our angel investors well and had been instrumental in them hiring me. He believed in MelaFind. We discussed the history of the program, the dreams, the realities, and the problems. I had every intention of telling him that I had done everything I could have done for the company and was thinking of moving on. I'd secured a binding pro-tocol agreement with the FDA so that the path to approval was cer-tain. I'd also lined up excellent investigators to execute the study. But at this point, I had too much opportunity risk at stake to wait around while the engineering team fixed the glitches and the bugs. I also didn't want to fight anymore, and it was going to be a fight with the founders to get this done right.

I was looking for the right time to say thanks, *sayonara*, and *hasta la vista*, when Barbara lunged across the table at me, grabbed my wrists, and pulled me toward her. She implored me—"Joe, you just have to fix this! We've put so much into this! You have to do something!" Not knowing what to stay, I sat there stunned staring at my wrists in her clutches. Adele turned to look at me, looked at Barbara, looked back at me, and then gently put her hand on Barbara's back. With her other hand, she grabbed one of Barbara's hands, trying to loosen the grip around my right wrist, and in a very soothing voice said, "It's alright. Everything is going to be okay."

I am a romantic, pure and simple. I think that heaven will be the first cup of coffee in the morning, sushi, and champagne, and perpetual states of infatuation. I have never thought of Adele as my wife, but always as my girlfriend, and I have always felt the need to impress "my girl." But what the hell was she doing? I didn't want to do it! I wanted to get out of the whole situation and proceed with my plan of a new kind of medtech/ biotech investment fund.

Once we got back to New York, I called all the investigators that I hadn't seen in New Orleans to tell them about the situation and that we had to address some problems with the equipment before the study could proceed. These were not pleasant calls to have to make. But these were my relationships now, and I had to break the news and deal with the consequences. One day, as I was walking from Grand Central to Penn Station to catch the train home, I paused in the middle of the street and said to myself, "My girlfriend thinks I can do it, so I'll do it." I decided I was going to own it, solve it, and make it work.

Diverticulitis in the Snow

ONE DEFINITION OF insanity is doing the same thing over again in the exact same way yet somehow expecting a different outcome. I wasn't going to do such a thing. The manner in which I'd observed the technical teams working—a Socratic approach that works in academia and even in the true "discovery" phases of development— wasn't going to get the job done. Our problems required a very specific approach, one that included: (1) specific problem definition;

(2) identification of multiple potential solutions; (3) testing of solutions independently and then in the context of solutions to other issues; (4) formal plans, complete with timelines and designated responsible parties; and (5) formal verification and validation of the solutions. In other words, they called for good old-fashioned project team management. I'd had a lot experience in that kind of thing from of my days at Cytogen, so I dove right in.

The first step was identifying every single problem. It's always a good idea to have a fresh set of eyes look at things with you, so I asked the team to identify the top companies in the electro-optical design and manufacturing space. One of the board members recommended a well-known company and the founders gave me another, one that they'd vetted from a longer list of a dozen candidates over the years. The first was in Ohio. So off to Ohio we went.

The company—I will call them OHIO—was a well-known electro-optical system development powerhouse. They performed work for NASA, the military, and many large private corporations. When we visited, we were required to leave all devices with picture-taking capabilities at security. The facility was maze-like, with multiple buildings connected underground, narrow hallways, no windows, and numerous double door security points. I have a reliable sense of direction, but the floor plan seemed purposely confusing, and there were no signs, no placards, and nothing with a map indicating, "You Are Here." And it occurred to me that I'd never be able to get back to the main entrance on my own. They didn't want you to know where you were, and you didn't. The walls were mostly concrete. Behind the few doors that were opened to us were discrete laboratories with no more than one or two people working. The equipment was new, and everything was clean, but it all felt a little dark to me.

The people we met with were serious and sharp, and they suggested a major technical review followed by a detailed report delineating the problems that they saw and their recommended solutions. I'd told our investors that I needed a little time to get my arms around the issues and develop a plan, but OHIO wanted more than I had, and I urged them to accommodate my time constraints. They offered a scaled-down 30-day process, with the caveat that there might be a few things that would need to be rethought if we decided to work with them after that point. I told them to proceed, thinking that at the very least, we'd get enough specifics and definite overall gestalt of the situation to make it worthwhile whether we ended up with them as long-term partners or not.

The plan was for them to descend upon us with a team of experts and live with us for a full week. After that, they'd take two weeks to review matters internally while still engaging with the point people that we designated for the various areas under study. Then they'd visit us to present their findings. We would digest their synthesis and then circle back with them to determine what role they might play in moving forward. It seemed like a reasonable plan, and they started the next week.

During the visit, I began feeling quite ill, and thought I might have caught the flu. I had all the usual symptoms, including sweats, fever, generalized abdominal pain, nausea, and some body aches. This, at least, seemed a problem I could solve myself with Tylenol. But the next morning, the character of my abdominal pain had changed. It became focally intense on my lower left side and radiated to my belly button. I was hunched over, because if I stood up, the pain got much worse. When I pushed in my side and let go, I had severe pain—doctors call that rebound tenderness. I also noticed that there was something missing from the typical flu-like symptoms. I had no diarrhea, because my bowel had shut down. And then I realized what was happening. I had diverticulitis. In Ohio. In the snow. Wonderful.

I called Dr. Glen Mogen, a GI specialist from West Orange, NJ. Glen gives me endoscopies every few years, because I have had gastritis, duodenal ulcers, gastric ulcers, or acid reflux since high school. He had also been the attending physician at Morristown Memorial Hospital Clinic when I was in residency and had been a great mentor. Back then, I would see my patients and then present the cases to him along with my clinical differential diagnoses. And then one of two things would happen. If I were right, he would congratulate me. If I were wrong, he would teach me by telling me why my diagnosis was off the mark. This time, the case was *me*, but the process was the same, and when I was done giving him the diagnosis, I waited for the verdict. The good news: He congratulated me. The bad news: I had diverticulitis. He told me three things: (1) I needed to start taking triple antibiotics therapy immediately; (2) I must not eat anything until the pain had totally subsided, although I could drink small amounts of water; and (3) I needed to get home because I clearly had a focal peritonitis and more significant perforation was possible.

I went to the pharmacy, picked up my prescriptions, and popped the pills. But I wasn't going home yet, because we had to visit the other prospective partner. It was a 325-mile drive to Michigan, and it took us a very long time to get there because the roads were terrible, with snow, ice, traffic, and closures. I spent the ride hunched over in pain and nausea, and every so often I had to yell at our driver to slow down. My travel companions, two of the founders who were focused on the hardware end of the project, were of no help and offered no sympathy. At one point, they decided to stop at a roadside fast food joint. They ordered hamburgers, fries, soda, desert, and relished them as I sat there in pain, prohibited from eating. And I was their boss!

The second company—I'll call them MICHIGAN—had well-known expertise in manufacturing high-end precision spectro-photometric equipment. They were color experts and made products for several well-known consumer and professional manufacturers under those companies' brands. They gave us a detailed tour of a very impressive facility geared completely to manufacturing. The place was buttoned-up, with large clean rooms appropriately vented with laminar air flow, designated materials receiving and quarantining areas, obvious signage and doorways separating manufacturing from R&D and administrative areas, hard hat requirements in certain areas, and one-foot wide yellow lines painted on the floor delimiting authorized access areas. The white coats were white, the tools were state of the art, and everything gleamed. MICHIGAN was clearly run by exacting management, and everyone knew their place and walked with intention and purpose. Me? I walked with a hunch, my left hand pushing into my lower abdomen.

We had an excellent meeting. But they told us that they were not hardcore problem solvers for development stage products. Rather, they were top-grade manufacturers. To work with MICHIGAN, we'd first need to figure out our own issues, and then come back to them with our status. And then *they* would decide whether they wanted to undertake a manufacturing methods development effort with us, or merely bid on the manufacturing contract once we were ready for prime time. This all came out during the lunch that we had at a nice seafood place in a large cozy booth, with me unable to eat, pyretic and wincing in pain.

Once we got home, we began to prepare for the technical audit from our friends from OHIO. The team worked straight through the next weekend writing up results of experiments and performance tests and putting all of the appropriate documents in order. They had binders of information at the ready for the exercise, despite the fact that they were not at all happy about the decision to involve outsiders. But we had no choice. We needed help, and fast.

Parallel Tracks

THE PEOPLE FROM OHIO arrived with a very specific mandate. They were to perform a technical review designed to identify the problems and recommend ways to address them as quickly and efficiently as possible. I was elated because I could communicate with the lead engineer from OHIO quite easily, and he had tremendous scientific and technical resources behind him. Our hardware team, on the other hand, wasn't so thrilled to have an outside group looking in their drawers, so to speak. There was also a good chance they'd actually outbid and/or outperformed OHIO in their days working with the government, and now had to stomach a technical review of their work by that team. MelaFind was also a work of art, true genius, and the founders had won Discover Magazine's 1998 Christopher Columbus Award in recognition of the innovation. In fact, MelaFind had beat out "Deep Blue"—the IBM supercomputer that had defeated Bobby Fischer in chess— for the award! And now they were to be judged on it by a bunch of Midwestern outsiders.

Over the course of the week, OHIO paired up with the appropriate counterparts on our team, including electrical engineers, optical engineers, algorithm developers, and systems engineers. At the end of each day, they provided us a list of questions and requests for specific information and reports that our team would fill by the next morning. It was an intense but amicable visit, followed by a few weeks of emails, requests for further information, additional performance tests and measurements, and peer-to-peer discussions. They returned once more to resolve final points and questions, and then delivered their findings in a very polite and respectful manner. They had a high regard for our team, and were complimentary about the technology, but they also saw a number of things that had to be addressed to ensure success.

Some of the fixes were straightforward. And while they obviously got a few things wrong due to lack of understanding of some aspect or other, they had warned us up front that the "quick and dirty" process might result in a few mistakes. OHIO were very impressed with a number of the things our team had done, particularly the lens and its assembly fixture that our young optical engineer from Poland, Tomek Momot, had designed and then built by hand. In fact, each generation of the hand-held units, called "probes," was named after Tomek–T1, T2, and T3. (Leave it to a collection of geniuses to call a non-invasive camera a "probe," which connotes invasive exploration and pain, of which MelaFind requires neither. It's really just a camera that you use to take a picture of a mole.) OHIO also suggested we consider some recommendations that were not quick fixes, such as a redesign of certain elements of the system that would make manufacturing more scalable and more reliable, with fewer failures. These were "design for manufacturing" ideas that no one had really focused on to this point in the project. We agreed to digest their report and follow up with them regarding next steps.

Still, I felt I needed a third alternative to working with OHIO and MICHIGAN. Why? Because OHIO was not a manufacturing house and it would be too easy for a dedicated manufacturing group like MICHIGAN to blame the design developers for problems. While meetings with both had helped, I had concluded that it would be best not to split the design for manufacturing process and the manufacturing function. The guy who draws the plans should build the house, in other words. I was also concerned that our business would not be significant to OHIO, and worried that they might get distracted with other larger clients.

So at the same time that we'd met with OHIO and MICHIGAN, I had reached out within my own network for help. I knew a couple of bankers named Andy Ziolkowksi and Richard Steinhart from my days at Anthra. They were forming a fund and had signaled an interest in investing in MELA when they closed on their financing. They were very knowledgeable in the medtech space, having raised money and merged several related companies. Andy and Rich put me in touch with an experienced medical optics engineer who in turn introduced me to a group in Germany named Askion that developed and manufactured precision electro-optical systems.

Askion was located in Gera, a small town in the former East Germany. Very few people speak English in Gera, but there is considerable electro-optical engineering talent in the region in large part due the presence of Zeiss, a world-renowned manufacturer of the highest quality lens systems, in nearby Jena. The whole area was a cold war hot bed of clandestine electro-optical engineering for military purposes. Askion, which was run by Lutz Doms, an engineer who had worked at Bayer Diagnostics, had actually been spun off by Zeiss about 10 years prior. Among other things, Askion manufactured and serviced Agfa's one-hour photo machines. Askion represented the best elements of both OHIO and MICHIGAN for our purposes—a real R&D laboratory to engage in design for manufacturing experiments *and* optimization, and more formal, buttoned-up, large space manufacturing.

Askion also had something that neither OHIO nor MICHIGAN had—a significant appetite for the project. They were hungry for business and told us they were prepared to be our partner in the *entire* process going forward. They would give us a complete characterization of the prototype systems that we developed and had used in clinical studies to date. They would undergo a major redesign for manufacturing of all elements of the camera. They would develop robust manufacturing methods and precision fixtures. And they would guarantee commercial grade manufacturing under both ISO (European) and FDA (USA) guidelines. Askion also agreed to house several of our employees within their facility, something that OHIO wouldn't do. They estimated that we would need at least a year, if not two, to make the systems for use in our pivotal trial—systems that, if successful, could then be manufactured at scale with great quality.

By the end of March 2005, then, I had an excellent idea of the problems, comfort that the true breakthrough elements of the system were solid, and three alternatives for partners to get it all done—OHIO, MICHIGAN, and Askion. What to do? Should I have the company work with one group on design for manufacturing development (OHIO), and another on manufacturing (MICHIGAN)? Or should I have it work with a hungry group that would do both but was also an ocean apart with significant cultural and political differences from our founding team? And regardless of what I chose, would the founders act out against me or respond to my leadership on the issue? The pressure was on, and I needed to make a decision. And the board was anxious to hear what it was going to be.

The Green Memo

AFTER OHIO DELIVERED their report, I decided to give the team a few days to consider and debate the findings, and then talk to them about our options. To my surprise, though, our technical team summarized OHIO's findings and emailed them to me, as well as the Board. The email listed 10 items, with three or four lines of text describing each. While the end-run around me bothered me a little, that was nothing compared to the content of the memo itself. Not only did it trivialize the nature and extent of the problems, it also suggested that we could readily deal with them ourselves, now that we were focused on them. Setting aside the fact that "we" should have been focused on them all along, it was clear to me that "we" needed more help than the email suggested. Basically, its conclusions were 180 degrees from what OHIO had said!

I called OHIO's lead engineer and asked him whether he or anyone on his team had been in touch with anyone from our team after the presentation. They had not. I asked whether he had rethought any of his major conclusions and then advised anyone on our team of these changes. No and no. Finally, I read the first item of the Board memo to him and asked him what he thought. His reply began, "Well no, what we said was . . . " Then I read the second item, and he said, "Well, not exactly. What we were saying there is that . . . " I then read the third item, to which he replied, "No, that makes no sense."

I asked him if he would do me a favor. I wanted to send him the memo in a Word document, have him turn on "track changes" and then type in parentheses what he thought about each of the 10 items. When he sent it back a couple of hours later, I opened the email attachment and his statements were in green. They were much more in line with what I'd remembered from the presentation. And he was very pointed, mincing no words.

In early April 2005, I went to the board with what became known as the Green Memo, gave them my assessment of the situation and the way forward. I made the point that the founders, as gifted and wonderful discovery scientists and researchers as they are, were not, in my judgment, capable of leading the design for the manufacturing process of the hardware, which was absolutely critical before we could execute the pivotal trial. I was confident that the software and algorithm team was sound. OHIO's top algorithm people had used other known families of classifiers to try and replicate our software results, and theirs were nowhere near to what Nyq and Dina achieved. OHIO was impressed with them. So the baby was healthy, it was just the bathwater that needed to be changed.

I recommended that we work with Askion, a company like us—young, hungry, eager—and with complementary skills to our own where those skills were needed most, on the hardware end. (If and when we got to a point where we were manufacturing at scale, I figured we might use MICHIGAN as well. You never want to have only one supplier. But for the time being, Askion was my choice.)

My fellow directors asked me two questions: how much was it going to cost and how much time did I think we'd need? The time part was easy—a year, maybe two. The money? I told them if we were going to do it right, we'd have to start the whole design-for-manufacturing process all over again, and that it was going to take a lot of money—perhaps as much as $10 million.

Call me naïve, but I couldn't see how the angel investor syndicate wouldn't ante up. After all, they knew as well as I did that innovation is a bitch, and it is also expensive. I told them that I expected that they'd provide me with enough money to get us over the finish line; we'd agreed to this in principle when I took the job. But as I read the expressions on their faces, I knew that things had changed. They weren't going to do it. This was not what they'd signed-up for. This was not what they'd expected. They were thinking of pulling the plug entirely!

I told them that would be a mistake. The product worked, and they were going to earn their original investment back and more, but it was just going to take a little more time and cost a little more money to get us there. Their reaction wasn't surprising—accustomed to making money on either banking fees or short-term public investments, they were looking for a near-term return. Again, these were not traditional VC's with a five-to ten-year investment horizon. The way I saw it, the only way to give our investors enough confidence from bailing entirely was to attract *new* investors. So I told them that I would find an investor to continue the dream. "Go for it," they said.

Meanwhile, I took a look around me and realized that I had no allies—the founders hated me for shining a light on the problem and the investors hated me for making them realize that they'd misunderstood their investment. I had no one to talk to, no one to confide in, and no one that I could count on. And with neither side willing or capable of owning the problem, the onus fell on me. A couple of years later, Dan Lufkin, who had continued to invest individually, told me that he'd been amazed at my response to the situation and had wondered where it had come from—as if I'd been hit by lightning or something. I told him that "it" had always been there, but that I'd just never felt empowered to show it. But at that point, I did. Because no one else was going to.

Yeah, How?

I'D ALREADY BEEN talking to a number of venture capitalists in February and March 2005. We had the perfect profile for a blue chip venture capitalist to consider as an investment. First, we had several thousand patients worth of clinical data that showed the product worked. Second, the regulatory risk had been taken off the table by virtue of the protocol agreement (more on this later). Third, we had the support of top melanoma experts in the form of key opinion-leader dermatologists. Fourth, the fundamental technology had just been vetted by a significant technical review by leading electro-optical contractors. Fifth, I had an engineering partner in mind to finalize the product and make final systems for the pivotal trial and then commercial production. Sixth—and most importantly—there was the high unmet medical need disease state. Our product addressed a real life-or-death need. What else did they need to know?

A couple of venture capitalists were interested in principle, and I was pushing them to step up with a meaningful investment. And then I got a phone call from Jonathan Burklund, a banker I had known back in my days at Anthra, but with whom I'd lost contact. He'd tracked me down by searching for me on the Internet, and he'd also done some research on MELA and was extremely impressed. I took him through the same sales pitch I was giving the venture capitalists, and told him that I was convinced that with the mistakes behind us, the only thing left was execution risk. His response? "Let me take you public." WHAT?

Burklund proceeded to tell me that he'd just raised $35 million for a company called CABG Medical, which was developing an artificial graft for bypass surgery. Manny Villafana, a well-known serial entrepreneur, headed the company, so it had that going for it, but it also only had data from trials in *pigs*—not humans. Burklund said that CABG could have raised $50 million if they'd wanted to, and he felt that he'd just palpated a soft spot in the public markets for medtech companies that promised VC-like returns. He said that MELA represented far less risk but an equal return to an investor who might be looking at a biotech IPO. (Or a CABG Medical IPO, for that matter: CABG was dissolved in 2006 when the technology failed in FDA trials.)

I told him that I would think about it. But that didn't take long, because the venture capitalist that had been closest to moving forward soon told me that all investments were on hold pending administrative changes at the highest levels of his fund. I called Burklund and told him that I wanted to present the idea of going public to the board of MELA. He came to the next board meeting in June 2004 and we did just that.

The three directors representing the $9 million that had just been invested discussed it with their angel network. They liked the idea in principle, but they and the rest of the board didn't think that I'd be able to get it done. Without a viable alternative, though, they agreed to let me go ahead and try. To their surprise, we did pull off an IPO—an extremely successful one at that, raising $21 million from new investors for a $50 million post-IPO valuation—but I'll get back to that in chapter seven. So they didn't pull out their money. We'd dodged a potentially fatal blow, and found ourselves with another chance—a rare thing in the medtech realm.

Having informed the board that I was going to proceed with Askion, in May I asked Tomek and Nyq to move to Germany during the design for manufacturing process. (Tomek remained in Germany until he left the company in 2013.) I personally spent a week per month at Askion for just under two years. The challenge was not actually to build a *better* handheld, but rather a mass-producible handheld that matched the optical properties of the T1, T2, and T3 handhelds used in clinical studies to date. This is an important point: when you're starting from scratch, better is, well . . . better. But because we weren't starting from scratch, we didn't actually want Askion to make our design better or use better materials, because those would have provided us with a completely different optical profile. And a totally different optical profile wouldn't match the optical profile upon which the algorithms were developed and the vast clinical data we had amassed to date. We needed the new systems made with reliable, reproducible, and scalable methods, but with a final product that still matched the optical profile of the T1, T2, and T3 "probes." We needed *new*, *reliable*, and *robust*—but not *better*. Otherwise, we'd have to start from square one, which would have taken even more time and more money!

There was much Sturm und Drang in the process, and Nyq would often show me examples of how the new handheld prototypes were not consistent with T1-3, and then I would have to mediate those battles. When I wasn't doing the rest of my job, that is: attending banking conference presentations, managing the team back in New York, dealing with the board, maintaining goodwill with the dermatology community, and eventually overseeing the rebooted clinical studies to validate the new prototypes.

Askion made big contributions to the product, including changing the optical path from 90 degrees to a linear 180 degrees, designing a new optical block that matched the properties of the folded block, partnering with Zeiss to make the lens, and creating precision fixtures for highly controlled and reproducible manufacturing. Tomek worked hand in hand with the Askion hardware team, and Nyq developed all of the manufacturing software that controlled assembly, testing, and release, in addition to the algorithms that made the system operate. When in Gera, we ate lunch at a little sterile cafeteria on the research park grounds that was open for just a single hour and offered the exact same weekly menu every single week. All of us MELA employees that visited Askion called it The Communist Café. But we liked it—for a group that had suffered some unpleasant surprises, we all welcomed knowing what we were going to eat every single day of the week.

Innovation REALLY Is Hard Enough

MUCH OF WHAT we went through in the early days of MELA would be considered "standard" for development stage companies.

Challenges during the process are not so shocking. (They shoot horses, don't they?) Still, there's an important point to be made: if any one of the more than a dozen critical junctures outlined above did not break the way they did, the company would have been dead and gone by now. That's the norm, not the exception. Most companies fail because one of these turns of events delivers a fatal wound. The only thing that was not normal, not par for the course, and not entirely expected was the sheer *number* of problems that we encountered and overcame. The amazing thing is that we somehow got through it and MelaFind is on the market, saving the lives of people we will never even know. I get goose bumps every time I say that.

We encountered numerous engineering challenges along the way and we solved them. When we were selling stock to new investors in the IPO, we basically told them that we'd goofed; we knew we had something great but that we'd tried to get it done on the cheap and couldn't. We promised to fix the manufacturing glitches, execute the studies, get the product approved, and on the market. We said we'd solve our internal problems, and we did. Our investors stayed with us, too—during the two years it took us to get to where we needed to be to start the pivotal trial again, the stock held tight around $5.75 a share. By January 2007, we were back where we thought we'd been when we'd started the original trial. I'd learned a few things about making assumptions, I'd deepened my relationships with some of the key people at the company, and we had a technically robust product that worked and everything lined up for a smooth ride through FDA trials.

Once again, though, it turned out I had no idea what was about to happen next. If you'd listened to President Obama, you might have been excited for us. After all, he'd declared that, "transparency and the rule of law will be the touchstones of my Administration." When it came to MELA, though, there wouldn't be anything of the sort. Instead, the FDA would break several laws during our approval process, ignore a few others, invent a few more, and then try to cover it all up. We'd find a way to beat them in the end, but that came a lot later. In the meantime, we were faced with a lack of transparency the likes of which we'd never seen. The FDA was broken. It still is. But

I believe I know how to fix it. I'll get to that in chapter eleven, but before I do that, I'll show you just how broken it really is.

The rest of the book will lay out a number of setbacks that followed our getting back on course. Nothing had changed there. But the difference is that the earlier setbacks were our own fault. Those that followed should *not* have happened; *could not* have been expected; and will absolutely kill medical innovation if they are allowed to continue happening to other companies less lucky than us.

4

FDA Part I:
What's Supposed to Happen

What Did We Expect?

GENERALIZING ABOUT THE FDA approval process is like generalizing about snowflakes. While every medical device application shares some basic traits—they're all medical devices, and they're all seeking U.S. government approval—at root, every new device is ultimately novel (thus prompting the need for a new clearance or approval), and a generalization about those approvals (or rejections) will only get you so far in the end. I do so now for the sake of explication, to make clear what we had reasonable cause to expect from our efforts to get MelaFind from the trial stage and into the market. At the beginning, we thought we were better positioned than most, due to both a binding protocol agreement and designation for expedited review. We couldn't have been more wrong about that.

There are only two types of device approvals. The first, 510k applications, is for devices that are similar to others that have already been approved. The second is called a PMA, or premarket approval, for novel products or those that pose significant clinical risk. For 510k's, the applicant needs only to show "substantial equivalence" to a previously approved device in key properties and intended function. PMAs, on the other hand, require robust clinical trials to prove that the device is safe and effective.

The statute calls for products to be reviewed and approval determinations made in 90 "review" days for 510k products and 180 for PMAs (Source: FDA website). The review clock isn't much of a clock, as it can be temporarily stopped by the FDA almost at their whim (more on that later), so with respect to the actual calendar, 510ks usually take three-to six months while PMA's can take two to three years or more. The more novel and breakthrough the product, of course, the longer the review time can be.

In 2011, the year that MelaFind was approved, the average number of days for the approval of 510ks and PMAs were 140 and 266, respectively. Time to 510(k) approval has been steadily increasing in recent years—a disturbing trend that the FDA now says has leveled or even reversed thanks to a 36-point Plan of Action begun in 2011 (Source: FDA website). Most industry experts are dubious about these assertions. Time will tell.

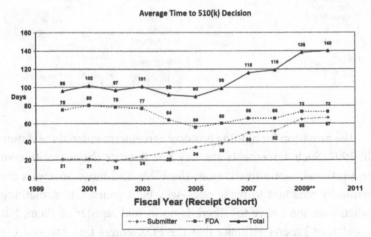

Average Time to 510(k) Decision

*SE and NSE decisions only: Averages may not sum to total due to rounding
** 2009, 2010 some cohort still open as of July 5, 2011 data may change

Because MelaFind represented a breakthrough technology for a significant disease, it was designated a Class III PMA device. This meant that we had a nominal review day target of 180 days, but because we were also granted an expedited review, meaning that the clinical, manufacturing and engineering aspects of the device were to be evaluated in parallel, and not sequentially, we thought that the actual calendar period might be somewhat abbreviated, perhaps getting us over the finish line in just one year.

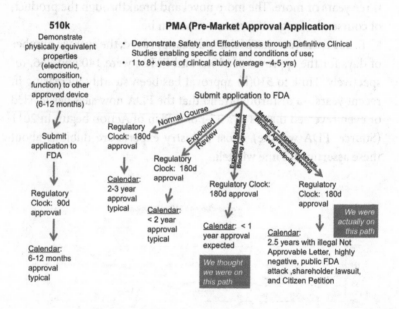

The provision for binding protocol agreements entered the statute in 1997. Such agreements are very rare because they constitute an institutional commitment from the FDA, and most reviewers are naturally reluctant to make one—why bind yourself to something when you don't have to? There is no formal register of them, but regulatory experts estimate that the FDA enters into just one (or perhaps two) each year. Because the agreements require extensive discussion with companies before a study begins and a definitive determination of the bases and thresholds for the determination of safety and effectiveness, they effectively constitute a "pre-review" without it being called such. As a result, a company that submits a complete PMA that fulfills the requirements of a binding protocol agreement, while also having the application designated for expedited review, might reasonably expect to proceed through the review/ approval process in under a year. That was us.

Our reasonable expectation didn't quite pan out. Despite the fact that we met *all* of our clinical endpoints, it took us two-and-a-half years to get through the process. The actual cost, the opportunity cost, the loss of goodwill in the dermatology community, and the impact on investors and shareholder profile of MELA Sciences caused by this senseless delay were enormous. And they continued to increase until the day that I left the company in June 2013.

The needless detours that we encountered were significant, caused by roadblocks and craters in the road that should never have been there, including: an unlawful Not Approvable Letter, deceitful and flawed FDA analyses of the MelaFind pivotal trial data, false public accusations by the FDA that the protocol was not followed (more on this in chapter five), as well as extremely negative public statements by the FDA that influenced investor sentiment, drove our stock into the hands of short-selling manipulators, and sullied the product in the eyes of the dermatology community. But MelaFind could not be stopped. Thanks to a Citizen Petition calling for transparency and adherence to the rule of law, a white paper by a left-leaning policy think tank, and a Congressional hearing at which senior FDA officials admitted that a mistake had been made (more on this in chapter six), we eventually arrived at our destination. Unfortunately, the car, which should have been running on cruise control, was still running out of alignment as of 2013, thanks to a broken FDA (more on this in chapter nine).

Establishing Rapport with FDA

THE FDA HAS recommended publicly that companies meet "early and often" with them before and during the review process. And they're right about that—building early rapport with the review team is absolutely critical. Before I joined MELA, a retired Office Director named Roger Schneider, during multiple meetings with the FDA's Office of Science and Technology, had advised the executive team. Several of those meetings included individuals from the review division within which the MelaFind PMA resided, what is known today as the *Division* of Surgical Devices (back then, it was the Division of General, Restorative, and Neurologic Devices) in the *Office* of Device Evaluation (ODE), in the *Center* for Devices and Radiologic Health (CDRH) of the Food and Drug Administration (FDA). If that sounds like a big bureaucracy to you, it should. Even those of us in the business can get lost trying to keep track.

MelaFind had been designated a "non-significant risk" device and, as such, the FDA had informed MELA that an Investigational Device Exemption (IDE) application to the FDA would not be necessary. That sounded great to the team, but not to me. For starters, an IDE is a very important method by which that rapport with the FDA is established. A big part of an IDE, which is essentially a request to the FDA for "permission" to begin studies of a new product in humans, is the clinical protocol. So the IDE process provides a level of confidence that things are headed in the right direction. With no IDE, you've effectively had no meeting of the minds on the protocol. And starting a big expensive study for the approval of a breakthrough product without getting significant FDA input beforehand spells T R O U B L E.

As I mentioned above, MELA had been speaking to the Office of Science & Technology. That was better than speaking to no one at all, but it meant nothing from a regulatory approval perspective. That division is charged with keeping a pulse on the state of evolving technologies so that the FDA can see the direction of medical science, anticipate it, and factor it into their planning with respect to the talent and expertise needed to review and regulate future technologies. But the Office of Science & Technology does not approve products.

Even more worrisome was that the protocol that emerged from those meetings was just 13 pages long. It wasn't very specific, nor did it include all of the critical requirements of a Phase III study, the part of the process that's designed to provide definitive proof of safety and effectiveness. If the review division had been formally involved in the discussions, the protocol would not have passed muster. And if the protocol had been part of an IDE, in my opinion, the IDE would not have been approved.

I had concluded during my original diligence process with the founders that the FDA was not taking the project seriously, and I needed to change that. So in January 2004, I called the FDA. No one called me back. I wrote a letter. I received no reply. I sent emails to the parties representing the review division in previous meetings. No one replied to those emails. I called again. Nothing. This went on for a month, and it was something that I had never experienced in my career.

I concluded that the review division was simply not interested in the product, and I attributed that to them not understanding certain basic principles of a diagnostic, that is *sensitivity* (the ability to detect when disease is present) and *specificity* (the ability to rule out disease when it is absent). How could I conclude that they might not understand the basic principles of a diagnostic imaging product? Well, that's the job of the guys down the hall in the Radiologic Health *Division* (in the *Office* of In Vitro Diagnostics and Radiologic Health), not the *Division* of Surgical Devices (in the *Office* of Device Evaluation).

I know that this sounds funny. How could people whose job it is to regulate products (a) not even understand them or (b) not be interested in them even if they did? Remember the bureaucracy! The left hand often doesn't know what the right hand is doing, and innovative products can sometimes get lost in the middle. What's more, there is obviously less accountability at this stage of the process—*before* a formal application for approval has even been submitted. My best guess was that the review division felt that they had already given enough feedback—a box had been checked, and no more work was required.

So why was the MelaFind application in the hands of the Division of Surgical Devices? Because all dermatology devices are in put in that division, without any more consideration than that. Get it? The confusion about which division the application belonged in was natural, mind you, because MelaFind was the first diagnostic device of its kind invented for use in dermatology. But it's the company's job to navigate the FDA—not the other way around. Ridiculous, but true.

Dr. Alicia Toledano, the statistical consultant that MELA had contracted with, worked at Brown University. A noted expert in the field of imaging-based diagnostic products, she was also on the team of external statisticians that the NIH (National Institutes of Health) consulted for the huge mammogram studies that demonstrated the impact of early detection of breast cancer. Even though she is barely five feet tall, Dr. Toledano is all that, and more—she's a special government employee, meaning that she's been vetted and cleared to consult for the government, and is often invited by the FDA to sit on advisory committees of diagnostic products. You can't get better than that—someone that the NIH consults with for the design of their studies, and someone the FDA consults with for product reviews. And our statistical plan was excellent.

Still, I remained concerned that we were talking to the wrong people at the FDA and that we should try to get the PMA moved to the *Division* of Radiologic Health. Why? Because I thought the reviewers in that division would better understand the product and the trade-offs between sensitivity (yin) and specificity (yang). It's easy to be 100% sensitive to melanoma—you simply consider *every* mole suspicious and therefore worthy of biopsy, in which case you will catch 100% of them. The problem is, your specificity will be zero. Or, you could consider no moles suspicious, giving you 100%

specificity but 0% sensitivity, i.e. you will miss every melanoma. When determining thresholds in a diagnostic test, it's all about the tradeoffs. Conversations like that happen every day in the Division of Radiologic Health, but not so much in Surgical Devices. That's why I wanted it moved. (See FDA Organizational Chart—Source: FDA website.)

Our consultants agreed with me. Roger Schneider told me that there was only one person he knew in Washington with the savvy and insight to get a PMA moved within the FDA—Mark Heller, a leading food & drug lawyer who had previously worked for the FDA and is intimately knowledgeable about device laws and regulations.

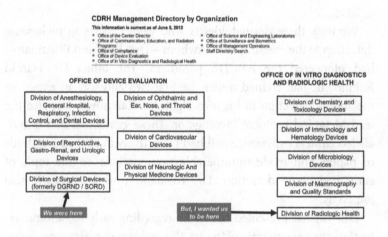

I hate lawyers.

I was schooled by Aileen Ryan and Bob McCormack *not* to involve lawyers when you're working with the FDA.

I had never used lawyers in meetings with the FDA.

I hired him anyway, and went to DC to meet with him on March 16, 2004.

A Funny Thing Happened on the Way to Moving a PMA

MOVING A PMA from one FDA division to another is not something that reflects well on the division from which it is moved, and it also raises red flags with the receiving division. But I truly felt that we needed to convince the FDA that the Division of Surgical Devices was the wrong group to review MelaFind.

Heller's efforts to set up a meeting to that end were about as successful as my own. After two months of nothing, I was by that point contemplating a different approach, he surprised me by informing me that he'd heard from the FDA and that they were open to a meeting. It was scheduled on a mutually convenient date—June 4, 2004.

We took three dermatologists who were experts in melanoma detection to the meeting, two of whom—Drs. Kopf and Friedman— had pioneered the ABCDE paradigm. The other, Dr. Harold Rabinovitz. had trained under the first two and was an expert in melanoma detection in his own right. Dr. Rabinovitz was also the lead MelaFind protocol investigator. These gentlemen had unparalleled clinical experience and had collectively published hundreds of papers and made innumerable presentations on the topic of early melanoma detection. Dr. Toledano (our statistician) also joined us.

Our experts presented the issues regarding early melanoma detection, the current state of the art, the problem of melanomas being missed at their earliest, most curable stages, and the high ratio of biopsies performed in an effort to identify (or rule out) melanoma relative to the actual number of melanomas found. They also presented the fundamental premise upon which the protocol design was based, which was that because melanoma is so difficult to detect at the earliest stages and that totally benign lesions can look like early melanomas, a biopsy of all the lesions in the study was an absolute must. (The alternative—using dermatologists' clinical impressions of the lesions—was an unacceptable basis on which to judge the performance of a diagnostic system. Because they weren't always right. That's why MelaFind was needed in the first place!)

We presented the eligible patient population, the study entry criteria, the protocol-specified procedures, and our primary endpoints, that is, what we were aiming to show. We also presented the plan for data acquisition and the plan to obtain interpretations of all biopsy results by a central expert panel so as to provide for a rigorous gold standard of comparison. And Dr. Toledano presented the rationale behind the proposed analyses.

As a Steven Covey fan, I always "begin with the end in mind." The end of the device approval game is the package insert, that is, the approved labeling of the product. And the most important part of the package insert is the claim or indications for use. All discussions about a protocol should flow from the desired intended use, which is the target that you're aiming to hit. The claim that we proposed to the FDA in 2004 was:

MelaFind creates multi-spectral digital dermoscopic images and performs an objective evaluation of the degree of disorganization of pigmented lesions of the skin. The system is intended as an aid to dermatologists in evaluating lesions that have one or more clinical characteristics of melanoma, but a decision to biopsy has not yet been rendered.

Seems simple enough, right? In other words, MelaFind is a tool to help *dermatologists* (this is a critical point—more on it later) when they're scratching their heads about what to do with a lesion. Moreover, it is intended to be used like an echocardiogram—when more information is needed—as opposed to an EKG—to screen for disease.

The people on the FDA's side of the table at our June meeting included reviewers, branch level managers, and the division of Surgical Devices Director, Dr. Celia Witten. Dr. Witten is a supremely smart and highly regarded figure. She moderated the meeting, and kept it under 60 minutes while listening quite skeptically. She was engaged as she clarified and crisply and accurately restated the points that her people were making and, with her own tilt, basically told us that what we were proposing was not likely to be acceptable to the FDA let alone stand up to review when the PMA was ultimately submitted.

That wasn't entirely surprising, in part because it was her very first exposure to the product, although several of her staff had attended prior meetings with the company. They asked some questions that underscored a lack of understanding of the practicalities of early melanoma detection—the way dermatologists approach atypical pigmented skin lesions—and even the clarifying responses of our three expert dermatologists did not seem to satisfy them. There were obvious points of confusion, a few things that we hadn't thought of, and the classic "go away" attitude I had seen first-hand many times in my career.

In short, it was the "Oh shit, close the company!" meeting that I referred to in chapter one. So it wasn't really that bad, as we were actually on familiar ground, and finally had something to work with! We also had someone to work with—Dr. Witten was smart, and smart FDA people (like Bob Temple) can be convinced with data and science. And we had the data and science. I was happy, of course, that we got substantive feedback and specific points of inquiry that were eminently addressable. And I was thrilled that I hadn't let the team start the pivotal trial before meaningfully engaging the FDA, because, as the day's events had just demonstrated, that would have resulted in a catastrophe. (I was also warming to the fact that moving the PMA might not be necessary for approval, but the next set of volleys would decide that.)

We went back home and attacked—hard and fast—all of the questions that had been raised. We prepared a succinct point-by-point rebuttal to their major objections, and included additional papers from the dermatologic literature to support the points that our experts had made in the meeting on June 4. We submitted a revised protocol on June 21, 2004 in which we addressed the FDA's specific issues with certain protocol procedures, added methods and provisions for independent 3rd party domiciling of all our results, and expanded the background section to better explain the state of medicine behind this disease. A second meeting was scheduled for August 6, 2004.

Just as I had expected, that meeting was drastically different than the previous one. There was a greater receptivity to the idea that the claim we were seeking was medically valuable and appropriate. I saw the proverbial light bulbs going off in their heads, the most important of which was Dr. Witten's. The FDA exhibited a deeper level of thinking about the various topics, specifically the ultimate intended use of MelaFind and the appropriate study population that would best validate that intended use. They showed an appropriate, rather than reflexive, skepticism, and raised more informed questions that we needed to address. If the meeting on June 4 could best be characterized by "go away," the meeting on August 6 could be characterized by, "Oh, that's what you meant!" Moreover, by the end of the August meeting, we were in harmony on the most critical points.

I asked Dr. Witten how to best to formalize our mutual understanding. What I wanted, in other words, was a formal "blessing" of the protocol by the FDA. This is typically done through an IDE application or an exchange of meeting minutes with the FDA so that their files contain your understanding and your files contain theirs, with the hoped-for result that both parties are satisfied with a mutually agreed-upon way forward. She said that she didn't want us to file an IDE because as a non-significant risk study, it wasn't necessary, but did advise a final follow-up phone call to tie up any critical loose ends as well as a subsequent exchange of minutes. We couldn't have asked for more.

Things were looking so good, in fact, that I felt that we might be eligible for one of those very rare legally binding protocol agreements with the agency. I wasn't familiar with the details of a binding agreement, and was concerned that adding one to the process could take more time—maybe six months or more—than whatever extra certainty it might provide was worth. I had promised our investors that I would have a relationship with the FDA secured by the end of June, and we were already in August.

But there was no harm in exploring the idea. "Hypothetically," I asked, "if I were to ask for a binding protocol agreement, how long would that take?" She replied that she felt very good about how the discussions between the FDA and MELA had evolved, appreciated us bringing our experts in twice, felt that we had reached strong fundamental agreement, and that she would agree to a binding protocol agreement. But she hadn't actually answered my question. And so I repeated it. Her reply: "If you keep the items of the agreement restricted to the most critical elements, we could do it in thirty days." Sold! I respected Dr. Witten, and knowing that the smoothness of any FDA approval process ultimately comes down to the people involved, I was optimistic about our chances with her. But this was something else entirely: a binding protocol agreement would effectively remove even the "people" risk from the equation. And if it only took 30 days, it was certainly worth the added time!

But that wasn't the end of the good news. Dr. Witten then said she thought MelaFind might be eligible for Expedited Review Status. On this one I didn't hesitate: I said that we would submit an application after the study commenced. I also asked Dr. Witten to designate a single reviewer on the team with whom MELA could maintain regular contact during the study so that when it was complete and the PMA filed, things could proceed as efficiently as possible toward a 180-day review and approval determination. Dr. Witten said that wouldn't be necessary since we'd had extensive discussions from the outset and had come to agreement on the critical items—and that the next time we'd need to get together wouldn't be until we had the data from the study.

The final point that Dr. Witten made was that MelaFind would be subject to an Advisory Committee Panel. In response to that, I laid out a case for the Panel to be supplemented with dermatologists—those who diagnose melanoma—rather than just the existing roster of the General and Plastic Surgery Devices Panel. She replied that they would most likely supplement the panel with members of the Dermatologic Drugs Advisory Committee. I asked that they focus on that process expeditiously because inviting and qualifying disinterested outside experts can be a lengthy process and having dermatologists with expertise in early melanoma detection was critical to the panel understanding MelaFind's capabilities. She said that they would do so.

This was all phenomenal news. We were speaking about panel meetings and panel constitution *before* the pivotal study had even started. We were in very rare territory. We had an incredible relationship with the FDA. We'd nailed it.

No Pain, No Gain

WE RETURNED TO New York and started working with great optimism and energy. Maybe too much energy. On a Saturday at the end of June, Adele and I were playing doubles tennis. She was lining up a backhand, and suddenly—crack!—she'd broken her left foot. I carried her to the car, took her to the emergency room, and an x-ray confirmed a Jones Fracture of the distal portion of the 5th metatarsal (the bones forming the arch of the foot that connect to the toes). It's a common sports injury. The orthopedist at the Hospital for Special Surgery in New York recommended casting and twelve weeks of rest. If it hadn't healed at that point, she might need surgery. We got Adele a Roll-a-Bout, an ingenious wheeled transport device like a child's scooter. It was quite substantial with four real tires, a tubular A-frame with a padded horizontal area on which to kneel, and a hand brake.

But one injury begat another: One day while getting out of the car, she lost her balance as she was waiting for me to get the thing positioned. I grabbed it by the top bar, lifted it with my arm extended in front of me and lurched forward with it, barely managing to get it underneath her before she fell. Me? I slipped, and suddenly experienced a terrible pain in my back. I couldn't move.

Crawling onto the MRI table at the hospital was excruciating. The good news: There was no structural damage. The bad news: I had severely strained the ligaments and muscles of my lower back. I couldn't sit. Driving was painful. The only remotely comfortable positions available to me were standing and laying flat. For the next 12 weeks, the only times that I actually sat down were during my 5:00AM drive to the Wilmington train station, and my 7:45PM drive home—a total of 24 minutes per day. I stood the entire trip on the trains, and I also worked standing up, using a tall file cabinet as my desk. I can't take Advil because of significant upper gastrointestinal issues, so if I made a false move, I felt it.

But the work had to go on, and so it did. We finished a memo addressing the FDA's final points, a revised protocol, and points of agreement under section 520(g)(7) of the Federal, Food, Drug, and Cosmetic Act, and requested a meeting to finalize the proposal for the binding protocol agreement. We submitted all that on September 2, 2004, and had a meeting with the FDA to finalize the protocol agreement on October 20. Crucial among the points of agreement: the size and entry criteria of the study, the determination of the basis of approval (demonstration of safety and effectiveness), and the threshold requirements for sensitivity (greater than 95%) and specificity (a statistically significant increase versus study dermatologists).

At the end of the meeting, Dr. Witten and I signed the binding protocol agreement. We now had a "relationship" with the FDA. Indeed, an October 29 letter from the agency, which contained a copy of the signed agreement, read, "We are in agreement that the following represents the most appropriate means for establishing the safety and effectiveness of the MelaFind device." And the punchline: "The agreement decision is binding both on the Center for Devices and Radiologic Health (CDRH) and the sponsor."

With the binding agreement in hand, our relationship was more like a marriage. It was a very rare, legally binding contract with the FDA—unchanging and immutable in the face of potentially changing review team composition, divisional and center leadership, and political or policy changes. The only way a binding agreement can be changed is if a significant new issue emerges, which never did. A binding protocol agreement doesn't address regulatory risk—it virtually eliminates it. At least that's what we thought.

Thanks to our lawyer, a funny thing happened on the way to moving a PMA from one FDA Division to another—the original division signed a binding protocol agreement!

Notwithstanding the above, I still hate lawyers.

The Honeymoon Phase

As I mentioned in chapter three, once we had the binding agreement in hand, we raised the second tranche of the Series C investment ($9 million), conducted an investigators meeting in New York, and started the pivotal trial. Even when we had to stop the trial due the technical difficulties I've already described, the FDA responded by agreeing to our plan to address any related concerns. The interactions with the FDA were appropriate and fair.

Nearly two years later, when our manufacturing partner Askion had completed the prototyping work on robust systems "designed for manufacturing," we submitted another report to the FDA. In it, we outlined some minor changes we'd made to the pivotal trial protocol, including adding a litany of melanoma risk factor questions we planned to capture for each patient. The questionnaire was designed by Marianne Berwick, PhD., and Nancy Thomas, MD, experts in melanoma epidemiology from the University of New Mexico and Duke University, respectively. We asked that the FDA confirm that the amended protocol was valid and covered under the auspices of the October 20, 2004 binding protocol agreement and if we were cleared to restart the pivotal study.

On January 4, 2006, we received notification from the FDA that "the revised protocol does not alter the pivotal study design but only improves . . . as, such, these changes do not alter the signed Study Agreement . . . and no additional response is required."

We conducted additional clinical studies with the new systems over the next several months, and then applied for expedited review of the MelaFind PMA on August 11, 2006. The FDA requires that a new product needs to meet just one of six criteria to qualify for expedited review. We received notification on October 4, 2006, signed by Mark Melkerson, the new division director (Dr. Witten had left by that time), that expedited status had been granted. We'd even met *three* criteria and not just one:

1. The MelaFind device described in your application does meet the criteria of a device intended to affect a condition that is life threatening and is irreversibly debilitating. Early or better detection of melanoma has the potential to reduce both life-altering surgeries and reduce mortality due to melanoma.

2. Use of this device has potential significant benefit to patients by reducing unnecessary biopsies for suspicious melanomas thus reducing patient anxiety as well as potential biopsy adverse events such as scarring, infection, and pain.

3. The MelaFind device is a breakthrough technology in that it uses multiple wavelengths of light to produce multiwave reflected optical signals for lesion diagnosis.

As I've already explained, the statutorily defined review period for a PMA is six months, or 180 days. But it is the rare exception, not the rule, that the 180-day review period is actually realized. The FDA has the ability to stop and start the review clock whenever they want through a variety of means, including "formally" asking questions (via letter), citing major deficiencies, issuing not approvable letters, requesting that sponsors submit amendments, as well as other means.

The questions need not be profound, and some of the deficiencies they cite can make one wonder about their definition of the word "major." Most often they're very simple and the responses are something like, "Table X in Volume Y, on Page Z of the original filed application contains a listing of_____." But it doesn't matter. If they ask it, the clock stops! And they do this, whether warranted or not, in an attempt to adhere to that 180-day review period. The FDA submits a scorecard to Congress as part of the User Fee Acts (PDUFA and MDUFA) showing their performance vis-a-vis the 180-day target review period for all sorts of applications (i.e., not just PMAs) as well as review targets for 510ks (90 days), and supplements. In this game, the cards are stacked in favor of the FDA. Both industry people and savvy investors know this.

So, in actuality, for a 180-day review, the norm is about 365 calendar days, but it's also not uncommon for them to take up to two calendar years. As amazing and ridiculous as this may sound, this is the system we've got. The law does provide for remedies when review times exceed the 180-day clock. (Which is an amazing occurrence, if you think about it, because the clock can be turned on and off by the FDA at their whim.) If a company's pursuit of approval has been deemed diligent, they can file for patent extensions covering the time lost during clinical testing AND FDA review. But the rules governing those extensions aren't really equitable, as only one patent in the patent estate can be extended. It makes absolutely no sense to not extend every patent in the estate but, again, those are the rules, for now. (I'll have a lot more to say about this later, when I outline how to fix the FDA.)

An expedited review does not shorten the review period "target." Nor does it stop the FDA from using all the tools at its disposal to stop the clock in order to make their scorecard as favorable as possible. Instead, it simply provides for parallel as opposed to sequential review by those FDA groups responsible for the different sections of the submission—clinical, manufacturing, and engineering. That said, it does generally have the effect of shortening overall review time.

One of the common complaints about PMA reviews (as well as those for new drug and biologics licenses), is that the FDA engages in "shifting the goal posts." This means that what the FDA told you would be acceptable before you started the costly, intensive, and time consuming clinical trials gets changed on the back end, after all of the work has been performed, the positive results obtained, and money spent. This is sickening, but it happens to companies every day. And it usually happens because of changing personnel on the review team, when the new people have a different way of thinking than the old ones. (Turnover at the FDA is a huge problem, mostly due to poor leadership.)

The way to mitigate the risk of "shifting goal posts" is to have a "relationship" with the FDA before you start. That is, to engage with the agency and have a meeting of the minds with your review team. Even better: if you exchange minutes of meetings with the FDA and both the Agency's minutes and your minutes say the same thing on the major points. Even better than that: if you have a letter from the FDA confirming that understanding. These are the typical ways that industry tries to cement the goal posts, but, in reality, they are usually set in sand.

We, however, had the Rolls Royce of relationships with the FDA in the form of a very rare legally binding protocol agreement. With expedited review on top of that, it was actually a Bentley, and it was purring. Our goal posts were not just set in stone. No, they were anchored to bedrock, to the very foundations of the world. Or so we thought.

Zooming Along with the Top Down

WE STARTED THE pivotal trial in January of 2007. Twenty-three investigators (dermatologists) from seven different clinical study sites enrolled patients and provided data. The clinical team was responsible for the conduct of the study. That included everything from compliance with good clinical practices (informed consent, source document review, data integrity) to facilitating a central reading of all biopsy samples by consulting pathologists (Martin Mihm, Harvard; Victor Prieto, MD Anderson; and Paul Googe & Roy King, Kentucky), blinded data transfer to the data custodian, and site auditing.

Regarding that data transfer, the study itself was "blinded"—that is, the dermatologists were not provided the MelaFind results lest their biopsy decision be influenced, which would render the comparison between dermatologists and MelaFind moot. Because the final MelaFind results were not provided, the Protocol Agreement stipulated that certain elements of the software did not have to be finalized until the study was completed. So while the study was being conducted and the biopsy readings were processed, Nyq, Dina, and the algorithm team were finalizing the final piece of software (the classifier), which would be invoked by the independent data custodian who would then provide the results only to the statistician, Dr. Alicia Toledano.

The study ended up including 1800 lesions from over 1300 patients. It was the largest positive prospective study in melanoma detection ever performed, and remains so to this day. On January 2009, top-line results were announced—MelaFind met both co-primary endpoints and all secondary endpoints, which is extremely rare in clinical studies. Even in successful studies, it's usually the case that only one of two primary endpoints is met. Or the primary endpoint is missed and a few secondary endpoints are satisfied. It's very rare that *all* the endpoints in a clinical study are met.

The pivotal study showed 98.3% sensitivity to melanoma with a statistically significant higher specificity than dermatologists when they weren't using MelaFind (10% versus 4%). A 98.3% sensitivity means that MelaFind detected 172/175 melanomas and "pre-melanomas" on the study. Consider this relative to the sensitivity of dermatologists, assessed in a parallel study with dermatologists not participating in the pivotal trial, which showed that dermatologists elected to biopsy just 18 of 23 melanomas for a sensitivity of just 78%. The FDA had suggested this adjunctive study—they wanted the investigators to take pictures of the lesions that were enrolled in the pivotal study to allow for additional confirmation of MelaFind's efficacy. When it came to specificity, MelaFind considered 6% more truly benign lesions to be clinically insignificant than did dermatologists, which would mean 6% *fewer* unnecessary biopsies than dermatologists would have otherwise ordered. The results were not only statistically significant, they were also very clinically significant.

We announced the findings of the study on February 13, 2009 and submitted the PMA application in June. The message of the PMA was simple—here is the binding protocol agreement specifying the hurdles for safety and effectiveness; here are the results of the pivotal study, which showed that those hurdles were cleared; here is the

expedited review designation; please send notice of approval immediately because we have lives to save and a company to build.

In early July 2009, we received a letter from the FDA indicating
that the PMA had been accepted for filing—a preliminary review
had found the application to be complete and capable of undergoing
rigorous review. In that letter, the FDA also affirmed that which they
had told us during the October 2004 meeting at which we had signed
the binding protocol agreement, namely, "A meeting of the General
and Plastic Surgery Devices Panel will be held at which your PMA
will be reviewed." (Much more on this later.)

Fantastic. The review clock had started—if it were not stopped
(low odds, yes, but one is allowed to dream), we might even receive
approval by the end of the year or in early 2010.

The advantage of an expedited review became apparent almost
immediately. Before we'd even received any questions from any
members of the review team, the compliance team had scheduled
audits of our offices (clinical data, design development, and manufacturing controls), our clinical study sites, and our manufacturing
vendors, including Askion in Germany. This was something that I'd
never experienced before in my career—the FDA was moving faster
than I had ever seen.

More Pain, More Gain

I DECIDED THAT I would be present at Askion in Germany during
the FDA audit, which meant flying out on a Sunday evening to
Frankfurt, taking a connecting flight to Leipzig, and a drive to Gera.
I also decided to play basketball that Sunday morning. And I broke
my left hand.

I knew that I'd broken it. I heard it crack, watched it swell, and
agonized as it throbbed. But I kept on playing. (My reasoning: if
I had left, there wouldn't have been enough guys to go full court.
So, I stuck it out. What can I say? I'm a team player.) I kept playing
so long that I wasn't able to get to th emergency room for an X-ray
before heading to the airport. Oops. I flew to Germany in pain; the

flight crew gave me fresh ice all night. Even the weight of the ice on the break hurt.

When the FDA auditor arrived at Askion, he laid out what we could expect over the next 48 to 72 hours—his desire to meet at the end of each day, and the expected course of the audit. Everything was pretty routine, and there were no surprises in the first three hours, so I decided to sneak out and get that X-ray. Lutz Doms, President of Askion, took me to the hospital. The X-ray showed an impressive break of one of my metacarpals, and the doctors recommended immediate casting and surgery back in the U.S. I emailed the X-rays to my brother, who is a surgeon-turned-rehabilitation medicine expert, who sent them on to a hand surgeon in New York City. He confirmed that I'd no doubt need surgery.

I stayed all week, with my hand elevated and throbbing, and met with the auditor at the end of each day. The audit was very successful—no torpedoes, all addressable items. We formulated a plan for how we would provide responses to the auditor's questions and enhance the quality system for the next audit. (These are the tedious yet mandatory and extensive formal policies and procedures that govern what you do, how you do it, how you record the what and how of what you are doing.)

I flew home and met with the hand surgeon. He was amazed that I had any grip strength, let alone was able to move my fingers at all. He decided that surgery might not be necessary, and instead put on soft casting and recommended some exercises that I need to do three times a day. They were very painful and rendered my hand quite achy for an hour after I did them. But they worked: after 12 weeks, my hand had healed such that I was able to use it without the soft cast.

The Day-100 Meeting

NINETY DAYS INTO a PMA review, the FDA is supposed to provide questions about the application. One hundred days into a PMA review, the FDA and sponsors are supposed to meet to discuss the application and review plan going forward. Our Day-100 meeting took place on September 17, but the 90-day questions didn't arrive until the end of the day on September 15, via email. So, the meeting really turned out to be a real-time response to those questions.

The questions centered on the design of the pivotal study, most of which had been addressed in the binding protocol agreement. We frequently reminded the review team that the study and the PMA review were occurring under the auspices of that agreement. I wasn't pleased that we needed to do this, but given that there were a few new members of the team, including a new division director, I wasn't too upset. It was simply that such questions were a waste of time.

We submitted our day-100 meeting minutes on September 22, which summarized our answers to the questions that they'd sent us just prior to the day-100 meeting, stressed the concept and legal framework of the binding protocol agreement, and reinforced our urgency regarding the timing and composition of the panel. On October 7, the FDA sent us a formal letter that stopped the review clock. This was upsetting because it was simply the day-90 questions, which we had not only already answered "live" at the day-100 meeting, but also had provided high level written responses in the form of meeting minutes on September 22! Not only that, the bulk of the questions were answered in the binding protocol agreement anyway. But what could we do? These are the review clock games that the FDA plays, and you just have to deal with it. Again, it meant more wasted time. We provided detailed formal responses to the questions on October 26, 2009.

And then came the good news. On November 23, 2009, I received an email from a member of the review team. It included this sentence: "It looks like we are heading toward a March date for the panel." The FDA had bought itself some review time by stopping the clock unnecessarily, but all was good in the end. Actually, all was *great*, because I had a call with several reviewers that same day about the timing of final approval. I mentioned that the next scheduled meeting of the General and Plastic Surgery Devices Panel was at the end of March. The purpose of that meeting was to discuss tanning booths, of all things, the very contraptions that bear significant responsibility for the rise in melanoma in young women. I thought I saw a chance for the FDA to pull off a real coup. On day one, they could introduce more regulation in the fight against melanoma. And on day two, they could move forward with a product that offered to help doctors improve their ability to detect melanoma when it's still curable. It could be a great PR opportunity for the agency, and for us as well. The timing couldn't have been better.

There's an important point to be made here. When it comes to most kinds of cancer, the single best way to reduce fatalities is through early detection. Why have deaths from breast cancer come down so much? Not because of chemotherapy, but because of mammograms. Why do people still die of ovarian cancer? Because they normally don't find it until it's the size of a grapefruit. Why are deaths from prostate cancer down? Because of publicity and a marked increase in screening. The FDA had recently approved yet another product that focused on late-stage melanoma and which only worked (i.e., prevented death) in about nine percent of those studied. But the potential for MelaFind was of an entirely different scope. If you catch melanomas early enough, *nobody* dies.

I asked the reviewers whether they might be targeting those same two days for the MelaFind panel. The response was typical—a "no comment" as well as an unnecessary reminder that they could schedule a panel meeting whenever they desired. My conclusion: they were planning our panel for the day after the tanning booth meeting in March. So I then asked, "*If* our panel meeting happened to end up on that same docket, and *if* there were no surprises, *might* we be in a position to suggest that final approval be issued on May 3?" They laughed. They'd had companies ask about being approved by Thanksgiving or Christmas Day, but never before on May 3. Was it my birthday, perhaps? I laughed in response. My birthday happened to be on May 4, I told them, but that had nothing to do with my question. May 3 was Melanoma Monday—the day that the American Academy of Dermatology would be kicking off Sun Season and Skin Cancer Awareness Month with free nation-wide screenings and events to highlight the risks of skin cancer—specifically, melanoma.

They were intrigued. I asked whether they thought that the FDA Public Relations office would consider a joint announcement by MELA and the FDA of the approval of a new diagnostic device for catching early-stage melanoma on that very day! They told me that it very well might. In order to be ready for the possibility, they said that they would endeavor to have all of the "paperwork" in order before the panel meeting so that if all went as planned, we'd likely only have to make some minor tweaks to it, and would absolutely be in a position to have final approval on May 3. I couldn't believe my ears! Still, just to make sure that I wasn't hearing what I wanted to hear, I asked what they meant by "paperwork." The response: "You know, the labeling." When you're talking about labeling, you're talking about a product that's nearly ready to hit the market, so the conclusion seemed obvious: Barring any disasters, we were on the final stretch.

We also talked about the need to supplement the panel with experts in melanoma. After the call, I provided the FDA with a list of all the dermatologists with whom we had ever worked—our investigators, our paid consultants, and our unpaid consultants with whom we'd had significant interaction, as well as those dermatologists who were recognized as thought leaders in melanoma but with whom we hadn't had any interaction. FDA rules stipulate that voting panel members must be disinterested and clear formal vetting, and there were a few melanoma experts whom I'd purposely never approached in clinical studies or even in general discussions about MelaFind in order to keep them eligible to serve in such a role.

We spent December preparing for a "MelaFind Summit" we'd scheduled in early January 2010 and to which we'd invited over 40 key opinion leaders (KOLs) in dermatology from all over the country. The goal of the summit was to educate them about the MelaFind data and hear their thoughts on the best ways to position the product as we prepared for commercialization following final FDA approval. We needed to identify KOLs who would be interested in presenting MelaFind data at scientific and medical conferences. The meeting was a huge success. We learned a tremendous amount and the top experts in dermatology (not simply melanoma) understood the data, got exposure to our team of scientific geniuses, and were in full support of the device. That kind of buy-in is critical for the launch of a breakthrough product. Everything was in place. We were doing it right. A big buzz started in the dermatologic community.

We were so focused on final preparations that we might have missed the January 2010 announcement that Dr. Jeffrey Shuren, the acting director of CDRH (Center of Devices and Radiologic Health), had been given the role permanently. Dr. Shuren had an aggressive agenda to completely revamp the device approval process, and he was unabashed in stating so. He also had a reputation for being somewhat anti-industry—that was the prevailing view in the medical technology world, and not just mine alone—but I'm sure he'd tell you differently. Anyway, he'd previously held various policy and planning positions within the FDA, and I believe he was given a mandate to change the device review process, with a particular focus on the quality issues with cardiac pacemakers, CT scans, and orthopedic devices that were in the news around that time.

His stated target was the 510k-approval process, but he also announced that he was developing new guidelines for all sorts of aspects of the device approval process, some of which crossed into PMA review. He added that the FDA would be re-reviewing already-approved products with an eye toward learning about ways to improve the review process and re-categorize certain classes of 510k devices. Reviewers aren't confined to 510K or PMA reviews—they work on both—so rewriting guidelines and re-reviewing approved products—even if most were 510k products—would have a significant effect on the PMA process. We didn't miss the news, but we also didn't think it really mattered to us.

After the MelaFind Summit, I called the FDA to ask about the timing of the panel meeting and the makeup of the panel roster. A reviewer told me that the FDA had decided they needed a few "more questions" answered before they could definitively schedule the panel. I asked them to send me the questions as soon as possible. I didn't know exactly what was happening—in hindsight, I'm convinced this had something to do with the new permanent director, the re-reviews of marketed products, and the new guidelines that were being drafted. Why? Because virtually the entire medical technology industry reported that their applications and discussions with the FDA fell off the track in January 2010, right around the time that Dr. Shuren was appointed. One example that garnered significant attention in the national press: Johnson & Johnson's sedation device, Sedasys, which received a non-approval letter almost at the exact same time that we soon did. (I'll return to the story of Sedasys in chapter six, when discussing how both MELA and J&J were featured in a 2011 article in *The Wall Street Journal* about the increasing unpredictability of FDA device reviews.)

In other words, there's a very serious likelihood that everything that followed had *nothing* to do with MelaFind whatsoever. We just happened to be in the wrong place (i.e., that particular point in the approval process) at the wrong time. Seen in that light, we were collateral damage, and it wasn't personal. Although it would soon become very personal indeed.

But I didn't know that in January 2010. Rather, I'd simply concluded that they really did need to extend the clock a little more—for whatever reason—and I was still hopeful that we'd be able to address their questions, have the panel meeting in March (or even April), and still obtain approval in time for Melanoma Monday. And if not by then, then at least in time for the summer.

That's what was supposed to happen.

5

FDA Part II: The Letter Bomb

Snail Mail, at That!

THE FDA'S STAFF is perfectly capable of getting in touch with you when they want to do so. I received an email and then a phone call on November 23, 2009 when they wanted to discuss the Advisory Committee Panel meeting in March 2010. So when they go radio silent when you're expecting to hear from them, you know something is afoot. It makes no sense to get upset with them. Losing a carefully collected reservoir of goodwill can only hurt your project when you do get it back on track.

We were told in January 2010 that they had some further questions for us. That was not unusual. What was: we didn't hear a peep from them for two months. Something was up. In November, the review team had communicated enthusiasm for *both* the March panel meeting and the goal of a joint May 3 announcement—on Melanoma Monday—of ultimate approval of MelaFind. And then we got a letter on March 19, via regular mail. And it exploded in our faces when we opened it.

The questions were there, but they were pretty much beside the point. Because the letter also stated that the PMA was Not Approvable at this time. It wasn't simply a few additional questions, but what is known as a formal FDA action letter. Action letters are supposed to come at the end of a review. By statute—that is, by *law*—MelaFind, as a breakthrough device, was due to be the subject of an advisory panel meeting, which is part of the review process. So the Not Approvable letter was not only premature, it was also unlawful. We were being denied our rights. What's more, from the standpoint of rational thinking, how could they have come to that view without obtaining the input of the medical practitioners who treat the disease? There was no similar device on the market, nothing like it at all. This is one of the main reasons that the statute requires advisory panel reviews for breakthrough products.

And, of course, the FDA had told us repeatedly—first in October 2004 at the protocol agreement signing meeting, then in July 2009 in the PMA "acceptance for filing" letter from the FDA, and finally during the November 23, 2009 phone call—that MelaFind would undergo panel review. It made absolutely no sense that the application would be deemed Not Approvable at that juncture. I felt that the surprise turn of events was in service of something that wasn't medical or scientific—structural or political, perhaps—some other agenda, and some other end.

When I read the seven questions—six of which were totally new and focused on the statistical analyses, and the seventh just a slight twist on something that had been discussed, asked and already answered—I became even more convinced that something sinister was afoot. And that it probably wasn't coming from the review team. I had a feeling that it was coming from much, much higher, and I thought I knew why. A few weeks after we received the Not Approvable Letter, the FDA announced new guidelines on how panel meetings were to be conducted. The final question of every panel meeting is something like this: "Does the panel vote in favor or against the approval of Product X for the following indication?" In other words, a formal vote by the panel that would serve as a "recommendation" of approval (or disapproval) of the product for the stated indications for use. In contrast, the new guideline stated that panel members would no longer be asked to vote on approvability. Rather, in addition to any medical questions that staff may have, the final question was to be replaced with three questions, focused on safety, effectiveness, and benefit/risk.

When I saw this, I had two reactions. The first was relief. The reason that they had issued a Not Approvable Letter, I figured, was to buy them more time. They knew that we could answer these simple questions very quickly, but they needed a 180-day stop of the clock. In other words, they didn't want us to go to panel until the new panel guidelines went into effect in May. I wasn't happy with the method by which they'd appeared to do so—a Not Approvable Letter—but the FDA simply does not care about the ramifications of its moves on sponsor companies, even if they are tiny, publicly-traded, one-product entities! Washington bureaucrats are immune to such mundane and practical matters, and can even have a deaf ear when it comes to regulation putting the brakes on the private sector in the midst of a horrible economic environment. The second thought was shock. What the FDA had done was against the law! The statute contains specific language that panels are to consider PMA's and make recommendations on the approval of the device. If they wanted to change the law, that was fine, but they should have made the change through the legislative process. You know, by asking Congress to do their thing. Jeff Shuren, the new director of the devices center, was both a lawyer and a doctor. He should have known that issuing a Not Approvable Letter for a first-of-a-kind device prior to an advisory panel meeting violated the statute.

Ed Harris Would be Proud

As ED HARRIS' character in Apollo 13 said, we "worked the problem." First, we scheduled and conducted a conference call with our lead statistical reviewer to address the six new questions. Our statistician was very surprised with the questions because the answers were obvious, several of them plainly contained in the

Statistical Report. Unbelievable! There are no words to describe how we felt about that, but I will try: How could they ask six new questions and call the PMA Not Approvable when they were effectively admitting that they hadn't read the Statistical Report? We submitted a complete response to the seven questions on May 7, 2010. Think about that: a complete response to issues that the agency said were the basis of the Not Approvable Letter was crafted and submitted within a month and a half of receipt. The responses required no new data, and no new analyses. What does this tell you? It told me, and every expert that I asked, that the statistics were not the real issue.

We also filed a Supervisory Review Request to Dr. Shuren identifying the transgression of law with respect to issuance of the Not Approvable Letter prior to a panel meeting, and demanded an immediate retraction. A Not Approvable Letter to a little public company is worse than a Supervisory Review request to an FDA supervisor, but that doesn't mean that the Supervisory Review Request wasn't causing them at least a little bit of consternation. It had its intended effect: Dr. Shuren's office contacted us and said that if we were to put the Supervisory Review request in abeyance, the FDA would schedule a panel meeting for MelaFind. My reply: "We can certainly do that, provided that the FDA also retracts the Not Approvable Letter." They replied that they would, indeed, retract the Not Approvable Letter. And so we went ahead and pulled the request. It had served its purpose, which was to get us back on track from a regulatory point of view. (On the other hand, the whole series of events did—irrevocably, I will argue—damage MELA in the eyes of the stock market. I'll discuss that in chapter seven.)

Alas, the regulatory problems weren't so easily solved. In the middle of planning and preparing for the panel meeting with the FDA (on May 26, they told us that it would take place on August 26), I inquired, yet again, as to when the Not Approvable Letter would be retracted. We'd done our part by retracting the supervisory request, after all. But the review staff informed me that something had changed—the Not Approvable Letter was *not* going to be retracted. Huh? I received no further explanation other than that "higher-ups" had dictated the decision. Amazing. This is not what is supposed to happen when the Office of the Center Director commits to something. Again, we couldn't do anything about it except play to win at the panel meeting. So that's what we did.

The first step was to prepare the pre-panel package of information that would be provided to panel members in advance of the meeting. I started in the industry as a regulatory affairs associate, assembling NDAs, PMAs, BLAs, 510ks, and PMAs. And I'd written numerous Integrated Summaries of Safety and Efficacy, the clinical theses of the approval applications. The best summaries pull the most important data from the program, the most relevant literature, and the latest healthcare statistics and then weave a very compelling story that leaves not a shadow of a doubt in the reader's mind that the product should be approved. These are typically dry documents, written in the fashion of a manuscript for publication, but like a review article, they are extremely well researched, referenced, and synthesized.

Naturally, we all thought our package made quite the compelling argument on MelaFind's behalf, but after reading through a late draft, I realized that it was too dry, too boring, and had no punch. We needed something *more*. We needed something that would grab the reader by the lapels and scream, "APPROVE THIS!" And we needed it to happen on page 1 of the Executive Summary.

So I recast the document, leading off with a picture of a melanoma that all of the dermatologists in our companion reader study had missed but that MelaFind had detected. And along with the image was a question: "Would you biopsy this lesion to rule out melanoma?" The point was that this dilemma is so common, and so frequently answered incorrectly, that one American dies of melanoma every single hour. I then told the MelaFind story in a very punchy and pithy manner. It was compelling literature! And just like a good short story, it was, well, *short*—but still comprehensive in presenting both the great data we had (meeting all endpoints and satisfying every item in the protocol agreement), and the significant unmet medical need. What else did they need to know?

Beware of Phone Calls Late on Friday Afternoons in July

WE SUBMITTED THE pre-panel package, along with all of the required attachments and forms, in early July. It is customary that the agency and the sponsor "swap" respective pre-panel packages more or less simultaneously. It is also customary for each side to provide comment so that obvious errors are corrected and a mutual understanding can be achieved on as many issues as possible before the panel receives any information. We repeatedly requested the FDA's pre-panel package. They repeatedly promised to send it.

They never did. Then, on a Friday afternoon a couple of weeks later, I received a call from the division director and his staff telling me that they needed to postpone the August 26 panel meeting because they needed more time to prepare their pre-panel package. I couldn't believe my ears. What about the review clock? What about the fact that *they* had selected the first panel date? What about the fact that we were a small, publicly traded, one-product company? Another delay would severely hurt the company's relationship with investors and public markets? What about public perception in the dermatology community, and with the panel members themselves? Of course, all of these outside stakeholders assume that the FDA is right, virtuous, objective, and fair, and that it is the little company that has once again done something wrong.

I begged. I explained what the delay would do to us as a company. What did I get? Nothing but a snide comment from a member of the review team in the Office of Device Evaluation. He said, "Don't bother submitting a Supervisory Review request to have the August 26th date maintained because this is coming straight from the top." What the heck did that mean? It meant that it wasn't coming from the review team; it meant that the action had been OK'd from on high. How high? I asked them to clarify how high. The answer: from the center director himself, Dr. Jeff Shuren.

What on earth was going on? I had some thoughts. The first one was that our pre-panel package was so damn compelling that they did, in fact, need more time to write their own. The second was that in May or June, the FDA had announced that a spate of new guidelines was forthcoming, including one on the determination of "risk/benefit." I surmised that they wanted the panel to occur after those guidelines had been released, so that they could try to ascribe a new standard or method of analysis, and thereby "move the goalposts" as they often try to do. Or third, they couldn't actually convene the panel on August 26 because of end-of-summer and back-to-school activities.

We immediately appealed to the ombudsman, whose job it is to mediate industry/FDA grievances. It was fruitless, though, as the ombudsman simply restated what the FDA was saying. But it wasn't *that* surprising, given that the ombudsman reports into the Office of the Center Director, and not the Commissioner. The Center Director had already taken a position on the MelaFind application by refusing to retract the unlawful Not Approvable letter when it came to his attention vis-a-vis the Supervisory Review Request. And the ombudsman wasn't about to go head-to-head with the Center Director—his boss—over the issue.

Whatever the reason, moving a panel date is very, very bad. The public markets and the dermatology community would assume that it was our fault. On July 21, we announced that the FDA needed more time and that the panel meeting was being rescheduled for November 2010. Investors didn't know what to make of the news other than to sell the stock, which fell 6 percent that day to $6.47 a share. The reaction was understandable, because the drumbeat of "good things not happening to MELA" that had started with the not approvable letter rolled on.

Cosmic Perversity

WE REQUESTED ANOTHER meeting with the FDA. We wanted to determine as quickly as possible where we agreed and where we did not agree so that we could best prepare for the panel meeting. A meeting might actually help the agency prepare their pre-panel package as well. As cosmic perversity would dictate, the meeting was held on August 26th! Well, why not? All of our calendars were open!

The meeting went surprisingly well. Normally, the FDA hurries you out of the room at the 59th minute. Not so that day. We went for 1 hour and 40 minutes with much of the staff, and I believed there was a definite meeting of the minds. Deputy Directors from the Office of Device Evaluation and the review Division Director were engaged and actually supportive after some clarification and initial pointed discussions.

There were three important outcomes from the meeting. First, we were told to present a claim to the panel that allowed for the use of MelaFind by *all physicians*, not just dermatologists. Recall that from the beginning we had proposed that MelaFind use be limited to dermatologists. The claim that we had submitted to the FDA in 2004 did exactly that. Second, we were told that the panel would vote on safety, effectiveness, and benefit/risk, and there would be only one vote. In other words, we could not ask them to vote on safety, effectiveness, and benefit/risk for alternative claims. I challenged this decision, because nowhere in the regulations are panels prohibited from discussing and even recommending the approvability and merits of alternative claims. In fact, it happens *all the time*. The member of the review team who'd told us about the single vote seemed to back down as we protested, but the issue was left hanging. Third, we were told that no new data or analysis could be presented to the panel—by us or by the FDA—from that point forth.

We left the meeting feeling confident. I requested a phone call with the agency to affirm and cement the major conclusions of what we came to call the "Panel Alignment Meeting." That call took place in early September and confirmed that everything was as we had left it on August 26th. So it seemed that we were of like mind. We prepared minutes of the meeting and the follow-up call and submitted them to the agency.

We were on a ridiculous roller coaster ride—up one moment and climbing, then down and almost thrown off the next, then back up and feeling secure, then totally off balance and dropping fast. I just took each challenge as it came, working the problem, and trying to move one step closer to the goal. I had never experienced anything like this in my career, nor even heard of anything like it. And it started taking a toll on me. People with whom I was close told me that I was "distant" and I wasn't enjoying things that I normally found enjoyable. My wife suffered watching me get tossed about, and just wanted it to end.

Feeling that we understood where things were with the FDA, we started working on our panel presentation. Notwithstanding the firmer footing that we felt we were on, though, I still knew that the panel meeting would be difficult and there would be even more surprises and angst to come. Little did I know that things were about to get much, much worse.

Fourteen Years of Work in Two Hours

THE WAY A panel meeting works is that the sponsor presents for two hours, followed by questions to the sponsor by the panel, then the FDA presents for two hours, and then also answers questions posed by the panel. Then there's a lunch break. The afternoon consists of follow-up questions from the panel to either the sponsor or the FDA, and then the panel debates over various points that arose during the morning presentations. After that, the FDA guides the panel through the consideration of their specific questions. At that point, the sponsor is permitted a final summation for ten minutes. Finally, the votes on safety, effectiveness, and benefit/risk are tallied and discussed.

The quality of your opening two-hour presentation at the panel meeting is absolutely critical. It must be clear. It must be compelling. It must be able to stand up to criticism and stand on its own because, unlike a trial where the defense attorney can object, question prosecution witnesses, and participate in most every step, sponsors can only speak during that presentation, when called upon by the panel chair, and during the ten-minute summation. The goal is to present an easy to follow, scientifically and medically robust story that anticipates obvious objections and the major assaults that the FDA might make.

It's a good idea to ask experts in the field to be part of your two-hour presentation. We were privileged to have a group of absolute all-stars who believed in the product, were impressed by the data, and were willing to say so. We asked one of the members of our Scientific Advisory Committee, Dr. Darrell Rigel (past president of both the American Academy of Dermatology and the American Society of Dermatologic Surgery, who along with Drs. Al Kopf and Robert Friedman first advanced the AB CDE paradigm of early melanoma detection at NYU) to present an overview of the disease, the problems in early melanoma detection, the unmet medical need, and the opportunity that MelaFind offered based on the data generated in clinical trials to date. Consistent with the new panel-voting framework, he would also present about the benefit/risk of MelaFind in the context of early melanoma detection.

Following Dr. Rigel, one of the pivotal trial investigators, Laura Ferris, MD, PhD (head of the Pigmented Skin Lesion Clinic at the University of Pittsburgh) would present the rationale for the pivotal trial design, and the specifics of the clinical study protocol. Dr. Clay Cockerell (University of Texas, Southwestern, and past President of the American Academy of Dermatology) would cover the results of the MelaFind pivotal trial. Dr. Cockerell is a melanoma histopathology expert who had reviewed slides of lesion biopsies from the MelaFind studies. Dr. Alicia Toledano was going to handle the results of all statistical analyses. Dr. Arthur Sober, head of the Melanoma Section at Harvard, was to present the rationale for reader studies in dermatology and the results of MelaFind reader studies. Dina Gutkowicz-Krusin, PhD, and I would also present. Dina would discuss the scientific background, development, and operation of MelaFind, and I would present what is referred to in the industry as the "regulatory history"—the record of our interactions with the FDA from the protocol agreement to the current day.

The panel meeting was set for November 18, 2011. Logistical coordination is a nightmare, so we began in earnest in the second week of September 2011. Experts of this caliber have tremendously busy schedules. Obtaining clear and focused time on their busy calendars for multiple meetings, phone calls, and slide reviews was not easy. We also scheduled a mock panel meeting with dermatologists who had equally impressive credentials for November 1, 2011. We needed to have the final presentations ready for the mock panel rehearsal so that we had enough time to tweak the presentations based on feedback. When you have "outside eyes" look at things, surprises and opportunities arise, so you need to build that into your plan. And we did. We had only seven weeks to work with our experts and get everything ready for the November 1 mock panel session. That's not a lot of time.

In order to set the mood of the mock session, we gave each expert a jersey of an NBA legend, and explained why each expert was given the jersey that they had received:

—We gave a Kobe Bryant jersey to Dr. Ferris—because Kobe has the most "perfect" basketball moves of all time, according to Jeff Van Gundy, and our protocol and protocol agreement represented the best, most rigorous in the history of the disease.

—Oscar Robertson was presented to Dr. Toledano—because "The Big O" had the best "numbers" of all time, the only player ever to average a triple double over a single season (he did it over a five season period!), and our statistician needed to have the "best numbers" and analyses.

—Dr. Cockerell got Michael Jordan's, because MJ is widely considered the greatest of all time based on his results, and our results were the best ever seen in melanoma detection.

—We gave Julius Erving's jersey to Dina, because Dr. J redefined the game and was responsible for merging the old and the new, and Dina had created MelaFind, our breakthrough product that would redefine dermatology.

—Dr. Sober got Larry Bird, because Dr. Sober was from Boston and was a deadly shot—he knew the literature better than anyone and could cite it without a Google search, having written multiple review articles on the disease.

—Finally, we gave a Walt Frazier jersey to Dr. Darrell Rigel, because Walt was the coolest player of all time, who often didn't break a sweat. As the expert synthesizing the case for the medical utility of MelaFind in the broader context of the disease, Dr. Rigel needed to be cool under fire.

We also gave players' jerseys to the experts on the mock panel that were pitted against our presenters, and they were purposely selected to represent a formidable "front line." They included Wes Unseld, Wilt Chamberlain, Bob Lanier, Bill Walton, and Bill Russell.

I didn't wear a jersey. I didn't need anything more to rile me up or get me motivated, and it was no longer fun for me. No, it was pure, insane stress and everything was riding on it. Just two-and-a-half weeks before the mock panel meeting, the presentations weren't ready. So we worked harder.

In the middle of this, I received an email from the FDA. It was a draft of their pre-panel meeting package. Recall that they'd had ours since we'd submitted it in July. In a word, it was a complete reversal, a 180-degree turn from where things had been left at the panel alignment meeting and follow-up phone call in early September. In short, everything that we'd agreed on in the protocol agreement from 2004 was challenged; every question that we'd answered in the back and forth of the PMA review over the last year was posed, yet again, this time as objections; we were accused of performing inappropriate analyses; we were accused of not following the protocol; and we were accused of not demonstrating the clinical utility of the product.

There were also some very aggressive statements about the FDA's position on approvability in the package. The most galling was the following: "The FDA review team has significant concerns this device has not been studied adequately for its current indications for use and therefore puts the health of the public at risk." I couldn't believe what I was reading. That was completely inappropriate as the FDA is not supposed to sway the panel publicly, even though everyone in the industry knows that FDA does pre-condition the panel privately. What's more, they were claiming concern over indications for use that they'd *insisted* we include—that MelaFind be intended for use by *all physicians* as opposed to just *dermatologists*.

(A less immediate, but equally egregious, outcome of such language is that it would surely scare at least some dermatologists away from MelaFind if we ever did get approved. "If the FDA says it can harm people," our prospective customer might think, "then maybe it could. What if I use it and get sued?" But that was a future problem we couldn't focus on at the moment.)

The purpose of a panel is for the FDA to obtain medical input. A pre-panel package is supposed to be neutral, and it wasn't. This was an unmitigated disaster. The very existence of the protocol agreement as the foundational definition of safety and effectiveness for MelaFind was being questioned! But it wasn't only offensive. It was *unlawful*, just as the Non Approval letter had been.

The document—which is supposed to be factual and contain no interpretation—was in my view also rife with misinformation, outright lies, and data presented deceptively so as to further a very clear agenda. Not only were the facts wrong, the FDA was in my view blatantly attempting to guide the panel to a negative vote. Repeating questions that were sent to us during the review is a very deceptive thing to do because there is no way that a panel member can dive into the details to the level that a reviewer can. In other words, even though we'd been asked many of the exact questions and satisfactorily answered them during our one-on-one sessions with FDA medical and statistical reviewers, they included them in the document as if they remained open. I believe this was a trick, of course, an attempt to create heft as if the sheer number of questions and issues, as opposed to the quality of the questions and insights, would sway the panel. It was ingenious, actually, because panel members do not typically dive deep, and they can judge books by their cover. (Or their weight.)

For the next several weeks, when we should have been 100% focused on panel meeting preparations, we objected with passion over each controversial point in the FDA's pre-panel package draft. There were many. They wouldn't allow us to amend the Executive Summary in our pre-panel package to address items that were raised in their package—this after having had our document to fashion theirs for three months! They did permit us to add an addendum, however, but it was placed at the end, and it was doubtful the panel members would even see it. It was a surreal and unbelievable experience. We didn't know what comments and changes they would accept in the final pre-panel package that was sent to the panel, but judging from the hostile tenor of the exchanges with us, it didn't appear that much would change, or change enough to affect the overall conclusion. So we had to re-strategize the presentation and redo almost all of the slides to take into account the unwarranted and unlawful attacks. All this with just a couple of days to go before the mock panel meeting!

But WHY?

I AM ASKED, literally, all the time, WHY? It is blatantly obvious to me that the FDA purposely and with volition and malice tried to poison the MelaFind panel, and did so in what I believe was a very sneaky and deceitful way. We had a binding protocol agreement and we'd met every endpoint. Again, "Why?" Why did the FDA want the MelaFind panel to be negative? The only rationale that the team could muster was that having sent a Not Approvable letter, which was no doubt a serious and egregious error that was driven by reasons that had nothing to do with MelaFind, and then deciding not to retract it, their best defense was justification after the fact.

In other words, a negative panel outcome would, for all intents and purposes, render the unlawful Not Approvable letter moot. The act of issuing the letter would still be "unlawful," but the "so what?" part of the argument would be abrogated. There would be no attention paid to an appeal of a rejected PMA if the panel were negative. So they had decided to do everything they could possibly do, lawful or unlawful, to drive a negative panel outcome. That's what we thought. An alternative conclusion was that in daring to question the Not Approvable letter through a Supervisory Request, and daring to get in the way of their grand plan to revamp the approval process, we had drawn the ire of the "higher-ups," who were responding by destroying our little company.

Another question I am asked all the time is, HOW? How did we go from planning a joint approval announcement in November 2009 to a Not Approvable letter in March 2010? How did we go from a panel date of August 26 to a panel date of November 18? How did we go from complete alignment with the FDA in September 2010 to a scathing treatise in October 2010? The answer to the first "How?" is the pursuit of an agenda and issues broader than the review of an innovative, breakthrough product like MelaFind. The answers to the second and third "How?" are the same as the answer in the preceding paragraph—they were intent on not letting facts get in the way of their larger agenda and plans.

It really did seem as if we were collateral damage in a bureaucratic phase shift at the FDA. Everybody has their own tales of bureaucratic nightmares, wherever they happen to work, but this was happening over the approval of a device that promised to improve the fight against a cancer that kills one American *per hour*. A cancer that is *visible on the skin*. It wasn't just frustrating for us; it was in my view unconscionable from a public health perspective.

I was in shock and disbelief. I'd spent my entire career working with the FDA. I respected the agency, despite the standard gamesmanship and mistakes that human beings make. I had liked virtually all of the people with whom I dealt at the FDA up to this point in my career. I believed in a strong FDA, and I still do. But their behavior was so egregious that I'd never heard of anything like it, even by the most vocal wronged companies in the industry.

In the middle of this strife, my own situation got even worse. I had to remind myself to eat. Adele didn't know what to do. She would bring home brownies, which are my weakness, and I wouldn't even look at them. Paradoxically, I had a tremendous amount of energy, and I would work out very aggressively every morning. I started writing poetry. At 2:30AM! (It wasn't Shakespeare, but it rhymed.) I began losing a lot of weight. At my nadir, a couple of months later, I had lost 29 pounds without even trying. I couldn't even drink a half of a glass of wine without being rendered unable to focus, so I cut out all forms of alcohol. And I drank more coffee than was wise.

One Saturday morning, the week before the mock panel, Adele tried to reason with me while I gazed off into the distance as we sat having coffee. She pleaded with me to end it, to just walk away, a caring sentiment that only served to anger me. And then she said, "I know the problem. You finally came up against something you feel that you might not be able to win, and this has never happened to you before." She went on to say that I had never thought of myself as a man but rather as a "force." But now, she observed, "You realize that you're not a force. And I'm glad about that. For your sake, and that of our relationship, I hope you lose!" At that point, our relationship turned to being just roommates. I'd wash her clothes or make her side of the bed, but that was it. We were nothing more than cordial. I basically shut my wife out of my life.

The Dress Rehearsal

PICTURE A DRESS rehearsal where the script isn't finished, and the costumes aren't fitted. That was our mock panel meeting. We were working with our experts until the wee hours of the morning even on the night prior to it. And I barely slept. I asked two former colleagues who had a great deal of advisory panel experience—Bob Maguire, MD, the smartest man I know, and Al Maroli, PhD, a very savvy and experienced clinical and regulatory expert—to attend. Al acted as mock panel chair. And as one of the few people from whom I can accept criticism without becoming defensive, Bob was there to provide us with a critique as well as recommendations for how to amend the presentation for the real panel meeting, the best arguments to make, back-up arguments to have at the ready, and the central themes to reinforce.

We emulated the exact conditions—the size of room, layout of tables (U-shaped), gallery and spectator areas, and, critically, the exact timing and order of the presentations. We also had two statisticians present on the mock panel. Both were part of the very small circle of experts in the analyses of diagnostic imaging products from which our statistician, Dr. Toledano, hailed. Quite often, the three of them find themselves on opposite sides in panel meetings—sometimes as panel members and other times as presenters of data generated by sponsors (companies or the NIH). We included generalist dermatologists, as well as non-dermatologist surgeons to best emulate what we believed would be the constitution of the actual panel. (Quite honestly, I believe that ours was much more qualified than the actual FDA panel.) We gave them our pre-panel package as well as the latest draft of the FDA's own pre-panel package that we were still "discussing" and protesting with the FDA.

We rented a huge projector to make sure we had the best way to show cases of melanomas that had been missed by dermatologists but detected by MelaFind as well as non-melanomas biopsied by dermatologists but "cleared" by MelaFind. That, after all, was a central argument of our case. A picture is worth a thousand words (and many statistical arguments), and we needed to make sure the pictures were good.

I was most concerned with the experts presenting our data—how they would perform and react to scrutiny, whether they would master the material enough to handle second and third-levels of questions, and whether they would honor their time constraints. Equally, and perhaps more important, whether they would revert to being doctors and thinking that they could handle any question on their own, or would they remember the rules of the game and clarify the question first, then get me involved in order to buy them more time to formulate a response, then confer with their fellow all-stars and Dina to prepare the best possible response while I either tap-danced or gave the answer, if I knew it.

That Saturday in early November was a huge success from the standpoint of learning how to make our arguments crisper, which slides to delete, and which avenues of discussion to abandon. The kinds of things that typically happen in a real panel happened at the mock panel, including side tracking on non-germane points, confusion, misunderstanding, and more. At the end, Al Maroli took a vote, just as takes place at the real panel. The mock panel voted in favor of the product. Of course, our team was thrilled, but I wasn't smiling. All I could see was all of the work that remained and the challenges in getting the experts ready. And there simply didn't seem to be enough hours to get it all done.

Dina, Kathy, Nyq, and I got together on Monday and reviewed our notes and recollections about the mock panel meeting. We debated strategies and the merits and risks of certain lines of argument and discussion. Mid-week, we received and reviewed Bob Maguire's critique and recommendations. We planned out the changes that we needed to make to each of the presentations, as well as additional tables and data analyses to have at the ready in case questions arose.

I then received an email from Al Maroli. After reflecting on all of the data and the critique and arguments that came out of the day, Al had concluded that MelaFind was not really a diagnostic test, like a lab test, rather it was an aid, an adjunct to the dermatologists' judgment. MelaFind doesn't take away a dermatologist's decision-making, he wrote, but is simply another input into it. That wasn't news to me. So why was he wasting my time when I had lots of work to do? And then, BOOM! He suggested that we simply present MelaFind as another "letter" in the "alphabet soup" of early melanoma detection, an ultra-sensitive letter to add to ABCDE, which could *only* help dermatologists, as the data showed. WOW. The idea was stunning.

Although the ABCDE paradigm had been around for 25 years, this new letter, the "M," the MelaFind result, had been studied in the most rigorous, prospective study ever done in melanoma detection. Just as the E (for evolving) was added to the ABCD paradigm a few years previously, it was time to add a new letter into the mix. In a word, it was a brilliant idea. We created a slide to that effect, and used it repeatedly.

Mr. Smith Goes to Washington

ON TUESDAY MORNING, November 16, 2010, I was in Penn Station, NJ waiting for the Amtrak train to Washington, DC. The night before, the FDA had released the pre-panel package publicly. They'd made few changes to the executive summary, despite our many attempts to correct the misinformation. My phone was ringing non-stop with funds and analysts trying to talk to me about the FDA materials. Of course, I couldn't talk to them about it, but the appropriate answers were in our panel package. With 48 hours to go until the panel meeting, I should have been focused totally on the panel presentation, not dealing with analysts, investors, board members, and employees. But that, of course, is what I had signed-up for when I took the company public. Solving one problem often creates others, and I suddenly understood why most pre-approval one-product companies don't go public! At the opening bell, the stock took a severe hit, and fell more than 54% by the end of the day. But the way to get it back up was a panel victory, so I remained singularly focused on that goal.

Once on the train, I opened an email that I had received that morning containing the FDA's panel slide presentation. The FDA had not given an inch—nothing was accepted, at all, as a factual given; there were no assumed "first principles." Virtually every fact, finding, protocol procedure, and analysis we'd agreed to with them was suddenly being questioned. If they were going to start by challenging the basic fundamentals of our research, how could an intelligent and insightful discourse on the main reason for the meeting—whether the product worked and would be a valuable tool in melanoma detection—ensue? This was a strategy to distract and simply not allow discussion of the product and its approvability to occur.

What's more, there were new analyses, new arguments, and new information included in their panel slides that I had never seen before that day. The FDA had told us that neither they nor we could present any new data or analysis at the panel. But they did so anyway. When companies perform post-hoc analyses, the FDA screams and moans as if your picture belonged on a post office wall. But when the FDA does it, companies have no recourse. How could things get any worse? And how much more of this could we take?

After getting through the FDA's slides, I needed to figure out what to do. I knew we had to tweak or significantly edit almost every single one of our slides, and this just 48 hours prior to the panel presentation. We'd have to devise a few new slides, too, and my own presentation had to be recast. I had originally planned to provide a history of the MelaFind regulatory review process in a dispassionate, factual, and likeable (think Jimmy Stewart) manner that inexorably and naturally led to the conclusion that MelaFind simply must be approved. But things had changed. At that point, I had to be James Cagney and present a "you dirty rats" bit in as even-tempered a fashion as possible.

What had they done? They'd used statistics to confuse the issue, even after we'd complained about it when we first saw it in their draft panel package. They couldn't change the results of the study itself—MelaFind had detected 112 of 114 melanomas eligible and evaluable for primary endpoint analyses, 125 of 127 melanomas eligible and evaluable for secondary endpoint analyses, and 172 and 175 melanomas and pre-melanomas eligible and evaluable for another secondary endpoint analyses, for a 98.3% sensitivity. The next step is to use statistics to extrapolate those results to eventual real-world usage. We'd used one method that our statistician had argued was the most appropriate for our type of study, and which was consistent with the protocol agreement and statistical plan. They decided to use several others, some of which were not appropriate for the kind of data generated in the study. And several of theirs put our sensitivity just slightly below the 95% lower threshold required. Could it have been an honest difference of opinion about statistical approach? Sure it could have. But it didn't feel that way.

Dr. Toledano would tackle that issue head-on, and I would deal with the numerous other misrepresentations and positions the FDA had taken that directly contradicted the binding protocol agreement. I found one particular move outrageous: they included in the sensitivity calculation melanomas for which MelaFind did not provide an output, and considered those missed melanomas in direct contradiction of the protocol, even though they weren't "eligible and evaluable" melanomas. Had it been a real-world situation, a doctor would be very much aware that MelaFind wasn't saying something wasn't a melanoma, but simply that it had no answer. In which case, it was up to the doctors to decide for themselves whether to biopsy or not.

I arrived at the Holiday Inn in College Park, Maryland around lunch and helped finish setting up the rehearsal war room, in which I would spend all but a handful of the next 45 hours. We could leave nothing to chance. The experts arrived in a semi-staggered schedule. The goal was to go over all of their presentations on Tuesday afternoon and evening, time the presentations, make sure that all jibed and flowed well, and get everyone comfortable presenting the material. Wednesday would be spent with further refining and timing of the presentations and then practicing the handling of objections. We needed to rank the back-up slides, sequence them appropriately, and catalogue them according to specific objections.

It was a nightmare of pure unadulterated stress. The many changes required also prompted a great deal of discussion and debate amongst the team. In the end, we'd never managed a single run-through of all speakers. The best we could do was work with each presenter individually. When the MELA team was alone, later in the night, we made final changes and strategized. At about 9:30 PM, I found myself sitting down with the first free moment I'd had in two days. I took a deep breath, put my hands on my face, said a prayer to myself, and exhaled.

But there was no rest for the weary, and no break for the boss. We never got to my presentation because the experts' presentations were not finished yet and we were still strategizing how best to take on a number of new things that had emerged in the FDA's slides. For example: their insistence on showing a sensitivity measurement for dermatologists on the study when it was impossible to measure dermatologists' sensitivity when all the lesions on the study were biopsied. And that point had been covered in the binding agreement. Or: their insistence that reader studies were not valid when it was the FDA, itself, that had asked us to take pictures of the lesions to allow for the additional reader studies later. All of their "new" points had been asked and answered *ad infinitum* with the FDA staff, but now were suddenly reemerging as if unaddressed. And how could we address them without losing time and steam on the more important points? I didn't get to bed until after 2:00AM and lay there for at least an hour. By 6:00AM I was back in the war room.

We were better off on Wednesday, though still harried, and still in a circus-like environment with parallel discussions happening simultaneously. Perhaps I just felt better because the plan was more or less coming together. The experts, having mastered their own presentations, helped each other, especially with slides containing arguments and data that were being presented by multiple parties in service of different main objectives. We timed each presenter several times, down to the second. It was very, very tight. I typically would delete more slides, but because of the FDA's obvious tactics designed to overwhelm and confuse the panel, I felt "more was more."

At about 5:00PM on Wednesday, the evening before the panel presentation, things were tame enough that I felt I would not be missed if I were to disappear for 45 minutes. I went to my room to finally put my presentation in order. When I came back down to the war room, our CFO knocked on the door asking to see me. I had put him in charge of dealing with everyone at the panel meeting who was not part of the presentation team—the board, investors, our investor relations and public relations team, employees, and counsel. I had told him that he needed to protect me, that I absolutely had to stay 100% focused on this and that I had no bandwidth for anything else.

For him to come to the door meant something was wrong. He informed me that a Class Action Lawsuit Solicitation had just gone out to MELA investors. It was based on the 54% drop in our price on Tuesday, when the FDA had released the panel package. I thought back to medical school when they had told us that if you practice medicine long enough, you would eventually be sued. The same thing goes for being a public company; it's only a matter of time before some ambitious lawyer gathers enough signatures to try and extort some money from you (or your insurance company). But I had no ability to concentrate on it, and there was nothing to do about it at that moment anyway. The best public comment on it would be a panel victory, which would almost certainly cause the stock to bounce back, thereby negating any investor complaints, so that's what I concentrated my efforts and energy on pursuing. (I was partially right about the stock—it was back up briefly by week's end. But I was wrong about the lawsuit. More on that in chapter eight.)

We continued into the evening with the experts and into the wee hours of the morning amongst ourselves. I never believed in all-nighters in school. I always had my studying done two days before a test so that the evening before would be very light refresher, allowing me a good night sleep so that with a fresh mind I would be able to handle the unexpected on my feet. No such luxury here. Because I'd only gotten about 2.5 to 3 hours of sleep a night for the past 12 weeks, I was used to it though. I ended up sleeping for only an hour.

Show Time

THE ANXIETY WAS palpable as we left our war room breakfast and headed upstairs to the Grand Ball Room. The room was set up as we'd expected, more or less, except the open part of the U-shaped table was closest to the audience and it was from that vantage point that presentations were made. In my past experiences and at our mock panel, the open part of the U was at the front of the room where the projector screen sat and there were two podiums flanking it—one on the right for sponsors and one on the left for the FDA. Here, there was a central podium in the middle part of the base of the U, and the screen was way off to the right. The presenters simply looked down the middle of the U where multiple TV monitors displayed the slides, rather than looking at the screen. Progress, I guess.

Two things surprised us. First, there were four statisticians present. I have never in my career heard of more than two statisticians on a panel. Statisticians are interesting individuals; typically a statistician who looks at his own work a year or two later doesn't agree with what he did! They're also very dogmatic and make great ado about formulas and treatment of data that, typically, in the end does nothing to affect the overall conclusions. They love "angels on the heads of pins" discussions. But the statistics in our data were quite simple—p values and confidence bounds—no angels, no pins. These were not esoteric or statistically complicated analyses. So the presence of *four* statisticians was a huge red flag.

We felt that the FDA, true to their apparent strategy of causing confusion to limit intelligent consideration of MelaFind, put those statisticians on the panel to weigh down the discussion. They were hoping to prompt such a volume of questions and distractions that on face value, one would conclude that the product was flawed in some way. An interesting side note is that FDA staff had actually called *our* statistician, Alicia Toledano, and asked her to be a panel member. She had to tell them that she was the company's consultant. Incredible. Note the irony: they wanted the very statistician who'd chosen our statistical analysis to be on their panel. But when she couldn't, they put four statisticians on the panel to try to argue that her choice of analysis was the wrong one.

Second, there were eight dermatologists on the panel, but *none* of them in my view qualified as melanoma experts. How could that be? How could you pick eight dermatologists and not have a single one be expert in the most important disease in dermatology and the topic of the panel? The panel had sixteen voting members. (In addition to the above, there was one pediatrician and a couple of general surgeons.) Panels usually have 11 or 12 members. Again, the reason for such a change was pretty straightforward to me: the more people, the more opportunity for misunderstanding, getting sidetracked, and erroneous conclusions based on lack of attention.

Finally, though, it was Go Time. The chair went through the perfunctory instructions and ground rules and overview of the agenda, then pointed our way. Our presentations were fabulous. Our experts presented the slides quite adroitly. Dina presented quite well, without losing the audience, and Dr. Toledano did a great job with the statistics. We had a big problem, however, as all of them had gone over their allotted times! That meant that I had to make up seven minutes on the fly. I did it with a combination of talking a bit faster in parts and omitting sections of slides in others. But I couldn't give short shrift to my two most important arguments. So I didn't.

For the first one, I laid out in detail the roots, foundation, and legal nature of the binding protocol agreement. I explained how it started with a claim that we had presented to the FDA in 2004, and which was included in the pivotal trial protocol. I then showed "smoking gun slide 1"—a slide that the FDA was to present shortly. On the slide, the FDA stated, "the panel will not be asked to address whether the sponsor had met the items of the protocol agreement but will be asked about the benefit/risk implication of the items." There were no two ways about it. I made the point that if they did so, the FDA would be instructing the panel to break the law, to ignore the binding protocol agreement, which stated that "this protocol is the most appropriate means for establishing the safety and effectiveness of MelaFind." Of course, safety and effectiveness are the bases upon which PMA approvals are based, as per statute, as per law. Wow!

It was a clear attempt by the FDA to diminish the importance of the existence of the binding protocol agreement, which should have been the starting point of the discussions. The FDA should have started off with, "this is what we agreed to with the sponsor before the start of the study regarding safety and effectiveness, and this is what the study showed." But they chose to trivialize the binding agreement instead. Because all of the endpoints were met, the panel meeting should have been focused on benefit/risk with respect to appropriate labeling of the product, which was precisely what the FDA had told us our panel was being convened to discuss all the way back in 2004!

My second one laid out "smoking gun slide 2," which was also to be presented by the FDA shortly. On it, the FDA decided to teach the panel the definition of safety and effectiveness. Only they didn't. Carefully and in my view deviously citing the Code of Federal Regulations on the slide, they advanced the statute's language for effectiveness as the definition of safety. Yes, I believe they purposely used the language of effectiveness proscribed in law as the definition of safety. The definition for effectiveness is a higher standard than safety, so they were, in effect, creating a higher standard for MelaFind, which was against the rules.

So, what definition did they provide for effectiveness? Well, it seemed to me that they concocted a definition that paved the way for a new analysis of the data. That's right, they devised a new definition of effectiveness that is not in the statute, yet, by the way the citation was placed on the slide, made it appear that this was the definition in the statute. The statute definition of effectiveness says, "In a significant portion of the target population, the use of the device for its intended uses and conditions of use, when accompanied by adequate directions for use & warnings against unsafe use will provide *clinically significant results*." The concocted definition, which is *not* in any statute, that the FDA would be instructing the panel to use was "how well a diagnostic test meets the intent-to-diagnose (ITD) analysis."

Why is this important? Because the FDA was trying to find a way to introduce a *new analysis* into the approval process, something that was not in the statistical plan or the protocol or the binding agreement. They wanted to include in the analysis all of the cases for which MelaFind could not provide a result but where use of MelaFind was attempted. This was nonsense. MelaFind has smart algorithms that tell the operator if it cannot provide a result; it doesn't guess, rather, it indicates that the lesion could not be processed. The population of lesions that would be included in the analyses was meticulously defined by our statistician in the protocol and agreed to by the FDA. It specifically excluded lesions for which no MelaFind result was obtained. So why did they want to do this? Because among the more than 100 lesions that MelaFind couldn't evaluate there were some melanomas. In their new analysis, these would be considered missed by MelaFind, which would reduce the device's sensitivity level to below the threshold required for the endpoint to be positively met.

The argument is, in my view, factually dishonest in two ways. Remember they told us that no new analyses were allowed. If this were a true concern of theirs, it should have been raised during the review and we would have addressed it—quite easily, in fact. This was the first that we were seeing of this point. But I also believe it was insane from a medical standpoint. One of our experts later commented that by this line of reasoning when a mammogram test comes back as "unable to be read"—something that happens often— the doctor would tell the patient, "Great news, your mammogram could not be read." But, no, that is not what happens. Rather, the patient is called and told that the mammogram could not be read so an MRI is probably required.

Somehow, I got all of my points in, but I had to be cut off by the panel chair. Still, I was pleased. We'd presented 235 slides in two hours and handled the questions from the panel very well. The questions afforded us the opportunity to make additional points, particularly high level points that we wanted to reinforce. I felt that we were in very good shape.

Act II & Intermission

THE FDA PRESENTED after us. Watching and hearing their presentation, which I considered factually incorrect and replete with purposefully misleading statements, as well as including questions about facts we knew that they knew, was much more painful than it was when I was simply reading them on the train. Moreover, the panel appeared totally confused and followed the trail of breadcrumbs.

One senior FDA reviewer from the Office of Device Evaluation, the same one who had told me not to bother to submit a Supervisory Review over the issue of moving the panel date because it was coming directly from Dr. Shuren himself, actually high-fived his peers when the panel appeared to accept pieces of misinformation and flawed analyses. I had never seen anything like it. Not only were FDA staff presenting things that they knew were wrong, but one official showed visible glee when the panel took the bait. Moreover, the purpose of a panel is to obtain the panel's objective medical and scientific input to use in forming a final decision, not to have already formed a final decision and then try to get the panel to agree with it. Let's set aside for a moment the sheer absurdity of going to a panel with a non-approvable letter extant (the one they'd promised to retract but did not). The whole tenor of the meeting was in my view literally "ass backwards" in the truest sense of the term. It was surreal to see the FDA acting like cheerleaders for a particular outcome.

Of the many, many things that were disgusting to watch, I remember three the most.

First and foremost, a dermatologist that appeared to be ordained by the FDA as the lead medical panelist by virtue of their seating location and extensive interaction with FDA staff was very damaging, and cast a doubtful and negative pall over everything possible. At one point, this panelist alleged that I had personally selected cases for one of the studies and made a big hoopla over how biased this was. But that was wrong—I hadn't selected the cases. Rather, the medical director of the study, Dr. Suephy Chen of Emory University—a reader study expert—had selected them. This was plainly stated in the protocol for that study, which was included in the panel package. Although I jumped up and refuted the allegation, speaking out of turn, the damage was done. And why would they have wanted to make that point? The results of the study were not the primary focus of the presentation or discussion. Not only that, the mere introduction of the word "bias" was in my view both reckless and antagonistic. "Bias" is scientific anathema, and when people hear that a study is biased, they simply tune out. It made me wonder whether the FDA had provided the panelist with a list of points to raise in hopes of tainting and discrediting the data.

Second, the pediatrician on the panel asked a perfectly legitimate and appropriate question: How many lesions and melanomas were found in patients under 18? The FDA presenter didn't know the answer and no one else on the FDA team seemed to be able to find the relevant table with the data and provide her with the answer. I was perturbed with that and with the lack of preparation on their part. It was the FDA, after all, that had invited a pediatrician to join the panel. If I'd asked a pediatrician to join, I would have had the data on pediatric patients at the ready. The answer, which I found a way of interjecting later, was 100 lesions, and MelaFind detected all four melanomas in pediatric patients. But by that time, the pediatrician very well could have already made up her mind (~against), or might not have even heard the answer, and simply concluded that it was not tested in pediatric patients. And that could have meant the difference between positive and negative votes.

Third, during the afternoon, one of the panel members suggested that a claim limited to dermatologists would go a long way to addressing many of the concerns. Remember, this was something we had been told by the FDA in September not to propose. What should have happened, but didn't, was that a supervisor from the FDA should have said that the FDA appreciated the feedback and acknowledged that we (MELA) had already agreed to such a claim, or indications for use. I have participated in panels where this kind of thing happens. By and large, the FDA tries to get it right; they are in the pursuit of truth. But that's not the way it seemed during our panel. Nope, they seemed hell-bent on assuring a negative outcome.

During the lunch break, we were not happy. Our dermatology experts were very upset because, in their words, the FDA had stated a total of 13 things that were flat wrong about melanoma, and the panel hadn't challenged the FDA on a single one. I guess that kind of thing happens when the lead medical panel member has an ax to grind against you and there are no disease experts on the panel. I explained to our experts that the afternoon would consist of the panel debating points raised by the FDA about the application, debating their own points, and asking both us and the FDA for points of clarification. I told them that we had only one more shot to present proactively and that would be the 10 minutes at the close of the meeting. I could request five additional minutes, which I did.

We faced a huge decision. Who should deliver the closing argument? Ninety-nine times out of 100, it would be the person in my shoes, and I had assumed that I would do it. But given the total lack of understanding of the disease as demonstrated by the 13 points enumerated by our experts, I now felt that maybe one or two of our experts should do it instead. So we split the difference: The plan was that a few of our team would stay down in the war room with Drs. Rigel, Ferris, and Cockerell making slides for the closing, while Dina, Alicia, Dr. Sober, and I went upstairs, listened to the afternoon session, and responded to questions. And we'd decide at the last moment. I ripped a piece of paper from someone's notebook and wrote down eight slide numbers from the master deck, asking the team to make a set of these slides for me to use on the off chance we decided it should be me.

Act III

THE AFTERNOON WAS a slaughter. I remember only one positive argument for our case resonating with the entire panel—it had to do with MelaFind's performance on lesions of questionable significance. But it wasn't a win on a key, central issue. I knew we were dead when one of the panel members, a dermatologist, said that he had significant concerns about the fact that MelaFind could not be used on the 10% of melanomas that were not pigmented. That was a blatant error—only 0.7% of melanomas have no pigment. But no one said a word. I wondered whether that was because none of the other seven dermatologists even knew that to be the case? Or was it that they didn't care, that the outcome of the meeting was such *a fait accompli* that it simply didn't matter?

With a half hour remaining before closing arguments, the team came back upstairs and whispered to me that they had the experts' slides ready, that they'd added a bit about pigment-less melanomas, and that the experts were ready and willing to do the closing. But then they also said that they thought the panel simply wouldn't care that 13—actually, at that point it was 14—facts that the FDA had presented about the disease were wrong. So everyone actually thought it best if I did the summation. I agreed, and asked the team for my slides. They then told me that they'd decided that two I'd requested weren't necessary, they'd replaced another, and added yet another. I would be getting up to speak not knowing what slide would be coming next! But why would the madness have stopped by that point?

Dr. Clay Cockerell then mouthed something to me. I disengaged from the team, took my ear out of the middle of the U, and squatwalked over to him so as not to be obtrusive. Hey, I was open to a good idea from anyone at that point! And Dr. Cockerell is a very, very smart guy. So, what pearl was he going to share with me? When I arrived at his chair he said, "I was asking you whether there even needed to be a vote." He was right, because at that point, it was obvious to everyone that it was over. What do I mean by "over?" Well, it wasn't like they were digging the grave. It wasn't like they were lowering our coffin into the grave slowly with rope. It wasn't like they were throwing the dirt back on top of the coffin. No, it was as if the grass on our grave already needed to be cut! That's how dead we were.

I went back to my chair. The team didn't have the other slide that I had asked for yet. I grabbed my notebook. I'd written down the most egregious errors on major points on one page. That page morphed into my notes for the closing summation—things that I *had to remember* to say, aside from the main messages indelibly etched in my brain. I turned to the team and said I knew exactly what I was going to do. I was going to look at each one of the panelists and say, "Shame on you, shame on you, shame on you, and shame on you . . . you have let the FDA confuse and confound you such that you have been distracted from the main point, which is . . . " Our counsel's reply: "Don't say 'Shame on you.' Just tell them they took their eye off the ball."

I had two thoughts. The first: nobody ever gets my jokes! Of course I wasn't going to say, "Shame on you!" to the panel members. (I was, however, going to try to make them feel shame at having been duped.) The second thought: I realized that I had never used the expression "taking [one's] eye off the ball" in my life, despite the fact that I love sports.

And then I was called up to the podium by the chair. I had no idea whether the new slide I had asked for was in the deck, just as I had no idea of the order of the slides. I ripped the page out of my notebook, and approached. My main goal, of course, was to win. But I had another goal, which was to get as much as possible into the public record, so as to lay the foundation for a lawsuit against the FDA. God willing, that wouldn't be needed, but by that point I had to think that way.

The Greatest 15 Minutes of My Life

IT WAS AFTER 5:00PM at that point. And it had been a grueling day of intense emotion. But I told myself that it would all be over soon. On my way up to the podium, I noticed that none of the panelists were focused on me. They were stuffing materials back into their briefcases, collating their paperwork, shutting down their computers, using their blackberries and telephones. I entertained some scenarios in my mind: this guy was trying to get an earlier flight, this one texting his daughter about where to find the front door key. They didn't care.

I had a conversation with myself, as if the devil were on one shoulder and an angel on the other.

The devil: *"They're not respecting you, Joe."* The angel: *"Don't you think I can see that?"*

The devil: *"Your usual style of talking fast and rattling off facts ain't gonna work here!"*

The angel: *"Don't you think I realize that?"* The devil: *"So what are you going to do?"*

The angel: *"Gravitas. Gravitas. I need gravitas."*

The devil: *"Where are you going to get gravitas, Joe? All the stores are closed."*

The angel: *"Don't you think I know that?"*

—The devil disappeared.

The angel: *"Who do you respect the most?"* Joe Gulfo: *"My father!"*

The angel: *"So be your father."*

My father is very formal. He speaks very slowly and deeply. He uses silence as a weapon. And he projects tremendous personal authority, standing totally upright at all times with a very forceful posture. I got smacked back to reality when the panel chair said, "Dr. Gulfo, you requested five additional minutes, which I will grant you, beginning now," as his hand came down and struck the timer.

So I did what my father would do. I stood silently until all eyes were on me. The clock was ticking, but I didn't care. The panelists at first looked up, and then just continued with their distracted behaviors. Then they put their bags and phones down and started looking up attentively. Several panel members had actually been friendly and helpful throughout the day. One of them had even stated that the protocol should have been considered the Bible and that we'd followed it chapter and verse. To those panel members, I mouthed, "Thank you," nodded, and gave a small crack of a smile. A few recalcitrant members still wouldn't give me their attention. To those two, I did what my father would do. I turned my whole body toward them and stared at them until they were attentive. The clock was still ticking.

I finally leaned into the microphone, taking a deep breath, and very, very slowly and in a very deep voice said, "Thank you, Mr. Chairman."

I proceeded through a very slow and methodical presentation of the claim. I started with the binding agreement which, I said, is a *contract*—a *pact*—and that we had lived up to every aspect of our end of that contract. And from that point forth, I simply don't remember anything else I said.

I do remember that not knowing what slide was coming next didn't really matter. Since I was pausing so much, it appeared as though it was by design! When I was finished with the slides, I looked at my single page of notes, quickly scanned them for the most important things that I had to say, and then tried to think of graceful ways to segue between the points.

Some of those segues weren't so graceful. I remember looking directly at the panel member who'd mentioned pigment-less melanomas, and saying, "About pigment-less melanomas, it is *not the case* that 10% of melanomas are pigment-less. Rather, *just* 0.7% are pigment-less." I paused, leaned back from the microphone, looked at every panel member, and then back to him, and said "Zero-point-seven percent." I got the pediatric data out as well.

I stated that we had listened with great interest to the conversation regarding use of MelaFind by all physicians, that we understood the panel's concerns, and that we wholeheartedly agreed that those concerns would only be obviated if the claim were limited to dermatologists, and that we would absolutely be willing to do so. I concluded by returning to the protocol agreement and repeating that we had met every endpoint. That we had done everything that we'd said we would do and to which the FDA had agreed. And that we felt we had unequivocally demonstrated the safety and effectiveness of MelaFind. And then I left the podium.

The Votes Are In

ANOTHER SURPRISE: The automatic voting system would not work. The panel voted on the safety, effectiveness, and benefit/risk of MelaFind for the claim that the FDA had told us to present—as an aid to *physicians* (i.e., not specifically dermatologists) in the evaluation of clinical atypical pigmented skin lesions. And they had to tally the votes by hand. This didn't bother me much because I was totally convinced that we weren't going to win, and by that point I was mentally preparing my comments for the press conference that would take place right after the vote. I was so convinced that we were going to lose that I wasn't really listening to what they were saying. And then I was told that we had just won "safety" by a vote of 10-to-6. When the first five votes for "effectiveness" were "yes," I started listening again. We won effectiveness 8-to-6, with 2 abstentions. But here's where it's all going to come crashing down, I thought, on "benefit/risk."

It was torture watching and waiting for the ballots to be revealed—each positive vote giving me great hope and anticipation, and each negative vote making me feel doomed. It literally came down to the last vote—at that point, there were 7 "yes" votes, 7 "no" votes, and one abstention. The tension was palpable. Everyone was on the edge of their seat. And finally, the last vote was revealed . . . YES! We'd won!

The FDA official from the Office of Device Evaluation, who'd been high-fiving his peers with each punch landed, was beside himself in disbelief. But our team didn't know how to react, either. I sat there stunned. We did surface a bit of a cheer, but had to settle down quickly because the reviewers had to explain the rationale for their vote.

As luck would have it, the first panelist rattled off some things that concerned her, but then said that if the claim had been limited to dermatologists, she would have voted yes to "benefit/risk." That basically set the template for the remaining reviewers. They explained why they'd voted as they did, and the ones that would have voted YES if the claim had been limited to dermatologists stated so. There was no official tally of these "exceptions," although three panelists said they would have voted yes if the claim had been what we'd proposed, and not what the FDA had made us present. That is, benefit/risk would have been 11 votes in favor to just 4 votes against.

Amazing. We'd won, and even on the claim that the FDA had tried to sandbag us with—a claim and argument that they'd clearly fed to the panel in advance of the meeting to try to effect a negative vote. But they'd failed. The vote was positive! And it would have been even more positive if it had been what we'd proposed.

Before I got out of my seat to talk to the whole team, I took my phone out of my briefcase, turned it on, and texted Adele: "Panel just voted . . . bad news . . . I am still a force!"

I walked over to the Division Director to ask about next steps. He told me that they would be in touch. Two members of the review team approached me with smiles on their faces, extended their hands, said a heartfelt and sincere congratulations, and then: "We look forward to working with you." They understood the promise of MelaFind and wanted to see it approved.

Those two, in fact, had been on the November 23, 2009 call when we were strategizing the joint announcement of approval for May 3, 2010. But here we were in November 2010 and 8,000 more people had died of melanoma since that call! I told the Division Director that I wanted to meet with the agency before Christmas to discuss the path to final approval. I also told this to the two reviewers who congratulated me, and they said that they would set it up. But that didn't happen. All I got, in fact, was a Christmas greeting email from one of the two.

No Words to Describe The Feeling

I ASKED THE dermatologists that had presented with us to accompany me to the press conference. When we got there, the analysts and reporters present wouldn't sit down. A reporter from *Medical Device Daily*, the top trade publication in medical devices, walked up to me and said he was astounded. "I have been doing this for 25 years and I have seen a lot of panels," he said, "but I have never seen FDA pre-panel documents as negative and damaging and as openly biased against a product as they were against MelaFind." (Another openly pessimistic Internet writer wrote the next morning that we were "back from the grave." So the FDA had shocked even those who had predicted a negative outcome!)

Even when the press conference was officially over, everyone, it felt, needed to speak to me despite the fact that I was numb, emotionally spent, and exhausted. They came one after the other—our investor relations people, our public relations people, our chief financial officer, employees, experts, and reporters. It just kept coming. Meanwhile, employees back at the office kept trying to call me and were emailing me. One of them, a very young engineer named Alexei Smirnov, texted me: "Joe, that was amazing. We were all watching over the Internet." I replied, "Yeah, we did it, feels great, see you and the team real soon." He texted again: "Joe, no, seriously, this was amazing—there are no words to describe it." "Yeah," I replied, "awesome, and now we'll really make it happen." But he wouldn't go away! He texted back, so I had to excuse myself and go off and volley with him a bit.

I went back to speaking to those around me and strategizing about the announcement we'd be making the next morning. We had a team dinner, and we tried to deflate, but we couldn't. The excitement was too great. As usual, I slept for only about two-and-a-half hours, then got up, worked out, and headed to a breakfast meeting with our counsel, our IR/PR team, and our CFO. I then took an Amtrak train home. I should have been ecstatic, but I was still numb.

6

FDA Part III:
Taking Matters Into Our Own Hands

Not Quite Basking in the Afterglow of the Panel Victory

IN MY VIEW, the FDA's blatant attempt to derail our panel meeting was not only inexplicable, it was irresponsible in the extreme. MelaFind worked, and it could save lives. We'd prevailed, though, and I looked forward to whatever brief period of celebration our team was going to be able to enjoy as a result. But I was in for another surprise.

As the panel team finally sat for a private dinner, one very important "stakeholder," who I shall refer to as "Master of the Obvious #1" said to me, "That was amazing, Joe, but I am not sure it was enough to win. So what's the next move with the FDA?" I wasn't even in my seat yet, and was actually leaning up against a wall to stop myself from keeling over due to exhaustion. The sentiment of his remark was correct—we did need to figure out our next move—but the timing could not have been worse. Did he actually think I needed to hear that, and in front of our employees, no less? Or that I didn't know there were more challenges ahead?

Of course, this particular stakeholder really did seem to think that he was being helpful, He also loved to call me and tell me what the Yahoo message boards were saying about our stock, despite the fact that I had told him many times in the past that our investor relations consultants, bankers, and investors had told me to ignore them. (Of course, I still read them. I couldn't help it. But he didn't know that.) So I ignored the question, and simply told him that my next move was going to be eating my dinner. When he rephrased his query, apparently thinking that I hadn't heard it, I nodded and added, "And after I have dinner, I'm going to visit my brother next week for Thanksgiving." At that point, he backed off.

Master of the Obvious #2 was even more pessimistic. He approached me in private the week after Thanksgiving and said, "That was truly amazing, but I'm afraid that it will be a Pyrrhic victory. People tell me that when the agency feels the way they do, and the panel is a split vote, they do not approve." I looked at him and said, "I've been fighting with my feet bound and my hands tied behind my back. But now I'm now a warrior with a weapon. Watch me fight, and you might learn something!"

That wasn't good enough for him, because he proceeded to repeat his comment in front of a larger group. I replied as I had the first time, and then asked him what percent of the vote the last three presidents of the United States had gotten. "Less than we'd received at the panel," I said without waiting for an answer, "and yet don't we still call all of them 'Mr. President?'" I then punctuated my soliloquy with something unfit for print, and a warning that if he ever raised the "Pyrrhic victory" garbage to me again, I would physically escort him from the premises. When I'm in "intensity mode," you're either on my team, or in my crosshairs. Guess which these two were in?

The company meeting on the Monday following Thanksgiving was one of the most memorable experiences of my life. (And came so soon after another, which was the panel itself.) I'd asked a number of employees to present to the company their own perspectives on the panel meeting so that *everyone* could take ownership of the monumental and historic success. I was also very interested to hear the take of the employees who'd been watching on webcast and those who'd been at the panel meeting but were not part of the presentation.

Jenna Glauda had come to the company straight out of college and had been with us for less than two years at the time. She told the story of how painful it had been to watch the FDA presentation and actually feel the entire panel moving against us. She'd been sitting about twelve rows behind the podium during the panel, and she told the story of how she'd wanted to talk to me, to be assured, and how at the lunch break she'd waited for me at the top of the stairs leading to the ballroom only to see me put my hand up to her from 100 feet away in the motion of a stop sign. She then said that when later in the afternoon I turned from the front of the room to smile at her, she'd known it was my way of letting her know that I was okay, and that I was sorry.

After another employee told a similar story, I made it "illegal" to talk about me. I told them that I wanted people to talk about themselves and what they saw and felt, and tell the others what had been going on around them. Nyq didn't listen to me—what else was new?—and asked me whether I had kept my note page from the summation, which I had. Later, and without my knowledge, he had it framed and hung at MELA's front entrance. He also told of how he and the others watching the webcast had been on the exact same rollercoaster ride we'd been on in DC: with all the cheering, jeering, and then ultimate pandemonium after the final vote.

As for me, I was still a basket case.

Promises, Promises

PROMISES ARE ONLY as good as the person who makes them. Take the FDA reviewer who congratulated me, expressed enthusiasm about working together to move things along, and told me that we could meet before Christmas. The following week, when he told me by email that our meeting needed to wait until the panel transcripts became available, after which there would be an internal FDA meeting to discuss the panel's comments, I believed him. And

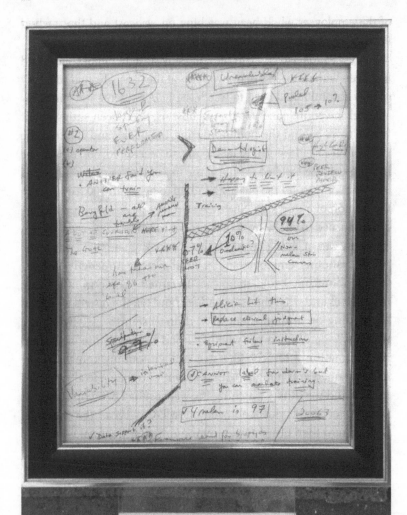

when he said he couldn't commit to a date in late December to meet, I wasn't that concerned. The end of the year is a busy time for the FDA. They often rush to issue as many final decisions as possible—approvals, usually—as the year comes to a close. But when I didn't receive replies to many emails and phone calls throughout the month of January, I knew something was wrong. And I was worried that it was once again coming from on high.

I was very concerned about the FDA moving to a final action without having another meeting with us. I was so concerned, in fact, that with each passing day my anxiety increased. The FDA loves to remind companies that, notwithstanding panel outcomes, they reserve the right to do what they feel is best, and feel no obligation to follow the panel's advice. It only made matters worse that we were now in the Internet era, and the FDA's negative arguments and analyses now littered the Internet.

All of which meant that instead of experiencing a turnaround as I should have, my physical and mental conditions only worsened: my mood sunk further, I couldn't sleep, and I even developed a dermatological condition known as alopecia areata, which is characterized by areas of focal hair loss, typically in a man's beard. I also needed to have an endoscopy due to intensifying epigastric distress. You might have thought I'd have been in a better mood given the panel victory, but the previous eight to ten weeks of wall-to-wall stress were also finally catching up to me. The combination of that strain finally beginning to manifest itself and the fresh strain I was feeling given the radio silence out of the FDA were almost too much to bear. My psyche was crumbling.

I asked a doctor I respected tremendously how he dealt with stress. He told me that I needed to do two things. First, I had to speak to someone schooled in matters of the psyche about getting some sleep. Second, I needed a hobby. I took his advice on both. The first resulted in me being prescribed a sleeping aid. And—voila—I started getting four-plus hours of sleep a night! I also started taking piano lessons. I bought a keyboard and headphones so that when I woke up at 3:00AM, I could practice without bothering Adele or my neighbors. I stopped taking the sleeping aid a couple of months later, but I'm still taking piano lessons. I have recitals once a year, along with my teacher's eight-year-old students! The way I see it, renewed sleep and the piano saved my life. Adele also forced me to go skiing, which brought me a pinch of happiness, but I will forever think of that time as my Dark Period.

Speak Softly and Carry a Big Slide

ON FEBRUARY 4, 2011, with the FDA still not responding to us, we went to the American Academy of Dermatology meeting in New Orleans. At a session about the FDA, we were shocked to see Dr. Peter Rumm, a senior staff member in the SORD Division, present a particular slide. Dr. Rumm had been one of the FDA presenters at the advisory panel. He had participated in the telephone call during which I was told that the panel date needed to be moved from August 26, 2010 to November 18, 2010, and he'd been present at the "pre-panel alignment" meeting where we'd been told to make the intended use for "all physicians."

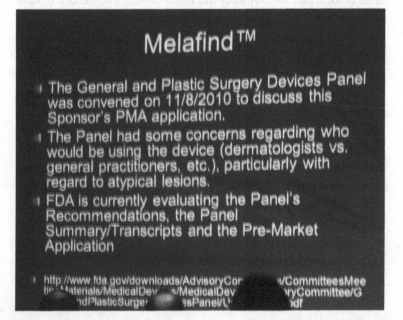

Melafind™

- The General and Plastic Surgery Devices Panel was convened on 11/8/2010 to discuss this Sponsor's PMA application.
- The Panel had some concerns regarding who would be using the device (dermatologists vs. general practitioners, etc.), particularly with regard to atypical lesions.
- FDA is currently evaluating the Panel's Recommendations, the Panel Summary/Transcripts and the Pre-Market Application
- http://www.fda.gov/downloads/AdvisoryCor   /CommitteesMee
ti   Materials/MedicalDev   /MedicalDev   ryCommittee/G
    ndPlasticSurge   esPanel/L   df

I'm going to set aside the fact that it's totally inappropriate for the FDA to comment publicly on active reviews. At the moment I saw the slide, I thought, 'Here they go again with an issue that is a total *non-issue*.' We had no problem whatsoever with the product being restricted to dermatologists. We'd suggested it from the start, but it was the FDA that had instructed us to change it. And you don't have to take my word for it: there were many witnesses to those conversations, and it has been put on paper multiple times. That notwithstanding, the panel had even voted in favor of the product for use by the broader group, and would have voted even more favorably on a putative claim limited to dermatologists. It should have been a non-issue by that point, but the FDA clearly wasn't going to let it lie. Rather, it appeared they might be planning to use it as a basis for rejection if not a wedge issue in future discussions with us. After we saw the slide, we called and sent emails with even more urgency to request a meeting or teleconference to discuss the panel outcome. NOTHING.

At that point, we reached an important conclusion: We desperately needed to go on offense. We needed to take matters into our own hands. And so that's what we did.

The first thing we did was negotiate with ourselves. On March 2, 2011, we submitted a PMA amendment in which we changed the intended use in the claim to "dermatologists" from "physicians." That's the kind of move one normally reserves for final approval discussions. Why is that? Because in the normal course of events, you'd wait to concede on certain things while holding the line on others as part of the larger negotiation—in other words, horse trading—for final approval. The way things were going, though, we felt that it was critical to do something—anything—to jumpstart a process that was clearly stalled once again. It would also force them to address the issue, while buying us more time if a final letter of rejection was actually in the works. It also gave us great "high road" arguments for later, in the event we decided to file a lawsuit against the FDA. In short, we were giving the FDA what they'd publicly said they were concerned about in the AAD meeting slide. No one could accuse us of intransigence.

I'd also noticed that the FDA had recently announced a new program for pioneering devices called the Innovation Pathway. The gist of it: the agency was going to speed up approvals for certain breakthrough products. We thought MelaFind was precisely the kind of product they were talking about. We'd actually followed all of the elements of the Innovation Pathway, without even knowing about it, and yet our approval process was being slowed—and nearly blocked—at every possible juncture.

Innovation Pathway – Priority Review Program for Pioneering Devices (Feb. 8, 2011)

Program Goals / Dr. Shurin's Quotes	MelaFind PMA
1. For "new medical devices that demonstrate the potential to revolutionize disease treatment, diagnosos, or health care delivery and that target unmet medical needs"; devices that offer "the biggest bang for the buck"	1. One American per hour is dying of melanoma because it is not being identified at curable stage. Treating in situ melanoma is 22 times less costly than a Stage IV melanoma
2. "Perhaps most exciting is our proposal to establish a priority review program for" these devices	2. MelaFind has Expedited Review—one of the 3 reasons is significant unmet medical need
3. The "key features of this pathway will be identifying and resolving" safety and effectiveness issues early in the process	3. MELA Sciences invested over 1 year to establish a Binding Protocol Agreement to establish the definition of safety and effectiveness before raising $130 MM and executing the largest prospective study ever conducted in melanoma detection, meeting all endpoints (See Arch. Dermatol.)

I saw the announcement as nothing more than a concocted response to the increasingly negative press and vitriol targeted toward the FDA (and Dr. Shuren in particular) by both the medical device and venture capital communities. And I wasn't alone. The consensus in the industry was that the Innovation Pathway was nothing but pure propaganda. Rather than simply expediting approvals and thereby reducing regulatory uncertainty, the FDA simply wanted to throw some words at the problem. I found the timing interesting, as well, given that the President's January 25 State of the Union Address had mentioned innovation over a dozen times while also outlining an explicit goal of reducing the regulatory burden on the private sector, the engine of innovation, and jobs.

Of Irony and Opportunity

THE IRONY OF the announcement was that Innovation Pathway program was and still is absolutely unnecessary. Why? Because the regulations that already existed in the books allowed for speedy review and approval if everybody played above board. In fact, the creation of a new program only meant more bloating of the FDA and could just as easily increase regulatory uncertainty as a result. All that said, I did consider joining them in the Innovation Pathway charade. Why couldn't they point to MelaFind as a model case for this new philosophy in action? It was an opportunity for both of us—kind of like the missed opportunity to announce the approval of MelaFind on Melanoma Monday—and might have had the additional benefit of convincing the industry that they really were serious.

We had, after all, successfully achieved all of the pillars of the program. We targeted a disease that kills one American (particularly young women) per hour but which is also 100% curable if detected early. We'd obtained Expedited Review. And we'd met extensively with the FDA early in the process to agree on the definitions of safety and effectiveness. We could be the poster child for the Innovation Pathway! The FDA could have held us up high as a beacon. They could have looked like superstars. But would they? Given their behavior to that point, it seemed unlikely, but we figured we'd give them a chance. When we next met with them, we thought, we'd try to plant that seed.

Another important thing happened in early 2011. In January, Adele and I bumped into Jonathan Rockoff, a writer for *The Wall Street Journal*, while sitting in JFK airport en route to the JP Morgan

Healthcare Conference. (Adele already knew him—she works in the industry too—and she introduced us.) A few weeks later, he called me about the FDA's review of Sedasys, Johnson & Johnson's product for monitoring anesthesia. J&J, he explained, had told him that they'd done everything that they'd been asked to do by the FDA and in his words they still were getting shafted, and it had reminded him of the elevator version of the MelaFind story I'd told him in January. Before I get into what we actually talked about, there's an important point to be made, and it's one that Rockoff addressed in the first line of his February piece, when he referred to J&J's direct appeal to the commissioner of the FDA—only the second such appeal in agency history—as a "rare public tussle between Johnson & Johnson and the [FDA]." In MELA's case, we felt we had no choice but to take the fight public, as we had run out of other options. J&J *almost never* engages in public spats with the FDA, but things had gotten so bad that even they felt that the situation required a public airing.

I knew nothing about the Sedasys situation myself, so Rockoff and I talked about the more general concept of the FDA's shifting of the goal posts, even when they seem cemented in the ground. He quoted me saying that, "[the] FDA is telling the market that the rules can change for any reason and at any time." In response, the FDA once again claimed that we hadn't followed the protocol and that the study hadn't provided conclusive enough data to determine the device's accuracy. Both points were patently false. But the FDA was suddenly feeling the pressure. Rockoff also quoted David Nexon, a senior executive vice president at the device industry trade group AdvaMed: "It's never been as bad as this." This wasn't a MELA-specific problem. It was affecting everyone.

Given that we weren't the only ones who thought that the FDA was killing innovation, we figured we might as well put ourselves up as Exhibit A, and continue to increase the pressure. Congress itself was showing some interest given the number of other medical device companies that were complaining. The timing was excellent because the legislative agenda for 2011 included reauthorization of the Prescription Drug User Fee Act and Medical Device User Fee Act. These statutes provide for application review fees to be paid by industry as well as setting review performance standards by the FDA. The problem was that while industry had been paying the FDA hadn't been performing. And we thought that we could use the experience of MELA to drive that point home by the time Congress was ready to vote on reauthorization.

We decided to create a communications plan to raise awareness of the case of MelaFind both in the industry and inside the Beltway. We knew we had to take the high road, though, and constantly emphasized to everyone we spoke to that we'd voluntarily limited our claim to dermatologists. We'd won at the panel meeting, after all, and didn't want to appear as if we were angry or complaining. There was a risk that we would appear that way anyway, but we figured the time had come to take the fight to another level.

And then it was our turn in the limelight: *The Wall Street Journal* published an editorial about MelaFind on March 30, 2011 entitled "Medical Progress, Please: Your Next Melanoma, Courtesy of the FDA." The writer, Holman Jenkins, questioned the credibility of the FDA in entering into a binding protocol agreement then failing to honor it as well as the fact that we supported limiting the claim to dermatologists.

Bringing a Knife to a Gun Fight

WHEN WE MADE the decision to go on the offensive, we knew that we would need a constant drumbeat of pressure from all corners—patients, dermatologists, industry, media, and policy makers. How does a little company pull off such a thing? For starters, I met weekly with our advocacy, PR, policy, and legal team in Washington. Olivia Pope from *Scandal* couldn't have assembled a better group of operatives. They had great ideas, including a grass roots letter writing campaign, desk side briefings with reporters that had an interest in the space, outreach to policy makers, and meetings with well-connected individuals and groups in the healthcare policy space in DC.

But the main objective was to raise awareness of the MelaFind story inside the Beltway. We all realized that without significant media coverage, the fight with the FDA would go into the back alleys, and we would certainly lose if that were to happen because they could just outlast us. That is, they could simply do nothing and watch us run out of money. No, we needed to bring the fight into Madison Square Garden. To that end, someone floated the idea of filing a Citizen Petition in my name. There was precedent for such filings in disputes with the FDA over patents or loss of exclusivity, but no one, to our knowledge, had ever filed one over an FDA review matter, let alone in the middle of an active review.

I asked our lawyers to draft it. The theme would be that the FDA had broken the law in two ways. First, they had issued a non-approvable letter prior to a panel meeting for a breakthrough product. And second, they had failed to abide by the terms of the binding protocol agreement. We added another argument as well, which was that the FDA had violated its own guidelines and laws in its procedural handling of the MelaFind review.

To be effective, the Petition would have to have everything in it—emails, letters from the FDA correspondence file, and minutes of our meetings with the FDA. If we did that, all of the information would immediately become public, making it a bold step for us to take. As we were preparing the Petition in April, we also drafted another PMA amendment to address another concern of the panel, about the training of the users of MelaFind. We had already committed to developing and implementing a formal training program and had even shown the outline of it at the panel meeting. Just as with the limitation to dermatologists, though, the act of actually including it in an amendment prior to sitting at the label negotiation table would give us even more high ground with which to work, while simultaneously extending the review clock. The FDA was obliged to review the amendment, after all, before issuing a final action.

Notwithstanding the fact that the FDA pretty much gave us zero response to emails and voicemails, I was still confident that they had read and listened to every one of them. With that in mind, on the evening before we filed the Citizen Petition, I called and left an urgent voicemail for the review team. "Believe me," I said, "You're going to want to talk to me tonight." The way I saw it, we were giving them one last chance to move the product toward approval before we forced them into the ring. But they didn't call back. We filed the Citizen Petition on May 9, and the second PMA Amendment a few days later.

Ding, ding.

Transparency and the Rule of Law
vs. Kafka and *J'Accuse*

ON JANUARY 21, 2009, President Obama famously declared, *"Let me say it as simply as I can: Transparency and the rule of law will be the touchstones of this Presidency."* But here we were in May 2011, and everything that we had experienced with the FDA up to that point (as well as in the months that followed) was anything but transparent and lawful. Let me state my view again: the FDA broke laws, rules, and guidelines, and cloaked their activities with deception, misinformation, and deceit.

The FDA had never accepted any responsibility, whatsoever, for the sorry state of affairs of the entire medical devices industry at the time, and still hadn't done so by the writing of this book. In Dr. Shuren's State of the Center talk in early April 2011, he offered his own explanations for why device approvals were down dramatically and why investment in the medical devices space was dropping precipitously on his watch. First, he blamed the recession for causing economic uncertainty, which in turn had made the industry unusually sensitive to regulatory uncertainty. Second, he blamed the increase in review times on the quality of the applications that industry was submitting. Third, he stated that the applications were becoming increasingly complex, with the result that additional expertise was required to review each document. Fourth, he suggested that a lack of funds for the FDA meant that the agency was being outpaced by advances in new technologies. Fifth, he blamed an inundation of requests for meetings with the FDA for extending review times. Sixth, he lamented a *high staff turnover rate.* (He was right about that—turnover on the device side was almost double that of drugs and biologics. But it wasn't his fault. Of course not!) And then, for his seventh and final point, he claimed that the Innovation Pathway represented a complete "sea change."

Numbers 2, 6, and 7 make me laugh the most.

#2: Could it be possible that the day after he took control, companies like Boston Scientific, Johnson & Johnson, and Medtronic had suddenly forgotten how to draft a quality application? Seriously, the walls in those places know what to do!

#6: I led MELA through tremendously uncertain periods, often with no more than a year to 18 months of cash, and yet we experienced no significant defections of key people. Zilch. Nada. How could he admit to a turnover rate that was twice that of the other two centers at the FDA and not see a leadership problem? I was astounded.

#7: This was no sea change. It was propaganda, a "we're doing everything right" defensive deflection. Amazing.

I was interviewed on Bloomberg Television on May 21, 2011, soon after the Citizen Petition had been made public. During the interview, I explained that I had filed the Petition to invite FDA Commissioner Margaret Hamburg to shine the biggest spotlight that she could find on the MelaFind PMA review and called on her to enforce the FDA's own laws and regulations. And I pointed out that I was simply asking the agency to do as the President himself had promised, which was to be transparent and to follow the rule of law. I added that I was confident that once Commissioner Hamburg had taken a look, our application review would be put back on track.

I explained the whole imbroglio to one Beltway insider who has worked in several agencies, the White House, and is now on K Street. He looked at me and exclaimed, "Why, this is Kafka-esque."

That's right. What the FDA had done to us, and continued to do, was akin to what had been done to Josef K in *The Trial*. It certainly felt like we were at the mercy of a big untouchable bureaucracy that was manipulating the rules and being anything but forthright. And like Josef K himself, we had been driven into nightmarish desperation and helplessness.

The insider also pointed to the air above my head, said *"J'Accuse!"* and then urged me to keep the faith and continue the battle. I had no idea what it meant, but a few days later I was in the Spy Museum, killing time prior to my flight back to New York, and came across a display about the *Dreyfus Affair*. In short, Emile Zola had written an open letter to the French government on the front page of the *L'Aurore* newspaper on January 13, 1898 that accused the government of judicial errors and lack of serious evidence in the wrongful imprisonment and persecution of Alfred Dreyfus, a military officer, for espionage. Emile is my kind of guy. As was the Beltway insider, apparently. I'd actually been afraid that he was going to say, "Welcome to DC. Call me when there is a dead girl or a live boy." But he didn't. He was truly shocked. Maybe others would be, too. So we needed to keep pushing our message out as aggressively as we could. He even offered to help us do so.

I'd just launched my own *J'Accuse* by filing a Citizen Petition against the U.S. Food & Drug Administration in the middle of an active review. The only question was whether, like Zola, I'd be forced to flee to England as a result.

Speaking of Europe . . .

IN EARLY MAY 2011, we filed an application with the European authorities for CE mark approval to market MelaFind in Europe. The CE mark approval process is much more straightforward and efficient than the FDA process. Many excellent products are approved for use in Europe years before they are approved (that is, *if* they are approved) by the FDA. Both the medical device industry and elected officials representing states with significant medical device constituents have pointed to this disparity a great deal in trying to get legislation that would expedite the FDA approval process passed.

To be fair, in many cases CE mark reviews are not as in-depth as the FDA's. But there's also no evidence to suggest any greater incidence of adverse events related to approved products in Europe compared to the U.S. Nevertheless, in January 2011 Dr. Shuren claimed that the European regulatory system allowed Europeans to be used as "guinea pigs," and that the use of notified bodies (private regulatory authorities) allowed device makers to "forum shop" their applications. And in February he said that the European review system lacked adequate public accountability. His comments greatly upset the Europeans, who sent a letter to FDA Commissioner Margaret Hamburg that ended with a challenge—let the European authorities know if the FDA had any evidence whatsoever "that certain medical devices, which were not safe and risked compromising the health and safety of patients or users, were brought on the EU market while [the] FDA [had] rejected them." Of course, there were no examples. Dr. Shuren had tried to add an entire continent to his roster of people other than himself to blame for the FDA's failures, and he'd gotten the reaction he deserved.

While I'm making a generalization here for the sake of brevity, I think it's fair to say that the CE mark process is usually more stringent from an engineering perspective but lighter on clinical aspects than an FDA review. But our design specifications, which are the starting point of the engineering review, were thresholds for sensitivity and specificity, not voltages and currents and other physical measurements. So our CE mark approval was based on clinical data, and we gave them a tremendous amount of it. The CE mark process can take under six months, so with a little luck, MelaFind could be approved for sale in Europe by September 2011. The sooner, the better, as far as we were concerned. Not just for its own sake, but because we could also then leverage that approval with the FDA, throwing a little more fuel on the fire.

The Poster Child

THE CITIZEN PETITION attracted the attention we'd hoped it would. The media picked up on it immediately, and I gave in-depth interviews to top trade publications, including *Medical Device Daily, The Gray Sheets, BNA (Bureau of National Affairs)*, and *Mass Device*. I was a quote machine, extolling the virtues of MelaFind and the largest prospective positive study ever performed in melanoma detection.

We became the example every writer cited in stories about what was wrong with the FDA. I was even asked to comment about FDA medical device review issues that had nothing to do with MelaFind whatsoever.

One writer working on a wrap-up of the 10th Annual MedTech Investing Conference (which I hadn't even attended) reached out to me via email on June 1. My quote—"The MelaFind PMA, which is predicated on our rare binding Protocol Agreement, is much bigger than just the MelaFind PMA; a denial would indicate that the rhetoric around U.S. (medical) innovation is mere propaganda and its approval would turn the rhetoric into reality."

On June 2, 2011, Dr. Shuren testified in front of the House Oversight & Government Reform Subcommittee Hearing. At one point, he was asked whether there was "a better way." His reply: "[The] FDA recognizes that it can do a better job at managing its premarket review programs. We continue to look for ways to improve our ability to facilitate innovation and to speed safe and effective products to patients. We know that medical device development is expensive. And we agree that, in many areas, insufficient clarity, consistency, and predictability on our part contributes to those expenses." He further stated that the FDA strives toward a "reasonable and fair approach to regulation that will foster innovation in the medical technology industry."

Medical Device Daily ran a story about his testimony in its June 6, 2011 issue. The first sentence: "Joseph Gulfo, MD, says he applauds the federal government's efforts to improve the medical devices approval process and to increase transparency in that process. But, he says, there is a 'tragic disconnect' between the FDA's intentions and the agency's actions." I was also quoted saying, "I applaud Dr. Shuren. I really do. He's admitting there are problems . . . he wants to make it better and I'm thrilled . . . I think the first step in change is problem recognition and I want to work with him and we've demonstrated that."

A few days later, at the Medical Device Manufacturers Association Conference in Washington, Dr. Shuren clearly thought he was being funny when he told the attendees that if they were having summer parties for their children and needed a piñata, he'd be happy to come. He was making light of the onerous regulations, massive uncertainty, and difficulties that industry was having. Amazing.

He also urged members of the audience to take their problems up a notch if they believed their reviewer's demands were irrational, promising that, "nobody is going to retaliate against you." And also this chestnut: "We're not always going to get it right, but we can't get better unless you come talk to us." And another deflection: "The increasing adversarial environment that we're in is getting in the way of having successful improvements in our pre-market programs. He also complained of difficulty in hiring people because of all the ill will expressed toward the FDA, adding that he'd "never seen this level of rhetorical poison in Washington."

I cannot stress enough that all of these problems either emerged or were exacerbated *after* the arrival of the new leadership of the FDA. The whole industry was thinking the same thing, but they were (and still are) afraid of retaliation. The real problem was (and remains) leadership, pure and simple, not a lack of guidance documents, attempts to engage reviewers, poor quality of applications, or acrimony in DC. It was surreal. And because the MelaFind application and review process had it all, we were invoked in articles, news pieces, and editorials as the beyond-the-pale example of everything that had gone wrong with the FDA. To this day, I still cannot reconcile the things that the FDA was *saying* with the things they were *doing*. To us.

The Turning Point

IN OUR SEARCH for Beltway insiders who would not only understand, but also care *and* be in a position to do something about it, we met with Dr. Michael Mandel, a Ph.D. economist who was working with the Progressive Policy Institute, a left-of-center think tank. Michael specializes in government regulation, innovation, and growth. He was the former Chief Economist for *Business Week* and a Senior Fellow at Wharton's Mack Institute for Innovation Management. Titles of pieces he'd written included 'Pebbles in the Stream: 'Does the FDA Slow Medical Technology Innovation?' (December 4, 2010), 'Reviving Jobs and Innovation' (February 2011), and 'Michael Mandel on Innovation, Growth, and the Regulatory State' (December 26, 2010).

When I met with Dr. Mandel in May 2011, he told me that he'd been in search of two things. The first: the beyond reproach/can't shake a stick at it/unassailable case of FDA over-regulation stifling breakthrough medical innovation. And second: a CEO not afraid to tell his story. I knew that he had both standing right in front of him. But he needed a little convincing.

He asked to me send him everything—the panel transcripts, study reports, and all the background information we wanted to provide. That was easy because the panel transcripts were readily available and the Citizen Petition contained everything else. I didn't hear from him for weeks. During that time, though, he not only read everything, but also performed his own statistical analyses. When he finally called me, he told me, "You're the one I've been looking for!" And asked to meet with me again.

In June 2011, Michael issued a white paper from the Progressive Policy Institute entitled, "How the FDA Impedes Innovation: A Case Study in Overregulation." The six-page masterpiece, singularly about MelaFind, laid out the fundamental problem as he saw it, which was that the FDA didn't even understand what innovation really was! He contended that innovation is incremental and needs to be fostered, not feared and blocked. It wasn't the tack I would have taken, but it was his paper, not mine. And it worked.

At the very same time, many people in the venture capital community were stepping up their fight against the capricious actions of the FDA that were causing an environment of extreme regulatory uncertainty, which was in turn reducing investment in the sector and killing companies and innovation. They didn't care how high the FDA wanted to make the regulatory hurdle. They only cared that the hurdle be clearly defined.

That said, they argued, they could no longer countenance two things. The first: hearing the FDA say, once again, "We're preparing guidance documents on certain aspects of the process, and we'll make them available as soon as possible." The second: having the hurdle raised at the end of the process. The result was uncertainty at both ends of the investment decision. At the front end, they couldn't even be sure that there weren't already rule changes in process that they hadn't been informed about yet. That made them reluctant to invest in anything. And at the back end, after all the work had been done and all the money spent, there was an increasing chance they would be told that the agreed-upon steps were no longer acceptable. And this made them reluctant to continue to fund companies and products already in development. I am stupefied as to how people in government couldn't see what was happening. Or, from a more cynical perspective, didn't care.

Timothy Hay, a writer for Dow Jones' Venture Wire, published an excellent article addressing these very issues on June 23, 2011. Its title was "Medical Device VC's Link FDA Dysfunction With Company Shutdowns." Among his findings:

- Nine venture capital firms were preparing to "wage war against the FDA, bringing to light damning evidence that directly blamed a dysfunctional agency for the failure of multiple start-ups";
- The investors alleged "that FDA regulators are inconsistent and un-predictable, keeping promising treatments in limbo for months or years";

- "At least four companies [had] recently shut down due in part to a daunting FDA process," including Acorn Cardiovascular ($110 million in funding; main VC investor New Enterprise Associates) and Luminous Medical ($50 million in funding, main VC investors De Novo Ventures and Draper Fisher Jurvetson).

That same month, the *Boston Herald* ran an interview with Senator Scott Brown who recalled a meeting with FDA Commissioner Margaret Hamburg in which he'd said, "Listen . . . you're crushing business in Massachusetts. We have the most innovative, intelligent work force potential in the world . . . and you're putting a big wet blanket over them and crushing jobs."

The Congressional Hearing

MEANWHILE, THE U.S. House Committee on Energy and Commerce's Subcommittee on Oversight and Investigations continued its series of hearings on the problems at the FDA with a hearing on July 20, 2011: "Regulatory Reform Series #5 - FDA Medical Device Regulation: Impact on American Patients, Innovation and Jobs." Dr. Shuren was present to testify before the committee as he had done on June 2. But this time, Michael Mandel was also invited. Congress wanted to discuss his white paper on MelaFind.

I watched the hearing via webcast from our lawyer's office. Rep. Michael Burgess (R-TX), who was a practicing physician before seeking office, and Rep. Brian Bilbray (R-CA), whose daughter had advanced melanoma because it went undetected when it was curable, asked the most questions of Dr. Shuren regarding the MelaFind approval process. There are two profoundly important quotes from Dr. Shuren worth noting.

The first: "I think in this case, there were issues with the data that were sent to us. What we are doing now is going through the data provided . . . and keep in mind, the manufacturer more recently, a few months ago, changed the indication they were looking for. We're trying to see, does the data support what the manufacturer would like to do, or something close to it? And if so, then, we would approve that device."

The second: He was asked, "Why was that device basically denied the ability to go through a review process, a review panel?" Dr. Shuren replied, "The decision the first time around to not have the device go through the advisory panel was wrong. The staff made the wrong call. It should have been allowed to go to advisory panel; it eventually was. It was supported. It was a very slim margin; it was eight-seven."

This testimony begs many questions:

—What was wrong with the data? We had hit every endpoint and satisfied every element of the binding protocol agreement.

—Why didn't Dr. Shuren retract the *unlawful* not approvable letter when we submitted the Supervisory Review request on April 15, 2010, instead of waiting seventeen months to admit that it was mistake? Why did it require Congressional intervention for him to do—actually, only to *say*—the right thing? Is that how "transparency" was supposed to work?

—Why did he not take responsibility? He'd made a mistake, as well, by not retracting it when we'd asked him to, which would have greatly limited the damage to the company.

—Why add the gratuitous comment about the vote being slim, when he had to have known about the unlawful and inappropriate lengths to which staff had gone to sully the product in pursuit of a panel rejection?

Journalist Tory Newmyer adroitly combined the MelaFind story with the venture capitalists' anti-FDA argument in a September 2 story in *Fortune* entitled, "Is The FDA Killing Innovation?" He quoted Jonathan Fleming, a well-known venture capital investor from Oxford BioSciences stating, "The policies of this administration without question have caused a loss of economic growth, a loss of jobs, a loss of American lives unnecessarily, and in the future, when we have to buy new advanced technology and drugs, we're going to be buying them from foreigners, because they can't get approved here. That's why I'm changing my politics."

Fleming also suggested that I had "effectively [committed] career suicide" by speaking out against the FDA. Newmyer quoted me in response: "Transparency favors those with the data and the research and the results. We've got it. There's not a stronger case out there, and the more light that shines on this, the more peoples' jaws drop."

Back on Track . . . Maybe

TWO DAYS AFTER the Federal Register announcement of the July 20 hearing, I received a call from the FDA inviting us in to meet with them to discuss how to put the MelaFind PMA back into approvable form. There was a new Acting Director of the Office of Device evaluation, Christy Foreman. She was in a particularly difficult spot. Normally, reviews are managed at the Division level, and so it is the Division Director that shepherds them through. Ours had now been bumped up a level higher, to the person (in this case, Ms. Foreman) to whom the review divisions report. She could not have been conversant in the details of the program and the history. A meeting was scheduled for September 7, 2011 and we started the process of reviewing labeling, post-approval study requirements, and the training program outline.

MelaFind received European CE mark approval on September 6. Consider: we'd filed the CE mark application in May 2011, and received approval to market in Europe by September—just five months later. On the other hand, we'd filed the PMA in June of 2009, and had not yet been approved by the FDA twenty-seven months later! The timing of the CE mark announcement was quite auspicious, to say the least.

We invited the dermatologists who had presented at the panel meeting to the September 7 meeting with the FDA. We also invited Dr.

Elizabeth Tanzi, a dermatologist in DC who had missed her own melanoma, and Dr. Clara Curiel, a dermatologist at the University of Arizona who was an expert in the development of dermatologist training programs. It was meant to be a working session with the agency, in the hopes of finally coming to agreement on all major outstanding issues so that a label could be finalized in short order thereafter.

We rehearsed the evening before the meeting, covering the major items that were discussed at the panel as well as the significant points raised by FDA reviewers. I never take anything for granted, so I tried to keep both the team and myself sharp and focused. The rehearsals and slide preparations went late into the night.

When we arrived at the FDA the next morning, there was a literal army of FDA staff in the meeting room—approximately 25, by my count. The reviewers who had been very supportive of MelaFind were there, but so was the one who had gleefully high-fived his fellow FDA staff during the panel meeting. There were also a curious number of faces that I had never seen before. It was neither what I'd been expecting nor what I'd experienced during past label negotiation meetings. "Keep cool," I thought. I wasn't alone, after all, but we were still significantly outnumbered.

It soon became apparent that we'd been wrong again. This wasn't a label negotiation meeting; rather, it was a mini-panel meeting. We relived and had to endure many of the same fallacious and flawed arguments from the FDA. We, on the other hand, were armed with irrefutable facts, the binding protocol agreement, the statistically significant and valid data, and the positive panel vote. But it really was like Groundhog Day, all over again.

I'm sure it was very difficult for Christy Foreman to have the MelaFind review dumped in her lap like that. And she probably wanted to show her team that she was going to be objective. Whatever she was thinking, I wish she'd told me that it wasn't going to be a simple label negotiation. Seven hours later, hoarse and exhausted, we finished. And we'd done well.

The Homestretch

OVER THE NEXT several weeks, we had many exchanges with the reviewers over matters discussed at the meeting. And then, on September 26, 2011, we announced the receipt of an Approvable Letter from FDA. *The Wall Street Journal* ran an article on page 3 entitled, "New Tool In Skin Cancer Fight," with the whole MelaFind saga and battle with FDA laid out for good measure. It bears mentioning that by this point, the issuance of the approvable letter was as big a relief to the FDA as it was to us. They'd been getting a lot of negative press over MelaFind, and that would be coming to an end.

An approvable letter signals a firm meeting of the minds on the most important matters, and that final approval could be expected after last-minute administrative housecleaning on things like labeling and post-approval study protocol finalization. We wanted—no, we *needed*—that final approval as soon as possible because we needed to consummate another financing. But there was a hitch: We were "encouraged" to withdraw the Citizen Petition if we wanted a quick turnaround, because the same review staff that would otherwise be working on the final approval would instead be working on the response to a Citizen Petition filing that is mandated within six months. They had us there.

There were other hiccups along the way. We didn't agree with many of the items that the FDA wanted in the labeling, as we felt that they added no useful information, were misleading, and would be confusing to dermatologists. We also didn't agree with a number of things in the post-approval study.

Of particular concern to me was the fact that the FDA would not let us use the term "early melanoma." They contended that we hadn't shown that MelaFind leads to *earlier* detection. Their statement was true. The study did not show that, nor was it designed to show that. But we weren't referring to catching it earlier than you otherwise might. We were referring to the stage of the melanoma itself. More the point, the use of "early" as an adjective modifying "melanoma" is all over the literature. "Early melanoma" means melanoma at the stages of melanoma *in situ* and minimally inva-sive stages. Our trial had focused predominantly on these types of melanomas, so much so that the FDA made us put a warning in the label that MelaFind had not been tested on "advanced melanomas." By that logic, we should have been allowed to use the words "for the detection of early melanoma." All of the dermatologists in the room told them so. What's more, the Expedited Review letter (on FDA letterhead) has used the phrase "early detection." But denying us something that we wanted seemed their *modus operandi* at that point. A parting shot, as it were.

In an ideal world, we would have kept fighting on these and other points. And we would have won. I have had many labeling discus-sions with FDA reviewers in my career, the majority of which came to happy and appropriate conclusions. But the timing of final ap-proval was critical with respect to raising money. Amazingly, the FDA still didn't seem to feel too much pressure to act expeditiously. Prudence being the greater part of valor, we stopped fighting when we had something acceptable if not necessarily ideal.

And then it *finally* happened: We received final approval, and an-nounced it on November 2, 2011. I almost couldn't believe it when I read the headline from the Associated Press. Eleven words that had taken nearly eight years: "MelaFind, Device That Screens for Mela-noma with Light Approved by FDA."

The statutorily defined six-month PMA review had taken 29 months. But it wasn't over yet. Before we could launch the product in the U.S. and Germany, we needed to create the training program, the outline and parameters of which had been approved by the FDA. We also needed to run beta studies with users to finalize the user in-terface (an interactive computer screen) since the system we'd used in the studies was "blinded" and therefore didn't show the MelaFind result on screen. We also needed to prepare for large-scale commer-cial production of MelaFind. So we had a lot more work to do before we could launch. But the fight with the FDA was over. We'd done it.

On November 21, 2011, I was interviewed again on Bloomberg TV, providing the happy news that MelaFind had finally been ap-proved, and talking about the importance of detecting melanoma at its most curable stages. I didn't even use the word "early!"

Over the ensuing months, MelaFind won a number of awards—an Einstein Award, a Wall Street Journal Technology Award, the American Business Awards Business Innovation of the Year, and a Cleveland Clinic Top 10 Innovation of the Year. I won the American Business Awards Maverick of the Year (Silver) and was a finalist in Ernst & Young's Entrepreneur of the Year. The irony? We were winning *innovation* awards for a product that the FDA had done everything in its power to kill at the same time that they had rolled out an "Innovation Pathway."

I didn't really get a chance to revel in our victory either. Perhaps it was because I was still in shock and disbelief. Or that there was still so much more to do and I couldn't let up. Or that I was not yet whole as an individual after the trauma. I still wasn't myself at that point, although I was sleeping better—unaided—and had regained some of my lost weight.

Adele wanted me to resign right after the approval. I actually liked the sound of the idea, but I felt an obligation to continue, as well as a desire to see MelaFind actually saving lives, in the real world. You know, the one where people put more importance on the saving of human lives than on their own bureaucratic bullshit?

Even today, I still can't believe what we had to go through with the FDA. From the perspective of industry, it's shocking that a breakthrough device that had been proven to work in the largest study ever performed on a disease (at the time) would not have been approved had it not been for a congressional hearing. From the point of view of the citizenry, it is equally shocking that transparency and fair play had to be forced upon our government. The FDA was broken. And it still is.

7

$160 Million the Hard Way

"Nothing in the world can take the place of persistence. Talent will not; nothing is more common than unsuccessful men with talent. Genius will not; unrewarded genius is almost a proverb. Education will not; the world is full of educated derelicts. Persistence and determination alone are omnipotent."

—CALVIN COOLIDGE

Money, Money, Money, Money!

THE THEME SONG from Donald Trump's NBC series, *The Apprentice,* just about sums it up. Moving a truly breakthrough medical innovation from concept to reality takes a lot of money. As I pointed out in chapter two, it comes from various sources in different amounts, depending on the development stage of the technology and perceived length of time required to get it to market. But the total amount required is always substantial. With a true first-of-a-kind breakthrough technology, even more money will be necessary, and the methods by which that capital gets raised will usually be novel as well.

Before I joined MELA, I had wanted to create my own venture fund to invest in a limited number of companies (4 or 5), with one team running all of them. The thought had occurred to me in 1998 when I realized that everything that I had worked on to that point with Aileen Ryan, Bob McCormack, and Bob Maguire (and later, on my own) had worked. I figured that if I could pick them, guide them through FDA approval, and run them, the only thing left was to finance them.

As I started speaking seriously with MELA's early private investors at the end of 2003, I thought that the division of labor was quite fair—the founders would engineer the product, the investors would pay the bills, and I would oversee late stage development and shepherd it though FDA approval. And then a big company would acquire the company for a huge sum. I loved the idea of not having to be responsible for raising money for start-up companies again and again. For one, I'd already been successful at doing so, so that challenge wasn't particularly alluring from the standpoint of gaining experience. More importantly, it's extremely difficult and time-consuming. Doing the other things is much more fun. (At least it usually is. Of all the words I might use to describe my time at MELA, fun is nowhere near the top of the list.)

When the founding team did not fully engineer the product for manufacturing and the investors no longer wanted to commit the amount of money required to do so, the company effectively became "mine." And along with that came the responsibility for raising money.

I tried to get a well-known venture capitalist into the company but a deal that I nearly lined up fell apart at the last moment. At that point, I didn't have time to get others interested. The current private investors were about to demand their money back if I couldn't show them a clear line of sight to a significant financing in the short–or immediate term.

I often reflect on what would have happened if I'd managed to get VC investors involved. In that event, we wouldn't have needed to complete an initial public offering, or IPO, until we'd completed late-stage development and the real commercialization phase was about to begin. That means that the company wouldn't even have been public as of the writing of this book in 2013. If we hadn't been publicly traded during the development phase, the FDA saga outlined in chapters five and six, and the commercial development phase (which I will discuss in chapter eight), we wouldn't have been buffeted about by the public markets. Our image would not have been degraded, tarnished, and sullied to as great an extent as it was. And I would not have had to spend time courting public investors and analysts. I could have just focused on the work to be done.

Another important thing that a venture capital syndicate would have brought us was validation. That's a gift that keeps on giving, too. On several occasions, while raising money from public-market investors, I was asked the question, "Who are/were the VCs?" Potential corporate partners and/or acquirers asked the same thing. Why? Because the world is full of followers, and it's easier to follow a leader than to think for oneself and blaze a new trail. Investment funds and corporate entities were looking for validation, to know that someone (that is, the VCs) had already performed deep-dive diligence, helped nurture the company, found the right people at the right time, and shepherded through its early growing pains.

I'm quite confident that if we'd secured a $50 million to $75 million round of venture capital investment before going public, we would have been in a much better position to raise much more money in any particular financing, and probably would have attracted a marketing partner, if not an acquirer, along the way. Furthermore, I'm also confident that even when the company was suffering through the capricious and unlawful activities of the FDA, the stock performance would have been much, much different had the company had investors with a strong medical-products venture capital pedigree.

Of course, there's no guarantee that a VC syndicate would have kept investing in the company through the ups and downs either. They likely would have forced me to find some "new money"—that is, new VCs—to participate along the way. (That, or their funds could have been fully invested and they might not have been permitted to invest in us from funds of later vintage, which often happens.) In addition, I have my doubts as to whether they would have had the desire or courage to back some of the decisions we made, in particular the filing of the Citizen Petition in the middle of an active review and our media campaign regarding the FDA. While venture capitalists are "owners" of their portfolio companies, they also own lots of them at once. By taking MELA public, I'd assumed complete responsibility for it; it was my sole focus, and that allowed me to stay the course even when the going got tough. There's simply no way that venture capitalists can love each and every one of their companies the way that I loved MELA.

But that kind of love cuts both ways. The good: I kept breaking down every wall, refused to take no for an answer, and made some extremely novel and outside the box decisions. The bad: the company totally consumed my being. For me, at least, the two entities (Joseph Gulfo and MELA) became one and the same. I remember introducing myself to someone by saying, "My name is Joseph Gulfo and my initials are M E L A!" So it's possible that taking the company public was the only route that would have resulted in PMA approval. We'll never know.

But that's enough contemplation of alternate realities and wondering about things that did not come to pass. What matters is that in 2005, I knew that being in a VC portfolio would have been best for the company, but it wasn't to be. We felt we had to go public, and that was that, despite the inherent difficulties and challenges of being a publicly traded single-product medical device company. Given the choice, I would have stayed private. But I wasn't given the choice.

"It's Not the Years, Honey, It's the Mileage."

THE QUOTE ABOVE was Dr. Indiana Jones' reply to Marion Ravenwood Jones in *Raiders of the Lost Ark* when she said to him, "You're not the man I knew ten years ago." The rest of this chapter is about raising $160 million as a publicly traded single-product medical device company with no blue chip medical-products VC pedigree. When you're selling stock to the public, it takes the same amount of work to raise $10 million as it does $75 million. So it's not just the total amount raised that matters in the end, but also the number of financings. In this metaphor, the years would be the amount of money and the mileage would be the number of financings it took to do so. We raised $160 million *the hard way.*

What goes into each and every deal? Here are the steps:

1. Identifying the bankers with whom you wish to work;

2. Arguing with the lead bank to treat the co-lead well as they quibble over who is "running the books" and other such nonsense;

3. Negotiating the banking fee and the bankers' legal expenses;

4. Undergoing underwriter's due diligence of all sorts;

5. Taking a phone call from the co-lead bankers after the process has begun during which they'll tell you how the lead bankers are jerks and should be replaced by the ones calling you;

6. Preparing presentations of the technology and business;

7. Performing roadshows for actual deals as well as non-deal road-shows throughout the year to stay close to your investors and keep your company fresh in their minds. These include multi-city national trips, as well as banking and industry conferences;

8. Running the business while you're quibbling with bankers and responding to diligence questions;

9. Taking another call from the co-lead urging you to throw out the lead;

10. Conducting follow-up phone calls with funds that you have met on the roadshow to answer questions and provide them more materials (published papers, slides, the latest news pieces, topical issues in the news);

11. Dealing with auditors who always seem to run right up to the deadline for finishing their audits on time or introduce some ridiculous completely immaterial surprise that must be dealt with before they will issue their final audit letters so that the deal can be consummated;

12. Working with your legal team to prepare offering memoranda or prospectuses (or both) or to amend a shelf registration;

13. Working with your investor relations and public relations teams to prepare S.E.C. filings and press releases; and then, finally;

14. PRICING NIGHT. What is pricing night? It's when the deal "comes together," that is when the specific number of shares and terms that each fund wants in order to commit to the financing are made known. It occurs after market close (hence, pricing NIGHT) or before the morning open. This is the most stressful part of the process, as you are faced with a choice. You can either take the deal that the bank's capital markets people are telling you is doable, leave money on the table and take less, or issue more shares (if you have them available) to take more. This is a board-level discussion, too. Once the decision has been made, the money is almost in the bank;

15. Wait for confirmation in the morning that the bankers received all of the signed subscription agreements;

16. Issue a victorious press release and make S.E.C. filings;

17. Wait for the money to appear in your bank account three days later—minus, of course, the bankers' underwriting fee (which is usually a hefty 6%) and legal expenses.

Again, the crucial point I want to make is not that the above is too much of a burden in exchange for receiving millions of dollars in outside investment, but that you have to do the exact same amount of work for a deal that raises $10 million as one that raises $75 million. The net is not cast any wider or narrower, the presentations and diligence are no different, and the paperwork is neither more nor less cumbersome. The only things that change are the amounts invested by the institutional investors and the number of institutional investors participating.

In the eight years that I ran MELA as a public company, we consummated 11 separate financings (see table). That's almost unheard of. Normally, companies try to raise at least three years of anticipated cash needs per financing. If MELA were a multi-product or platform-based biotech, biopharma, or even medical device company, we probably could have raised $160 million in no more than three financings. But because we were a single-product medical device company, and had gone public far sooner than was ideal, we had no choice but to raise the money in 11 separate transactions.

Why is that? Because the milestones for device companies tend to be more compressed in time, and so investors prefer to hand over as little as possible in any single financing, taking a "come back and see me again when you hit the next milestone" approach. In addition, no matter how many times you try to explain it to them, most investors think that all devices are 510ks, where the real value inflection point occurs when the device hits the market, and not like a drug or biologic where significant value is realized upon FDA approval. Given its inherent novelty, a device that is designated for PMA is like a drug or biologic, but when investors hear "device," they tend to want to wait to invest not at approval but after it's actually for sale.

Because we consummated more transactions than is typical, we also had to participate in many more non-deal roadshows and banking conferences in order to stay close to our investors. I never had a "holiday" from investor engagements. Smart companies look to bolster their accounts when they're approaching 15 months of cash remaining, so when management is able to raise three-plus years of cash, they don't have to think about another financing for 18-24 months, and can focus on actually running the business in the interim. Not so with MELA. Because we were only able to raise an average of 12 to 15 months of cash at a time, our focus had to return to raising capital once a year or so. I always tried to make sure we stayed above 15 months of cash, too, especially after one investor told me that when *any* holding of his gets close to 12 months of cash, he invariably sells his position, knowing that the company will soon be coming to market to raise more, and he can then buy back in at a discount. He would have done it with his MELA stock, even though he actually believed in the company. And could you blame him? Who doesn't want to make instant, nearly risk-free profits?

MELA Sciences, Inc. Public Financings

Pricing Date	Type	Shares Sold (MM)	Amount Raised (MM)	Price	Market Discount	Warrants	
						Issued	Price/Coverage
10/28/05	IPO	4.26	$21.3	$5.00	N/A	150,000	$6.25/3.5%
10/31/06	PIPE	2.31	$13.2	$5.70	Market	346,587	$6.70/15%
7/31/07	PIPE	2.00	$11.5	$5.75	≈12%	500,051	$8.00/25%
7/31/08	Registered Direct	2.09	$11.9	$5.68	≈7%	N/A	
7/16/09	Registered Direct	2.40	$15.0	$6.25	≈16%	N/A	
2009/10	CEFF	2.23	$20.6	$9.22	≈7%	200,000	$11.35/5.9%
6/30/10	Public Offering	2.20	$16.5	$7.50	≈10%	N/A	
12/15/11	Public Offering	5.00	$16.2	$3.25	≈18%	N/A	
6/5/12 – 2/5/13	At the Market	6.58	$14.4	$2.19	≈VWAP	N/A	
2/11/13	Registered Direct	6.10	$7.9	$1.30	≈23%	N/A	
3/4/13	Venture Debt	0	$6.0			693,202	
Total Raised			$154.6	In the public markets			

. . . And The Terrain . . .

INDIANA JONES TALKED to Marion about years and mileage, but what about terrain? Anybody can rack up mileage on the highway. It's different and varied terrain that really wears on a vehicle. We consummated six different types of transactions—our IPO, PIPEs (Private Investment in Public Equity via unregistered shares), registered direct offerings (similar to PIPEs, but with registered shares, usually off a shelf registration), a CEFF (Committed Equity Financing Facility), an ATM (At The Market transaction), and a venture debt financing.

The only major financing type that we did not consummate was an announced public follow-on offering, specifically the type in which a public company issues and then sells new shares into the market. This is actually the most preferable form of follow-on (i.e., post-IPO) financing from a balance sheet perspective, as the shares are sold at the market price of the stock on the day of the deal and not at a discount. This is because follow-on public offerings are typically done from a position of great strength—when pre-announcement of a financing and a week of marketing are not likely to drive the stock price down. Investors can always buy your stock in the open market, but when they want *a lot* of stock, their own purchases can push the price up, and a follow-on public offering offers them a chance to buy in bulk at the market price. But you need that demand to be there for the follow-on to work, and you need to *under-satisfy* it—meaning many more investors want to be in the deal than there's room for, and the amount each one wants is more than they'll ultimately receive.

Larger companies can tap the markets for a variety of reasons, but a key element to a successful follow-on offering for a small company such as ourselves is that the company plans to raise such a significant amount of money that the markets have confidence that it will more than likely be the last time for the foreseeable future that shares will be issued. In other words, the company should be raising enough money to take it to profitability or to some other major and significant value inflection point, such as an acquisition.

A successful follow-on offering of this sort serves to obviate "financing risk," which is the downward pressure on the valuation of a company that occurs when investors hold off buying stock or, just as likely, sell shares they already own because they think that the company will likely issue shares in the near future at a discount to current market prices. Even if they like the stock, why wouldn't they lock in profits at a higher price and then buy again at a lower one? That's their job.

I had hoped to float a public follow-on offering right after the FDA conducted the advisory panel meeting in the first quarter of 2010 or, perhaps, a few days after the proposed joint FDA/MELA announcement of approval on Melanoma Monday, May 3, 2010. The company was valued at $300 million—with shares about $12 a piece—in January of 2010. If the stock had risen on the good news of the panel meeting or the announcement of approval, the shares could conceivably have been trading between $15 and $20 a share, and we might have issued 5 to 7 million shares, raising $75 million to $140 million in the process. A number of our investors even told me that we *needed* to do a public follow-on offering, and that they would be buyers when we did.

But it didn't happen. Instead, because of the FDA's unlawful actions and their subsequent attempts to cover them up, the next time we came to market, in June 2010, we were only able to raise $16.5 million at $7.50 a share. Between June 2010 and February 2013, we issued nearly 20 million shares at an average price of just $3.86 a share, for a total of $55 million. Clearly, the markets were holding that financing risk over our heads every step of the way. Had things proceeded as I believe they should have—panel meeting in March 2010 followed by approval in May 2010, there's no reason to think we couldn't have pulled off a significant follow-on offering to fund us all the way through the commercial launch of MelaFind. But things didn't happen as they should have, and the company was forced to scrape by on what meager amounts we could raise when we absolutely needed to do so.

And that, in a nutshell, is the real crime that the FDA perpetrated on the company. It was a double whammy, starting with the unlawful not approvable letter and then followed by lies, misinformation, and wantonly negative statements about the company that still live on the Internet. The FDA destroyed significant shareholder value and then continued to do so even when called to the carpet for their mistakes. MELA was given a Scarlet Letter followed by an albatross around its neck. It was as if Nathaniel Hawthorne's Hester Prynne and Samuel Taylor Coleridge's Ancient Mariner had a child and named it MELA!

And that's only what happened to the company in the capital markets. The FDA's actions also soured our relations with potential customers—dermatologists—and potential partners—corporations with significant dermatology franchises.

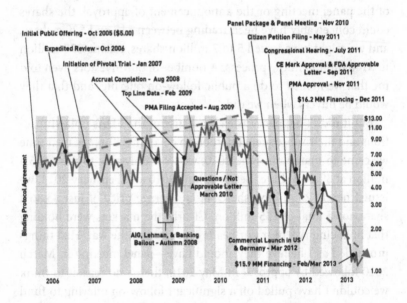

Consider a chart of our stock price performance. We had a clear upward trajectory—the green line—before the FDA's unlawful not approvable letter. And a clear downward one—the red line—afterward. There's an important disconnect to consider here as well. As far as the business itself is concerned, things have proceeded pretty much as they should have once the whole FDA imbroglio finally came to a head, from the ultimately positive advisory panel, to CE mark approval, FDA approval, product launch in two markets, excellent clinical results in a real world setting, and a Cleveland Clinic Top 10 Medical Innovation award. We sold 150 systems in our first year on the market, after which a MelaFind device was within 75 miles of 63% of the US population. But the value of the company has continued to decrease steadily and progressively in the face of that good news. The land mines that the FDA placed in our path completely destroyed both the car we were driving and the road we were traveling on.

More than a few analysts have told me they believed that the FDA's unlawful not approvable letter drove long-term institutional investors out of MELA, which not only destroyed the valuation (stock price), it also compromised our ability to raise the kind of money we needed to continue with our business plan. And the FDA's subsequent behavior, which included spreading of misinformation in an effort to cover up their mistakes, I believe attracted the shorts. And once the shorts assumed near-total control of the trading of the stock, they sent it over a cliff.

To demonstrate this point, consider several dramatic changes in ownership of MELA shares by three institutions with a long-term investment perspective starting with the issuance of the unlawful not approvable letter in March 2010, followed by the ensuing public drama over the next 18 months (change in panel data, pre-panel documents, panel presentation, Citizen Petition filing), and the eventual receipt of the approvable letter in September 2012:

—Fidelity investments, which owned 965,907 shares as of March 31, 2010, had disposed of *all of them* just six months later, a 100% reduction.

—UBS Global Asset Management, which owned 999,743 shares as of June 30, 2010, owned just 59,899 shares a year later, a 94% reduction.

—Susquehanna International, which owned 630,533 shares as of June 30, 2011, owned just 51,735 shares as of September 30, 2012, a 92% reduction.

When the good guys bail from your stock, and you still need more money, you start having to deal with a markedly shadier crowd. When I said we had to raise $160 million the hard way, I wasn't joking.

The IPO, Part I — the Prospectus and the Pitch

WHEN THE BOARD and I made the decision to take MELA public in 2004/2005, we first worked long hours with our lawyers preparing an IPO prospectus, which is included in the S-1 registration statement filed with Securities Exchange Commission. An IPO prospectus contains a description of the company, its business, its capital structure, and risk factors that investors should consider. Meanwhile, the lawyers representing the underwriters (that is, the bankers) performed exhaustive diligence of all types—patent, business, technical, clinical, legal, and regulatory. It took us over two months of intense work.

The role of auditors in an IPO is quite significant, and burdensome provisions of the recently passed Sarbanes-Oxley Act (2002) complicated matters further. Under Sarbanes-Oxley, any accounting firm that has provided consulting services to a company is barred from acting as an "independent" financial auditor. As the time we planned to file the S-1 rapidly approached, our auditors realized they'd overlooked this conflict—and they suddenly told us that because they'd been providing consulting services for us, they couldn't serve as independent financial auditors for the company's IPO in early May. So we had to find another independent auditor, give them time to do their work—life at MELA seems like it was one delay after another—and, yes, we had to pay for two audits.

While I understand the desire of legislators to protect the investing public, I am not alone in thinking they went overboard in some parts of Sarbanes-Oxley, which was passed in the wake of the Enron scandal. The above rule about consultants being barred from auditing means that companies essentially need two accounting firms. One helps prepare the company's financials and needs to be available to answer day-to-day accounting questions, and another needs to review that work. This adds great cost, wastes time, and, in my opinion, does nothing to protect shareholders. In fact, it hurts them by adding unnecessary administrative costs.

Our *new* auditors—whose official opinion would be included in the S-1—also proved problematic. Their issue was this: the private investors had agreed to a reverse stock split if the IPO proved successful. (This is common, and had been approved by the board.) We were planning to file immediately after Memorial Day in 2005. But then the auditors informed me late on Friday of the holiday weekend that they couldn't provide their opinion until the stock split had occurred. The problem was that if there were no IPO, there would be no stock split. But if the IPO were consummated, there would be one. But with no official opinion, there could be no IPO. We had a classic chicken and egg dilemma on our hands. We resolved it on a call with several audit partners that lasted until after midnight on that Friday night. We filed the S-1 on June 3. And I consumed more Tums than I should have.

Dina and I went on the IPO roadshow in late July and early August of 2005 while our chief financial officer managed the SEC review of the S-1 with the lawyers. The seven main points we made on our roadshow were:

1. Our founders, off-the-charts geniuses that had developed computer vision systems used by the Pentagon, had created a device for melanoma detection that worked, based on clinical data from 2,000 patients to date. That addressed the notion of *technology risk*;

2. We had a very rare and legally binding protocol agreement that covered all of the critical items for subsequent approval determination, most notably the parameters for proving safety and effectiveness. The agreement protected us from staff changes, leadership changes, and political changes at the FDA, and in doing so, addressed *regulatory risk*; I, Joe Gulfo, had been responsible for the approval and launch of a number of products and I had managed two advisory panels, so showed a solid profile when it came to *execution risk*;

3. A group in Germany, the optics capital of the world, was going to manufacture MelaFind, which addressed *production risk*;

4. Some of the best and most renowned melanoma experts in the world were participating in the program, which addressed *medical risk*;

5. Dermatology was (and remains) a booming specialty and there was a completely unfulfilled and significant medical need. That took care of *business risk*, and so;

6. There was only one risk left, Mr. Investor. That was *financing risk*, and that is what we're asking you to help us address.

We visited close to fifty funds all over the country with our bankers. We thought it was a great pitch, and many institutional investors seemed to agree.

The IPO, Part II —The Deal

EVERYTHING SEEMED TO be going great. And then we started hearing rumors that Ladenburg Thalmann, our lead manager (banker), might get out of the investment banking business or be acquired. Ladenburg had just done a great deal for CABG Medical, and its chairman was a well-known and successful pharmaceutical executive, Dr. Phil Frost, so the news was certainly a surprise. But nothing had been easy so far, so why should we have thought the IPO process would be any different?

When we finished the IPO roadshow, the funds that were interested made it clear that they wouldn't participate in a deal in which the lead manager's future was unknown. So we had to suspend the process, wait until after Labor Day, choose a new lead manager, give them time to perform their diligence, update the S-1, and then go out again. In late September and early October, ThinkEquity, our new lead manager, accompanied us to another 50 or so presentations, a little more than half of which we made to the very same investors we'd visited on the first go-around.

In retrospect, this turn of events probably sounds straightforward enough and is surely something that other companies have had to deal with in the past. That much is true—we weren't the first, and we won't have been the last. But it wasn't as simple as finding a new co-pilot because the first one had fallen sick. We had on our hands what bankers call a "broken deal." And broken deals leave a horrible taint. Even though it wasn't me (or anyone else at MELA) that broke it, we ended up the ones who smelled. It doesn't really matter how you got there; if your deal is broken, your company is suddenly "flawed," and in a real and meaningful way. At the conclusion of the first roadshow, we were eyeing a $10 a share, which would have meant a $50 million IPO. With the taint of a broken deal, investor demand fell to such an extent that at the end of the second roadshow, we were looking at just $6 or $7 a share. And nothing had changed for the company whatsoever.

We'd planned on pricing after the close of trading on Tuesday, September 27. After making calls to all of the funds that had expressed interest, ThinkEquity's capital markets honcho informed me that he couldn't put a deal together and apologized for having wasted our time. What the hell? We'd given the funds exactly what they'd asked for—new bankers and a significantly reduced offering price. And now the deal was dead? I was crushed, angry, and shocked all at once.

I took the red eye from San Francisco to New York and couldn't sleep a wink. At 8:30am, I was working out on a Stairmaster, my heart rate in the 160's, when my phone rang. It was one of the private investors who'd played a part in hiring me. He asked me what I was doing. I replied, "Trying to kill myself in a socially acceptable manner!" Once I'd blown off some steam, I called the bankers in San Francisco and told them, with great passion, that what MELA was doing was important and we simply could not fail. I told them that we had to take another run at it, and I needed the list of all of the funds that were warm to us so that I could win them over. They thought I was nuts, but gave me the list anyway. And I started dialing (and visiting) for dollars.

One of the funds was full of very smart and shrewd guys that had played good cop/bad cop and bad cop/worse cop with us during pricing discussions. I implored them, sharing my passion and vision as best I could. I kept hounding them over the next couple of days and managed to get them speaking to the bankers again. At that point, though, they insisted that the deal be limited to a certain number of investors with every single one committing some minimum amount. They also wanted some insider participation. In other words, they wanted a very "tight" deal. In IPO financings, they told me, the concern was that some funds would come in simply to get the stock on the cheap. Assuming it traded up—which bankers practically promise you will happen while they're trying to convince you to take an even steeper discount than they'd originally said was necessary—one or more of them would then vacate their position, having made their fast money "playing the deal," and leaving others holding the bag.

It's hard to overemphasize the preposterousness of hearing this from them. These were the same people who had driven the price down from $12 at the start of the first roadshow to $10 at the end of that process, and also the ones that then drove it down to $6 to $7 during the second roadshow. And now they were worried about other less "principled" investors simply looking to flip our stock? But that's where we found ourselves, and we had to do what we had to do. They eventually came in for $5 million worth of stock, at $5 per share. And a few others followed. We got the deal done on

October 12. Despite the lower-than-hoped-for stock price, it was a victory. There was only one other publicly traded, pre-revenue medical device company that was public at the time—NxStage Medical.

MELA started trading at $5 per share on Nasdaq. If we'd had venture capitalist investors, we wouldn't have bothered raising money after the first attempt at $10-12 a share came up short. Instead, they would have funded the company for another six months or year and then taken another run at the public markets when market conditions were more favorable. But we didn't have that luxury. I remember Dan Lufkin and Ken Langone, who supported me through the process, taking me out to lunch to talk about the deal. They told me that we never would have gotten it done if I hadn't taken the whole process personally and made it happen come hell or high water. Truth be told, nobody, including them, had thought we'd get the deal done at all. I thanked both for their support. I also thanked Dan for providing the insider participation, which he also did in several subsequent financings. Sitting there at lunch with two titans of business is a memory I will never forget.

Guess what happened next? The fund that was so concerned that others would leave them holding the bag sold their entire position at $7 per share about six months later, for a 40% profit. We later visited with them on a roadshow for a subsequent financing. On the night of pricing, I told the bankers not to let them have any influence on the deal. The result: they didn't participate. A few weeks later, I bumped into one of them on a street corner. He grabbed my arm and said, "You pulled off a nice deal." Should I have felt good about outplaying an experienced fund manager? Maybe. But I didn't. Instead, I felt angry and disillusioned. This was all a game to them. I'm not so naïve as to think that the investors in MELA were my friends, but after all we'd been dealing with at the FDA, it was exhausting to endure yet another powerful group of people who are ostensibly working *with* you but in reality have objectives that frequently diverge from your own.

My last dealing with that particular fund occurred three years after the IPO, when I happened to run into one of them at a banking conference. This guy was "good cop"—the one with whom I felt a good connection during the first IPO roadshow—but I hadn't run into him in subsequent visits to the fund. I asked him what the heck had happened to the investors who'd seemed to be sincerely interested in our company and its prospects.

His reply? MELA had gone from being a promising investment to a really good "trading stock." What this meant was that there were enough shares trading hands each day and enough volatility in the stock that they were making money coming in and out of MELA on a regular basis. (And, obviously, participating in deals and then selling their position a short time later.) These guys were adding no value to the enterprise. They were taking minimal risk. They weren't developing a product that could save lives. No, they were subsisting off our work. There's a good half to Wall Street and a bad half. The good half helps finance promising ideas and also acts as the lubricant to the system. The bad half is nothing more than a leech attached to the real economy.

God Bless Fundamental Investors

A "FUNDAMENTAL INVESTOR" is one who invests with a long time horizon, and either holds or adds to his position over time. These are not the leeches. A fundamental investor is someone who looks at what's going on in the company as the driver of their decision, as opposed to external factors such as volatility in the stock. In other words, they're bottom-up stock pickers. Which means that they're attracted to good stories, and not simply stocks that trade in such a way that they can buy and sell them ten times in a single day.

Of course, if there is a sudden or unexpected marked increase in the stock price, they may sell sooner than planned to lock in a gain. Or, if there is a sudden and unexpected change in a company's prospects, they might sell because their original investment thesis no longer holds true. Either one of those outcomes is completely understandable. But otherwise, the fundamental guys try to spot a real business with real prospects, get in early, and enjoy big profits down the road. One of the funds that participated in our IPO was this kind of investor. They participated in multiple rounds, trimmed their position occasionally for portfolio balancing, increased it at other times, and apparently did quite well. I was later told that they'd gotten out at an average of about $10 a share.

As you can see in the table of MELA's 11 public financings, our stock performed incredibly well for the first four-plus years. And that made perfect sense: the markets were rewarding us for steady operational progress. Four of the five financings that followed the IPO were consummated at progressively higher prices, and the other one was just 7 cents lower than the one that had preceded it. After investors recovered from the financial crisis and bank bailouts of late '08 and early '09, MELA continued to climb. And our fundamental investors did what fundamental investors do—they bought stock in financings and even added to their positions between them.

As far as I'm concerned, the smartest financing that we ever did was the Committed Equity Financing Facility in late 2009 with Kingsbridge Capital, a private investment group. We had the right to sell stock to a single investor at a price that would be calculated from the closing price over eight consecutive days, subject to certain discounts. In exchange for that, we paid a small quarterly maintenance fee, closing expenses, and provided a small amount of warrants at a premium to the closing price on the day that the deal was signed. It was a not a commonly used type of financing, so we performed a great deal of analysis and homework before taking the plunge. Our bankers tried to talk us out of it. They said they were concerned for us, but in my view they were also quite clearly concerned about the fact that they would earn no fees from it. Because it was a non-traditional financing vehicle, they said, institutional funds would see our use of it as a sign of weakness. They warned that that it would put downward pressure on the stock. We saw it differently, as a tremendous insurance policy. And I had no intention of using it in lieu of a traditional financing unless we actually needed it.

It was an interesting vehicle, to say the least. Once you hit the button, you could not un-hit it, and the pricing of your deal was going to be based on the closing prices over the next eight trading days, irrespective of stock price moves and events in the macro environment. So when you pushed that button, that is to say, when you sent a letter stating that you wished to issue a target number of shares in a cycle, you were locked in. But the higher our stock price, the lower the discount that Kingsbridge would receive. We were not compelled to use the CEFF in lieu of other financings; in fact, in July 2009, we consummated a Registered Direct offering of 2.4 million shares at $6.25 apiece. The funds that participated in this financing were true fundamental investors—they had no problem that the CEFF was outstanding, in contrast to what the bankers had told us.

When and if we used the CEFF, we knew that Kingsbridge would not hold onto the stock for long, so it would be best to use the facility when there was a lot of natural demand in the marketplace, and we did. We "tested" it in August 2009, and it worked quite well—we saw no ill effects in the trading of MELA, and the logistics were quite straightforward. The stock had started moving very nicely after we announced top-line data from the pivotal trial and then the PMA filing. Funds were reliably accumulating the stock in the open market, with occasional pullbacks for profit taking, after which the inexorable march upward continued. We were placed in market indices as the price climbed, which further catalyzed institutional buying and the stock's upward march. And rather than perform a financing that might put the brakes on that trajectory, we decided to use the CEFF. We were taking nearly two weeks' worth of pricing risk, of course, but as far as we saw it, the risk of eight consecutive days of pricing and closing was low because the stock was in an upward trajectory. When we went ahead with it, too, there were no signs, whatsoever, of selling pressure—the stock price kept rising. It worked brilliantly. With the stock price on the rise, we issued over 800,000 shares in September 2009 at an average price of $9.25. We continued using it in the 4th quarter, ultimately issuing more than 1.8 million shares at $9.24 per share in 2009 and then a little more in 2010. I take great pride in this financing, for thinking out of the box, going against conventional wisdom, and using this vehicle for the optimal benefit of shareholders. The CEFF was a very inexpensive financing, raised at the highest price, and yielded the most money we ever raised—over $20 million at $9.26 per share. At the time the unlawful not approvable letter was issued, we had amassed a war chest of $45 million, in large part due to the CEFF.

The Scourge of the Markets—The Shorts

WHEN THE CAPITAL markets are working properly, young and promising companies can find investors that believe in them and that will finance their growth through to profitability. If you've got that kind of investor in your stock, it's hard for others to manipulate it. But if you don't, it's easier than you'd think.

Which brings me back to the outrageousness of the FDA's behavior. Things had been going swimmingly until the moment we received the unlawful letter from the FDA. But then everything started moving in reverse. That letter—and the subsequent campaign of misinformation—didn't just delay the approval of MelaFind. It drove the long-term investors out of our stock. Before long, MELA was on its way to becoming a highly volatile stock, which is the bailiwick of short sellers, fast money traders, and technical momentum investors. The pressure on the company—and thus the stock—that started the very day that the unlawful not approvable letter was issued continues to this day.

Because of that pressure, we were forced to accept steeper and steeper discounts in subsequent financings. Except for the financing immediately following the financial crisis, those with the steepest discounts (18% and 23%) came after the unlawful not approvable letter was issued.

Moreover, when the CEFF expired in May 2012 and we put the ATM (At The Money) financing facility in place in June, the experience was nothing like the CEFF. True fundamental investors had vacated MELA, and were not accumulating the stock in the open market. The deal-playing and fast-money traders had no interest in our stock for its own sake, and in my view simply participated in our financings because of their ability to drive the price down beforehand. So the ATM was far less effective a source of financing than the CEFF had been. We'd used the CEFF before the FDA's unlawful letter; the ATM came after it. Long after it, in fact—after the eventual FDA approval—and we naturally thought that the stock would perform. But with an entirely new investor makeup, it didn't.

I place much of the blame for the reduced stock price, significantly discounted financings, and lack of effectiveness of the ATM relative to the CEFF squarely on short sellers and the havoc that they create. I don't think that I could ever explain fully how much damage professional short investors can do to small companies. These funds stop at nothing to try to make your company go out of business. And that's no exaggeration. Your ruination is the ultimate win for them.

A short-seller, of course, is making a bet that a stock will go down and not up. The way shorting works is that the short seller first borrows shares from an investor and then sells them. If the stock goes down, they can then buy the shares in the market at a lower price than they'd borrowed them, and return them to the lender, thereby "closing out" the short. In order to make money, the difference in the prices of the stock in those two transactions must not only be positive, but also meaningful enough to cover the interest that the short seller pays over the borrowing period. In an inversion of the traditional dictum, shorts look to sell high and then buy low.

There's nothing wrong with taking a point of view that a stock will fall instead of rise. It's when they start trying to manipulate your price to their advantage that things turn ugly. In lieu of actual bad news, short sellers can—and do—try to "shape" any news that comes out of a company to negative effect, by overemphasizing small pieces of bad news in the hopes of overshadowing good news. If they're successful at that, they can increase volatility in a stock, and also trade in and out of it as other investors work through the confusion. And if there are no fundamental investors in a stock, that volatility is much easier to produce. There's a lot of money to be made in that particular game, and all it results in is back-and-forth trading in a stock with no real purpose.

The shorts are also well-practiced at getting so-called "technical" trading activity to kick in—the kind initiated by computer programs when a stock moves sharply in one direction or another—thereby adding even more volatility to trading than there otherwise might be. There are market manipulators on the long side, of course—so-called "pump and dump" scam artists that seek to generate unwarranted enthusiasm about a stock, pushing the price up so they can dump shares they'd bought in advance. But those scams are usually aimed at otherwise worthless companies. Some shorts have no qualms about spreading misinformation about an actual company doing actual things, and can wreak devastation in the process. Their influence can be so pernicious, in fact, that a fundamental investor once asked me whether I thought that the shorts had an inside man at the FDA. I don't think they do. On the other hand, there have been several cases of insider trading by FDA employees. So you never know.

(I said above that short sellers seek to actually destroy companies, and that's literally true. If you go out of business and your shares stop trading entirely, the cost of "returning" those shares is effectively $0. There's nothing to return.)

What's more, shorts and their partners in manipulation also put into place elaborate put and call options schemes that seek to limit the range within which a stock trades, with the goal of obviating any risk of a short squeeze—a situation in which a rapidly rising stock sends shorts scrambling to "cover" their positions, which can then send the stock up even more. Remember, a short seller needs to buy your stock again to give it back to the people who lent it to him. So if a lot of them are looking to cover at the same time, a stock can soar as a result. The most famous short squeeze of all time happened with Volkswagen in 2008, when short covering temporarily resulted in the carmaker becoming the most valuable company in the world. But the shorts tend to focus more on small companies, where it's much easier to manipulate stock prices. (That's why I am calling for the SEC to make shorting of small companies unlawful, which I will address in chapter ten.)

Once the shorts (and other manipulators) were involved with MELA, we couldn't even catch a break when we had good news to report. In December 2011, right after we *finally* received PMA approval, we decided to go back to the market for more money. But the stock dropped from $4.56 to $3.97 during the three days that the deal was being confidentially marketed. This had never happened to us in any previous financing. But the only people who had any interest in MELA stock at this point were those that made a living "playing deals," and they were clearly up to no good: that deal was done at $3.25 per share (28.7% off the $4.56 price at the start of the week and 18% off the day's close of $3.97). Worse yet, we couldn't raise enough money to satisfy investors that we wouldn't need *even more* money in the near future. Financing risk, in other words, still weighed down on the stock right after we'd shown that we were *able to obtain financing*.

There were other factors, too. Because of the disappointment associated with many overhyped biotech product launches and the time required for adoption of new disruptive technologies (like Intuitive Surgical's DaVinci robot or Dendreon's Provenge), a "short the launch" strategy came into vogue in which investors seek to capitalize on hype by betting against it. Again, there's nothing wrong with such a strategy per se, but when the tactic is mindlessly applied, it simply adds to overall volatility in companies' stocks at the time when their prospects are getting more promising.

Long-term investors now know, for example, that Intuitive Surgical did not become profitable for three-and-a-half years after the DaVinci robot was launched. And some of them knew it back then too. Because the best long-term investors have a long enough time horizon to look at early milestone achievements as reasons to have continued confidence of future business success. They do not expect or look for significant sales and profitability in the first year or two of a launch. But without long-term investors in MELA, the shorts and manipulators were able to create enough confusion about even our most positive news that the price of our stock stayed extremely volatile and downwardly trending, sometimes precipitously so.

And then there was the utterly ridiculous "continued skepticism"—to quote a vocal short blogger following the announcement of the approvable letter in late September 2011—"over [MelaFind's] accuracy and clinical utility." It was apparent to me that those seeking to cloud the issue of MELA's future simply flooded Internet message boards with complete nonsense and recycled unlawful FDA information, had their minions write skeptical "research" reports, and generally distorted the news flow about MelaFind. Having no long-term investors allowed short investors and stock manipulators to have their way with MELA, particularly in the commercialization phase. And we suffered for it. With no long-term investors in the stock to gobble-up the shares that the shorts were selling, MELA was driven progressively lower and lower.

The emergence of so-called "dark pools" has made short investors even more dangerous. These are trading environments within which the identity of those buying and selling stock are not visible. Why on God's green earth, in Obama's Age of Transparency, with so much hype about Wall Street reform, would something called "dark pools" be allowed? There have been a number of articles calling for their abolishment, including one by John Thain, the former CEO of the New York Stock Exchange, but there's been no action yet, and the lack of transparency continues. As an analyst once told me, "When it comes to trading stocks, if someone is trying to hide what they are doing, it's probably not for noble reasons."

Some of the market's most influential long-term investors don't even bother investing in small companies. When you've got a ton of money under management, you'd have to buy so much of a tiny company to make it a meaningful part of your portfolio that it becomes something other than one of many pieces of many companies that you own. Other funds promise their investors that they won't play around in the stock market's little leagues, and those promises are often included in their charter. So if your market value is less than $50 million, you're already dealing with less than 100% of those investors who might actually be interested in your stock were you worth $250 million, $500 million or more. Recall that MELA was worth $300 million before the FDA's letter bomb arrived. At that level, we had interested from a very large number of funds. A few years later, however, we were worth just $50 million, despite finally having gotten MelaFind approved and on the market.

Because of the activities of the shorts and dark pool trading, even those long-term investors that are able (by charter) to purchase stock in companies with $50 million in market capitalization (which was where MELA traded in the months before I left the company) are reluctant to take a chance on a risky venture until they can see real and sustainable growth in revenues and earnings. Why is that? Because the shorts and their band of "research analysts," bloggers, and message board participants can distort even excellent news such that an investment thesis can be based on concrete business performance metrics—increasing sales, earnings, business ratios. In the early days of a commercial launch, you can't deliver these kinds of results, so the fundamental investors steer clear. The shorts know it, and exploit it.

Lest you think I'm seeing goblins behind every corner, I'll point you to the so-called "short interest" in MELA's stock. At any point in time, there were up to six million shares of MELA sold short— even when we only had 35 million shares outstanding. There's a measure called "days to cover," which is the ratio of short interest and average daily trading volume in a stock. The higher the ratio, the "riskier" a short can be, because when fewer shares are trading, the more pressure a sudden burst of short-covering can have on a stock's price. As of mid-August 2013, MELA had the 29th highest days to cover ratio of all stocks trading on Nasdaq. The shorts like it so much, they've stuck around even though the risk of a short squeeze is really quite high.

So, goodbye, Mr. Fundamental Investor, we were sorry to see you go. It was a nice ride while it lasted, and we might have had one hell of a public follow-on financing in mid-2010 if the FDA had done what it said it was going to do, rather than lie and then try to cover it up. We could have raised $75 million-plus and launched the product correctly, without financing risk and without the shorts and manipulators being able to hurt us. But that's not what happened. And the company has never recovered from your departure.

The last equity financing I was involved in at MELA took place in February 2013. A similar thing happened as had happened in the IPO—we had a tight deal and no fundamental investor as our anchor. Because of that, pricing was once again a bit of a nightmare. We were up until after midnight on two subsequent pricing nights before we actually had to postpone the deal. Several days passed, and the deal was about to fall apart completely, when something I should have expected happened: one key investor offered to throw us a lifeline but demanded a 23% discount to the day's close to make it happen. (The other funds had been happy with an 8% discount.) But they also demanded more shares than we had available for issue. What to do? Did we cut back the other funds' allocation? Of course not. The only option: I could forfeit my own stock options (until such time as shareholders authorized more shares), and so I did. We did the deal at $1.30 a share, a 23% discount to the day's close.

Look, I'm not naïve. Institutional investors of any stripe will take advantage of every opportunity to make money, whether they're fundamental investors or not. Some are more aggressive than others, but even a fundamental investor will take his profits. Funds don't care about saving lives, they care about making money. Raising money is a difficult proposition for any small company, because enough bad breaks exist in the general day to day of business—for example, banks going out of business in the middle of your IPO, unavoidable delays in execution, macroeconomic events that affect customers, and natural business cycles—that picking the perfect time to sell new stock is nearly impossible. When you're a high risk, pre-revenue breakthrough product company, it just makes it that much harder. It's a sizeable enough challenge that it certainly doesn't need to be compounded by government agencies. Simply put, the FDA created an opportunity for predatory funds to victimize MELA, which drove out our institutional base of fundamental investors, which set in motion the whole cascade of events described above. Your banker going out of business is one thing. Your government lying to you, breaking the law, and covering it up is another.

Pimps and Johns and Whores

I OFTEN BROUGHT an operational executive with me on road-shows. Dina did the IPO with me and several employees from the commercial side of the business did others. I remember explaining to one of them how the process worked, including the difference between our bankers and our investors, but it wasn't sinking in. I needed an analogy. I came up with the idea that bankers are like pimps. They put two parties together—one party "has the goods" and the other party "wants the goods." The investors are the johns—they've got the cash, and they're looking to spend it. And just like johns, most investors are looking for a quick thrill, no long-term commitments, and definitely no marriages. When the thrill is gone, they are too. And we were the whore.

How do you know which investors are in your stock for a cheap thrill? One way to identify them is if they're overly focused on catalysts for stock price movements—including new data, papers, conferences, earnings reports, and product launches in foreign markets. They'll also want to know how much money you have in the bank and your burn rate. They're usually trying to determine why they should invest now, as opposed to in your next financing. And they'll try to play the volatility around those catalysts—they know that stocks tend to run up in the lead up to them, and then sell off afterward. (They'll actually help make *both* of those things happen.) Jumping in and out of the stock, or participating in a financing to get the stock at a discount knowing that catalysts are near is how hedge funds make money. While fundamental guys also ask for your catalysts, they also want to understand the company, the product, the strategy, and the management team. Sure, they want to know what the value drivers look like, but they want to know that to determine the potential ultimate value and return, not to determine whether there will be enough "trading action" in your stock to make messing around with it worthwhile.

The "johns," on the other hand, look for catalysts to give them opportunities to make some quick money (cheap thrills) as your stock bounces around. They participate in the grand buffering system that keeps stocks within a certain range with massive amounts of shares trading hands.

The Importance of Simultaneous Equations

MUCH OF THE mechanics of raising money revolve around three sets of what is known as a simultaneous equation—one for the funds and two for the company:

a. **FUNDS:** Knowing a fund's minimum threshold size (in dollars) and maximum percent ownership of a company (in shares) that their charter allows can instantly tell you whether they can buy stock in your company. Suppose that their minimum investment size is $5 million and their maximal percent ownership is 2.5%. In that case, they can only invest in companies with a market capitalization of $200 million. When a company's valuation increases, they can buy more, and they do. That's what happened to us as the valuation of MELA increased (which was helped by being added to various market indices)—the big funds kept buying. But when your stock price is falling, many funds *have to* trim their positions, regardless of the reason behind the stock decline, which drives the price down further. That also happened to us. And here's the main problem with the above: short sellers and other stock manipulators know all of this, and desperately try to keep a company's valuation below the level at which the bigger players can get back into the name. Once you're in their clutches, it's like quicksand.

b. **COMPANY:** The most important simultaneous equation relates to the amount of shares outstanding that are available to be issued in a financing and the amount of money you want to raise. Often, the funds dictate how much you raise—they want to see you have X number of months of cash to burn on

hand. If your stock is $2.50 and you have 10 million autho-
rized shares available to sell in a financing, you can raise $25
million at no discount. So if the funds want to see you have
18 months of cash and you're projected to burn $1.38 mil-
lion per month (for a total of nearly $25 million), you're fine.
On the other hand, if you're projected to burn $2 million per
month, the funds won't be happy, so you either need to trim
the burn or supplement the financing. (We did the latter with
venture debt.) Asking investors to authorize too many shares
to be available for future financings can send the wrong signals, too, so there's quite a balancing act to pull off, especially
for small emerging companies.

c. **DEAL**: The tighter a deal—that is, the fewer the number of
funds solicited—the less likely it is that a stock will trade
down during its confidential marketing. Why? Because
there's less likelihood of the news leaking, which results in
selling designed to lower the price in the days leading up to
a deal. On the other hand, the tighter the deal, the greater
the likelihood of significant discounting on pricing night,
especially if the parties are not long-term investors looking
for significant gains over significant lengths of time. (If a
long-term investor thinks a stock is going to $20 a share,
they're not that concerned if they buy it at $12.25 or $12.20
today.) So, it's all about who is in the "book"—the ideal
scenario is a tight deal with long-term investors—which
should result in no leakage, no down trading in the days
leading up to pricing, and no surprises on pricing night
itself. Our deals that were post-IPO but prior to the not
approvable letter were exactly of this sort. But those that
came after the not approvable letter didn't go so well. Three
examples illustrate the point:

  i. *Our second attempt at an IPO, with the "broken deal
  stigma" from the first, left us with just a few long-term*

guys in the book, so it was a tight deal. Fund #1 had its way with us, driving the price to $5 from $7, because we didn't have enough others in the book to take up the slack. One important reason was that the others were limited by simultaneous equation "a" above;

ii. Our financing in December 2011, right after PMA Approval, was a widely marketed deal because we were looking to raise a lot of money. The precipitous drop in price on the day of the pricing suggests that several bad actors got wind of the deal and drove it down during the week and then quite significantly on the day of pricing;

iii. Our financing in February 2013 was among a very tight circle of players. On the night of pricing, with such a tight group, we could not withstand the aggressive terms dictated by one fund—there weren't enough other participants to increase the allocation of each of the others and leave that fund out. We couldn't negotiate effectively with a straight face, and that hurt us. If we'd had two to three years of cash in the bank, we could have dictated terms and certainly not acquiesced when things turned against us. But we didn't, and so we had no leverage.

Relationships Matter

DO YOU THINK your investment banker loves you? Of course you don't. But you could be forgiven for thinking that he has your best interests in mind. That would be a mistake. For starters, he's got other clients who might just have interests that don't coincide with your own. And while he may not love them either, he might be more loyal to them than he is to you. Take institutional investors, which includes everyone from funds with a long-term approach to hedge funds and short sellers. The banks deal with those people *every day*. And they only deal with you and your company once—maybe twice—a year. So make no mistake where you fall on the hierarchy of loyalties. Investment bankers will not do anything for you or your deal that risks their falling out of favor with the investors.

Once I realized how simultaneous equations influenced how institutional investors could (or could not) invest in our stock, I began leading off meetings on road shows with a pertinent question. Does MELA fit your portfolio with respect to your minimum bite size and maximal percent ownership? By my tally, four of the last six meetings I had on one road show were with funds that couldn't participate even if they'd wanted to do so. So I challenged the bankers about it. They told me that they thought it was smart to meet with the funds at that point, because they would already know us by the time our $5 stock was a $20 stock. It made enough sense to me, so I left it at that. What I didn't learn for another three years was that some of these funds thank the banks that bring roadshows to their offices by channeling trading through their trading desks. It makes you wonder why they're so eager to take you on non-deal roadshows.

Uninvited Guests Spoil the Party

THERE'S AN EXPRESSION, "The devil comes in the front door." Well, so do the shorts. They literally came in the front door of MELA the day after the not approvable letter was announced and they've been in the stock ever since. As fundamental investors vacated MELA in the wake of the not approvable letter, the FDA panel materials and slides, the public media battle with FDA, the Citizen Petition, and the Congressional hearing, the value of MELA continued to decline. Some of that decline made sense, of course— when your story gets this complicated, investors have every justification for moving on, looking for other, less complicated situations in which to invest. But when we obtained both FDA approval and CE mark approval, one would have expected the valuation to have rebounded and perhaps even exceeded what it was prior to the not approvable letter. But that's not what happened. And we can thank the shorts for that.

MELA was valued at $300 million when we were on the cusp of the FDA setting a date for a panel meeting way back in January 2010. It was then driven down to a valuation of just half that amount on the very day of FDA approval at the end of 2011. Think about that—from $300 million when your product hasn't even been reviewed to less than $150 million when you have FDA and European approval in hand! The further decline to just $50 million when I left in June 2013 was driven by what some investors clearly perceived as "underperformance" from a commercial point of view. I don't think we'd underperformed. We had 150 systems in place within a year of our March 2012 launch—a MelaFind within 75 miles of 63% of the U.S. population—and were collecting many stories of excellent clinical results. I was certainly pleased with this operational progress.

If we'd had blockbuster results, the shorts wouldn't have been able to color the news negatively. But we were launching a new and novel device, so things were naturally slower than what some investors were looking for out of the gate, and the shorts were once again able to overemphasize the negatives. It's really crazy, if you think about it. With many young companies, there's always a lag before market value catches up to true potential. But that gap normally narrows over time, when the results can speak for themselves. But when the shorts have taken over, the gap can actually *increase*, even in the face of that actual (if gradual) success. It's perverse, and isn't good for anybody but them.

A Golden Opportunity

DON'T GET ME wrong. Many companies end up with a sub-$1 stock price or sub-$50 million valuation for good reason, whether it's because of a significant problem with their product or a serious flaw in their business model. But others, like MELA, are simply "oversold." In other words, they are trading for less than they are worth. There is an excellent and high-return opportunity in identifying those very situations. All they need is to take a longer-term view than many investors seem willing to do.

When you've got a situation like the one we had at MELA, where pretty much every risk had been taken off the table other than that of financing, a sizeable investment at the moment the stock is oversold can do wonders for both the company and the investor. The company can then focus on its *actual* business—and not the business of raising money. With enough funding, the counterproductive cycle of alternating strength and weakness in the stock around periodic financings can be eliminated entirely, in the process giving the question "Why Invest Now?" an entirely different meaning. *Without ample funding*, the question is really about whether there will be a chance to buy in again soon, and maybe at a lower price, because the company will inevitably be back, hat-in-hand, asking the capital markets for more money. *With* ample funding, on the other hand, the "Why Invest Now?" question becomes squarely focused on the commercial prospects of the product under development instead of the interim financing needs of the company itself.

And that can start a cycle of positive reinforcement, the opposite of the negative cycle that short sellers find so attractive. Significant investment from longer-term investors will serve to validate a company, which will attract additional investment and ultimately bring the valuation of its stock closer to where it should be. And when that starts to happen, short investors and manipulators will quickly vacate their positions in the stock—it's much more difficult for them to have their way with a stock when a company is on strong financial footing. And at *that* point, a company can stop focusing on meeting shorter-term financing-related milestones that can come at the expense of longer-term plans. When investors make a significant investment in a company with an oversold stock, in other words, they are getting a discounted ticket to a story of long-term success. Odds are, they might not even have to wait around for that success to happen, as financially stable emerging medtech companies that are meeting their development objectives are prime candidates for acquisition at significant valuation.

When MELA found itself in the unfortunate situation of lacking sufficient financing to get us over the finish line despite the promise of MelaFind, I did everything I could to arrange for a financing that would capitalize the company appropriately. In the end, I could not make it happen. But the experience showed me that long-term investors are missing out on some amazing opportunities. And if they won't take them, I would love to by raising an investment fund to do just that—separate the incorrectly oversold wheat from the true chaff, make significant investments as the anchor in recapitalization financings, and then help guide those companies we've invested in through success.

8

Let's Not Forget: This Machine Saves Lives!

Who Cares?

JOE NAMATH ONCE said, "While I'm out there playing football, other guys are playing 'kill the quarterback.'" I had a similar experience as I navigated MELA through the gauntlet of challenges it faced over the course of a decade, most of which simply should not have happened. Why did I continue, especially when I had only expected it to be an 18 to 24-month gig? For the simple reason that MelaFind saves lives. How could I walk away from that?

A banker I know who invests sizably in his own deals once said to me, "I would never invest in you because you actually care how you make your money." What he meant was that he knew there were certain things I wouldn't do to make money. I took it as a compliment. You bet I cared. Who else cared? I've put together a simple table of all the parties involved in MelaFind over the years, and ranked them on a five-point scale according to how much I think they cared (or didn't) about the life-saving aspect of the device.

STAKEHOLDER	Saves Lives	Rationale
Founders	+++++	The company was profitable in its first iteration as a defense contractor. The potential to save lives was the main impetus for the shift to medical development. Of course, it could also pay off big, but there was no guarantee.
Private Investors	+++	Many were melanoma survivors.
Public Institutional Investors	+, ha, ha	It's all about the money, whether they make it in 3 or 4 years (longer-term investors), in a financing (deal players), around catalysts (hedge funds), by driving the price down (shorts), or on sideways trading and volatility (traders and manipulators). The single + is for those rare investors who do endeavor to do well by doing good (advancing health).
Bankers	Ha ha ha	It's all about the fee. Two of our bankers actually felt good that they were raising money for a product that could save lives, but they were the exception. Nor was it the primary reason they were raising money for us.
Analysts	++.5	They are healthcare analysts for a reason, but funds beat them up over the performance of their "picks," so money is more important to them in the end.

(continued on next page)

(continued from previous page)

STAKEHOLDER	Saves Lives	Rationale
FDA	+	Should care a lot, but as a group didn't (except for Celia Witten a few reviewers, and Christy Foreman). As an organization, they care more about not making mistakes than truly advancing health. And there is no institutional appreciation of the implications of their actions on medical innovation. As regards MelaFind in particular, the Fast Track Innovation Program propaganda *versus* the treachery in the MelaFind review proved a lack of concern.
Employees	+++++	Everybody cared. We had no significant defections throughout the many battles and uncertainties, which pretty much proves the point.
Patients	+++++	In the development phase, patients reached out to us. Since commercial launch, they continue to thank us.

What about the dermatology community? And by that I mean both dermatologists and corporations selling products to dermatologists. Those two stakeholders require a more detailed analysis than this table provides.

Dermatologists' View of MelaFind

WHEN WE WERE concluding enrollment in the pivotal trial of MelaFind in the summer of 2008, I found myself on the phone with a top dermatologist and melanoma expert. I was providing him with the latest clinical information on the MelaFind studies for an upcoming talk he was giving at a major dermatology conference. One thing he said: "There's just one thing wrong with MelaFind . . . it isn't approved yet!" He told me the that the dermatology community had been impressed with the MelaFind data, had seen the company as it performed market research at the American Academy of Dermatology meeting for many years, and thought it was about time that they had the device in their offices. I told him that we were working on it!

We performed a great deal of market research including: (1) formal qualitative and intimate 60-minute one-on-one sessions at market research facilities; (2) one-on-one conversations lasting 10 to 15 minutes at scientific meetings; (3) conversations with investigators and advisors; and (4) quantitative, masked survey instruments. At the end of the qualitative market research exercises, we would ask dermatologists for their general impression. Virtually every time, they said something like, "This is going to save lives." Every time we heard it, we felt great.

Dermatologists will openly admit that they need help detecting melanoma. MelaFind was something they wanted—the market research was very strong in that regard. Of course, there are many elements to turning a breakthrough medical technology that physicians *say* they want into a product that's used in practice and a business that is successful. And it can take years. Many years, in fact, even in optimal circumstances. Unlike the latest smart phone, which can sell out before it hits the shelves, the time from introduction of a medical breakthrough to its routine use can take 10 years. The time from its launch to commercial viability of the business can take up to five years or more. That's why it's critical to have multiple years of cash on hand for the commercial launch.

But the starting point, the absolutely critical part of the equation, is that the physicians view the product as "better medicine." We had that in the summer of 2008. The whole dermatology community viewed MelaFind as a tool that could be very helpful in saving lives. We had that in January of 2009 at the MelaFind Summit. The dermatology community was waiting with bated breath to have MelaFind in their offices. And they were expecting it very, very soon.

When the FDA issued the unlawful not approvable letter, we lost something more important than time. The dermatology community was quite shocked and surprised. When the FDA released the pre-panel package full of untruthful and misleading statements and analyses that were picked up by the media and message board blog-gers, we lost a great deal more. The panel documents stated, "The FDA review team has significant concerns this device has not been studied adequately for its current indications for use and therefore puts the health of the public at risk."

I have difficulty writing that statement for many reasons, the most basic of which is that it had no place in an FDA review, espe-cially *before* a final action, and even *before* a panel meeting. I believe that they knew this, but they made the statement anyway, as part of an effort that was purposely designed to bring about a negative panel vote. By some miracle, we were able to make the panel look past their machinations, see the life-saving potential of MelaFind, and vote favorably. But there was still much damage that couldn't be undone. The day I left the company in the summer of 2013, the harm caused by that single sentence was still ongoing.

We performed the largest positive prospective study ever done in early melanoma detection under the auspices of a binding pro-tocol agreement with the FDA where all endpoints were met and the criteria for demonstrating safety and effectiveness were satis-fied. But the FDA decided to publicly state that MelaFind would put the public at risk. The dermatology community had been impressed with the vast amount of data that we had generated, and the large multi-year studies that we had performed. But the FDA took all of that away with 30 words.

And when the seeds of doubt are planted so deliberately, it can be hard to uproot them all. Prospective dermatologist customers asked me questions like, "What didn't the FDA like about it?" or "Why did the FDA turn it down initially?" In May 2012—two months after our launch—I made a presentation to a regional dermatology so-ciety. When I was done, the president of the society told me that the dermatologists in the room were still "pretty spooked" by the whole FDA mess, and that he was sure most of them would wait to see what happened before "taking the plunge." In other words, those same people who couldn't wait to use MelaFind a few years before were now taking a wait-and-see approach. But waiting for what? MelaFind had been approved. It worked. What else could I tell them?

I could point out, I guess, the obvious fact that the Internet is both a wonderful and a dreadful thing, simultaneously. All the mistruths that the FDA spread about the product live on the Internet and can be found in a matter of keystrokes. Not to mention that bloggers and many Internet analysts I believe are allied with the shorts and manipulators recirculate these arguments ad nauseum, so they actually exist in multiple iterations. The FDA had been quite favorably inclined toward MelaFind in early 2010, was ready to move to a panel meeting, and was even strategizing with us about a joint announcement of its approval for May 3, 2010. Then the not approvable letter, which Dr. Shuren admitted 17 months later to be a mistake, precipitated a cascade of events where untrue arguments saw the light of day. The ultimate approval of MelaFind did not erase those statements from the Internet.

As recently as June 2013, just prior to my leaving the company, a dermatologist who was a customer of MELA in Europe told me that he was very impressed with our website. He then said that while he'd been on the Internet searching about MelaFind, he'd seen the FDA's comments and had been taken aback. Luckily, he was already a customer. He probably wouldn't have become one if he'd known about all that garbage beforehand. He's in Europe, which is why he hadn't heard. Here's the problem, though: the entire U.S. dermatology community has heard all about it.

Dermatologists certainly want to save lives when they can. But the FDA review put a question in their minds as to whether MelaFind was all they'd thought it would be based on the data they had seen, themselves, up to the time of the not approvable letter and its aftermath. So the ultimate approval did not right every wrong. It did not put the tens of millions of dollars that we spent fighting the FDA back into our bank account; it did not return the valuation of the company to where it had been before the unlawful not approvable letter; it did not allow us to perform a big public follow-on to raise enough money at an appropriate valuation to optimally launch the product (and sustain the typical "short the launch" assault by fast-money funds); and it did not erase the perception of doubt in the minds of dermatologists placed there by the FDA.

Aside from all that, we were in great shape with the dermatologists!

With respect to the large companies with significant dermatology-related sales, the reason they are successful is because they are close with their customers. So it follows that they, being influenced by their customers, have also taken a wait-and-see approach with MelaFind.

In a series of meetings with one of the behemoths in dermatology in 2008, the year prior to PMA submission, I explained the unmet medical need, the concern that every dermatologist has about missing a melanoma, and the fact that MelaFind was a first-in-class product with no competition. The CEO of the company told me that we had exactly what his company had with one of their most successful products, one for which they had developed a category, taught dermatologists about a disease that they were not treating effectively because it was not easy to diagnose, and educated patients in the process. But he concluded the meeting by telling me, "I have absolutely no doubt that MelaFind would be a commercial success, I just don't think you'll get it approved." His company had just gotten through a long and tortuous battle with FDA on one of its products and he had just lived through the anti-innovation FDA agenda.

Three years after that conversation, when MelaFind received approval, he bought me a bottle of champagne at an AAD meeting. We drank it together. The obvious question on my mind: how might we work together in the commercial phase given the absolute confidence that he had previously expressed about MelaFind's commercial potential? But he still wanted to wait to see how warmly dermatologists took to MelaFind before entering into any sort of relationship.

Did the FDA's tremendous negativity factor into his decision not to proceed immediately? I find it difficult to conclude otherwise. Typically, big companies partner in one of three circumstances: (1) Early in development, usually driven by competitive forces; (2) In the peri-approval period. New products can be of great interest to customers and energize sales forces, which can also provide a boost to their existing portfolio; and (3) After a product is commercially successful in order to have instantly accretive earnings to fuel growth. But they don't typically partner in the midst of the growing pains of a launch before significant market traction can be shown. With a breakthrough product, you *never* see significant traction for at least a couple of years. So there is no doubt in my mind that the highly negative comments from the FDA and pessimistic view of the odds of MelaFind's approval right up until *it was approved* took away the peri-approval window for a partnership or acquisition, either with this particular company or others that might have considered it.

Business Success & Clinical Success, Perfect Together

IN ORDER FOR MelaFind to help save lives, it needs to be used. And if it's used a lot, then MELA Sciences will be successful from a business perspective—the company gets paid per use. But the devil is in the details. How do you get from launch of a breakthrough product to routine use? You get there in small bites, achieving qualitative successes initially, then progressive business success. At that point, everyone is happy—patients get better care, dermatologists provide better care, and the company thrives and reinvests, making the product even better, which drives even better clinical experiences and a more successful business. Capitalism and healthcare have always worked very, very well together.

We decided to study the successful product launches of three breakthrough medtech products that had come before ours—Intuitive Surgical's DaVinci robotic surgery system, Hologic's digital mammography and interpretation software, and Cytyc's ThinPrep automated cervical cancer screening device—to craft our own launch strategy. Here's what we learned from the trailblazers before us:

Intuitive Surgical reached profitability three-and-a-half years after launch. At that point, they had 220 systems placed, and surgeons had begun using DaVinci on prostate cancer, which really drove its adoption and use. Importantly, the device hadn't originally been used in prostate cancer surgery, rather, that only started to happen once it was on the market, as surgeons started thinking about its optimal uses.

Hologic had to wait three years following the launch of its system before a large study showing the benefit of digital mammography was published. The company enjoyed steady success thereafter.

Cytyc didn't manage to secure reimbursement from Medicare and private payers of its product at launch. That took two *more* years. Even then, real market growth didn't come until four years later. What's more, that success came not from the automated scanner, but from the novel way the Pap smear was applied to a slide (Thin-Prep). That was completely unexpected.

All three of their experiences were potentially relevant to us. As with DaVinci, we knew that dermatologists would need to play with MelaFind to figure out its optimal use. Like Hologic, we planned a large post-approval study to provide more data on clinical utility, which would hopefully drive adoption. And similar to Cytyc, reimbursement would be an evolving issue, a decision that depended in large part on how much dermatologists decided to charge their patients for using MelaFind.

We also studied a few unsuccessful launches in which the companies had product-related issues, including technical problems recalls, reworks, and manufacturing issues. We learned from studying both the successful and not so successful breakthrough product launches that a beta launch period seemed critical to helping MelaFind establish its niche, and for us to perform proper market segmentation. At that point, we could craft a strategy for rapid uptake (the alpha launch) and business success (significant and growing profits).

So we planned a two-part beta launch. I consider the beta launch as "developing the recipe," and the alpha launch as "making the donuts." Full-blown commercialization en route to significant business success would mean making "lots of donuts." On March 7, 2012 we installed our first system and started the deliberate and methodical initial rollout. We announced that availability would be limited to the northeastern and just a few cities in Germany. By design, we put out just five systems in March and April. This allowed us to address any technical and manufacturing issues without the possibility of a large recall. Thankfully, no showstoppers, or even show delayers, arose. We then expanded to cities outside the northeast, and in particular to our investigators—people we already knew.

The goal of a measured rollout was to develop our operating infrastructure, including technical support, installation, and sales. In the first 12 months, we placed approximately 150 systems. But the stock market expressed disappointment with this accomplishment because I had estimated that we would have 200 systems placed in the U.S. and 75 in Germany before MelaFind had national reach, that is, ready for the second part of the beta launch. I learned a lesson about saying anything quantitative in a beta phase—it was viewed as "guidance" even though I'd never represented it as such, and so we'd been judged as underperformers! It was my fault for giving the shorts something to work with, but in my defense, I would never have let MELA miss actual "guidance" by that much—it was not my first rodeo.

It's a fact of life that investors always want more. For us, that even included those who'd managed to see past all the controversy at the FDA. And some of them, unfortunately, were clearly disappointed with our progress. But they shouldn't have been. Throughout the planning and execution phases, our team consisted of professionals who had previously worked at Allergan, Pfizer, Merck, Bayer Diagnostics, Schering, Abbott, and Novartis. One of them, our senior vice president of Product Development & Innovation, told me, "When I was at my previous job, we would have been happy if we'd placed 50 new systems in the first year!"

Another absolutely critical thing in the first part of the beta was to refine the medical messaging and understanding of the product. You will recall that MelaFind is a first-of-a-kind device and a nuanced product. What I mean by this is that it is not a hammer, a tool that is needed in virtually every carpenter job, and it is not an awl, a tool that is needed in few but very specific carpenter jobs. Rather, it is akin to a Phillips screwdriver, a tool needed often, but which only works on Phillips head screws. A hammer would be a "screening device"—something a dermatologist could put on any and all lesions without thinking; an awl would be a replacement for biopsy; and a Phillips screwdriver would be comparable to using MelaFind on a common but defined set of lesions—clinically atypical pigmented skin lesions where a decision to biopsy has not yet been made.

Dermatologists practice differently—one dermatologist's definition of "asymmetry" (the first A of the ABCDE paradigm) doesn't always jibe with another's. (Pathologists are also different, so the interpretations of one pathologist reading slides for a dermatologist will not overlap perfectly with the interpretations of another.) Dermatologists needed to use MelaFind and learn how best to use it given the way that they practice. With more frequent use, we saw dermatologists really settle into a MelaFind sweet spot. For example, we knew of dermatologists who learned so well how best to use MelaFind that they were experiencing "low disorganization" readings up to 50% of the time. This is amazing because on the pivotal trial, this occurred only 10% of the time. MelaFind is measuring "disorganization"—how the cells in the pigmented skin lesion are arranged—low disorganization is highly correlated with the absence of melanoma, and high disorganization readings lead to detection rates of 98%. With practice, dermatologists really learned how best to use the product—which lesions to put it on to obtain truly valuable information that was useful to them in their biopsy decision. Without MelaFind, dermatologists find melanoma in only about 1 out of every 30 biopsies performed, so in addition to improving melanoma detection, MelaFind also promises to reduce the rate of unnecessary biopsies as dermatologists learn its sweet spot. And that's exactly how we positioned MelaFind—it helps dermatologists make a *better* biopsy decision. They just need to learn what a Phillips head screw looks like in their patients.

Dermatologists also don't listen. Okay, it's not just dermatologists—*most* physicians don't listen. Our training makes us arrogant. More importantly, dermatologists are very busy—they see five to ten patients an hour, they are behind seeing patients before they start in the morning, and routinely see three or more patients at a time (in multiple exam rooms) while likely talking to a referring physician or patient on the phone in the meantime. When you're busy and you're arrogant, messages don't sink in. No, they needed to learn it on their own.

It was critical then, in the early going, to work very closely with them and give them time to learn the product and how it fit into the way they practiced. We anticipated that various "archetypes" of MelaFind use would emerge. Once we had enough dermatologists of a particular archetype knowing and loving MelaFind, they could then teach their peers so that the learning curve for the next group of customers wouldn't be as steep.

That's part of the classic launch of a breakthrough product, and is known as the adoption curve. Patience and listening to the customer are critical, and so is making changes, as needed. One of the things that we needed to do was set expectations properly—those dermatologists that hadn't been swayed by the FDA's campaign of misinformation, we sensed, actually expected MelaFind to be the Oracle at Delphi, that is, to be knowledgeable about all topics and always correct. Well, it isn't. It only knows about the clinically atypical pigmented skin lesions that we trained it on, and even on those, it is extremely sensitive, but not extremely specific. So we needed to really hammer home the message that MelaFind only provided another letter to the alphabet soup of melanoma detection—the "M"—and then communicate how to use the M.

Part I of the beta launch (the first 12 months) was to get it out and get it understood. Part II (the second 12 months) was all about patient mobilization and awareness (lots of PR and strategic advertising), and to get dermatologists using it as much as possible. In our market research, dermatologists had told us that they faced the medical dilemma that MelaFind was designed to address about once an hour. We needed to figure out what it would take to achieve usage at that level, or 40 lesions per week. We were learning that as I left the company. The most successful users had MelaFind prominently displayed, challenged patients to perform self-skin exams to identify clinically atypical lesions, and proactively offered the use of MelaFind to their patients. In Part II, we were refining the messaging to patients and the tools for dermatologists to make that happen.

We enjoyed great media coverage, from national TV shows (*The View*, *The Doctors*, and *Good Morning America*), to national print media (2013 sun season issues of women's magazines, including Allure, Redbook, Prevention, and Self). We also launched a marketing campaign on WebMD. Just before I left the company, we were planning these kinds of things in Germany.

After 24 months on the market, which would put us in March 2014, we felt that we would have the recipe set and have started to taste it in the form of financial performance. We would then start the alpha phase—making the donuts, that is—a more intense rollout geared toward true commercial success and a line of sight to profitability. And it would only get better as the following milestones were achieved:

1. Data from ongoing post approval studies that would demonstrate that MelaFind detected melanomas that would have otherwise been missed, that MelaFind helped in earlier melanoma detection than was previously possible, and also showed a documented higher rate of low readings (thereby obviating unnecessary biopsies) than in the pivotal trial;

2. MelaFind entry into disease management guidelines promulgated by dermatologic societies and universities;

3. MelaFind use in residency programs where dermatologists obtained their training in the detection of melanoma; and

4. MelaFind reimbursement once a fair price was established in the marketplace and it was widely available.

That last one is a little complicated. It's never been clear to me whether it was even sensible to pursue a reimbursement code, given the state of Obamacare, Health Savings Accounts, Accountable Care Organizations, and large deductible catastrophic-coverage-only health plans. Reimbursement requires three conditions: widespread availability, a significant body of literature, and that the new product/intervention is contained in practice guidelines. It is very tricky, and once a reimbursement decision has been made and a price set, it is virtually irrevocable. So it's prudent with a new breakthrough product not to rush the process lest the way the product is initially used differs from the way it is used once it is "market tested." I felt that since we were in dermatology with a low price, we had more flexibility to wait until conditions were optimal. Cytyc's ThinPrep also started as a self-pay product, so, there was precedent.

That was the plan—very straightforward, very rational, well thought out, based on precedent, and modulated by experience. And we had the right team in place to execute it, people with relevant experience and excellent track records at great companies. When I laid out the general strategy to a fundamental investor in June 2012, he asked me in an accusatory tone, "Whose idea was this?" I told him it was mine. And he told me it was brilliant. So I asked him when he was planning to become an investor. He smiled and said, "You'll see." (While he never did become one, in part because he changed his focus to larger companies, the point is that he liked our strategy but he, too, was hesitant due to the influence of the shorts and the tiny market capitalization that resulted from it.)

Measuring Progress versus the Successful Comparables

INTUITIVE SURGICAL (PEAK market value over $20 billion), Hologic (peak market value over $6.3 billion), and Cytyc (acquired by Hologic in 2007 for $6.2 billion) faced some of the same challenges that we were facing. But they had some things we didn't have—blue chip venture capitalist backers, strong fundamental institutional investors throughout the launch phase, and strong balance sheets (including lots of cash) to execute their launches and render financing risk moot.

Now, to be fair, MELA had some things *they* didn't have, such as real data at launch on how the product performed! The DaVinci robot was a 510k device; there were no data, and there still isn't on pain, recovery time, blood loss, and outcome from surgeries performed with it (especially relative to traditional open surgery). Hologic's strong data on digital mammography relative to traditional mammography came out three years after launch. Cytyc had data on the automated system's ability to identify areas of interest in the automated reading, but no data on the use of the ThinPrep by cytopathologists, which is what made the company successful. None of them had significant commercial success in the first 15 months, by any means.

MelaFind was a PMA product with excellent data at the time of launch. Those others did not have that. But they had something absolutely critical—strong and savvy fundamental investors. Why is that important during a beta launch? Because quantitative success, that is, significant sales, impressive operating margins, and a line of sight to profitability are not possible at that time. Savvy fundamental investors know this, and short predators and their manipulating counterparts bank on it. Sure, Intuitive, Hologic, and Cytyc had some hiccups and valuation retrenchment during the beta segment of their launches, but the fundamental investors were there to see those as buying opportunities so that the negative "short the launch" effects were muted. At the very least, they rode it out, not bailing on the stocks entirely.

In January 2013, I ran into an investor who I consider to be long-term focused. I'd seen him at several conferences over the previous year, and he always had incredible recall of what I'd told him the last time we'd seen each other, as well as always seeming up-to-date on our latest news. I asked him when he was going to start buying our stock. He smiled and said that he liked me, he loved our story, and liked what he'd seen so far in the beta launch. And . . . he'd probably be a significant buyer when we moved into alpha launch, but not before.

Long fundamental investors understand many things beside launch dynamics. They also understand the macro environment. In 2013, America was truly waking up to the difficulties of implementing Obamacare, questions about whether it would survive or what parts of it would survive, and how it would be changed.

That made the already difficult challenge of launching a new break-through medical product into the market even more difficult than it should have been. And it wasn't just us: Because the most basic and essential underpinnings of the healthcare delivery model were up in the air, many companies in the biopharma and medtech space that were rolling out new products reported sluggish demand.

I am certain that when dermatology practices have had their partners meetings over the past few years, the bulk of the conversation focused on whether they should agree to have their practice acquired by the local hospital, or whether they should follow the large practice in the next county in not accepting some payer. And those are long discussions. After that, and only if they had time, would they have addressed the question of bringing MelaFind into the practice, getting a second or third MelaFind, or implementing programs designed to increase MelaFind usage. Fundamental investors would know this and not be frightened by the sluggish sales. They might, in fact, add to their positions in the event of stock price declines. But we didn't have fundamental investors. We had short sellers and fast-money hedge funds that exploited the situation, causing sideways motion in the stock, volatility, and further valuation declines.

Finally, long fundamental investors, understanding the dynamics of a measured, methodical two-part beta rollout, would focus on surrogates or predictors of future business success. These predictors would have "outweighed" the inherent vicissitudes of launches—e.g., not placing 200 systems in the first 12 months, or showing flat revenue growth flat in the quarter when part two of the beta-launch kicked in and we switched from a placement-centric strategy to a usage-centric one. I think fundamental investors would have focused more on the likes of:

1. public comments we made about one practice taking delivery of six MelaFind systems;

2. stories of actual dermatologists using the product and having excellent experiences;

3. MelaFind's winning of the Cleveland Clinic Top 10 Medical Innovation Award;

4. news of some practices beginning to use MelaFind at a greater frequency;

5. news that MelaFind was performing better in the marketed setting than in the trials (higher rates of low readings); and

6. reports that dermatologists experienced better performance with MelaFind the more they used it.

And I think their focus on all of that would have provided them with the confidence to stick around, with the result that MELA would have maintained a respectable valuation during the beta launch phase. And then it would have risen when sales and operating margins started to show demonstrable gains.

Ask anybody: disappointing the market vis-à-vis expectations happens all the time during commercial launches. Plans are made to be tweaked, of course, but you also don't plan on not meeting expectations. No one is happy when you do, even if it happens often enough that it should actually be expected and not the opposite. Unfortunately, a certain class of investor has learned to profit on such misses to the point that "shorting the launch" has become an investment strategy. Without significant cash resources to execute your plan, you can fall short of your goals. After I left the company, a research analyst called me and said, "I always knew it would take $100 million to launch this product correctly." It didn't matter where the money came from (the capital markets or corporate partners) or who was leading it (MELA or a partner). The adoption of a breakthrough product in this economy and healthcare climate, he thought, would take at least $100 million. And we didn't have $100 million.

Who Else Forgot or Didn't Care that MelaFind Could Save Lives?

I MENTIONED EARLIER that on the eve of the advisory panel meeting in November 2010, our CFO informed me that a class action lawsuit solicitation to shareholders was issued in connection with the significant drop in stock price following issuance of the FDA panel package. The basis of the shareholder lawsuit was the highly negative statements that the FDA had made about MelaFind.

When the paperwork was ultimately filed with the courts, several things struck me. First, the complaint referred to MelaFind as a drug and its approval application as an NDA (New Drug Application), whereas MelaFind was a device and its approval application a PMA. Mere details, I suppose. Second, the complaint alleged that the company should have known that MelaFind had no chance of being approved. I also couldn't believe that the complaint had even been filed given that the advisory panel had voted positively, directly addressing the second point above. Further, given that the not approvable letter was well known, as well as the fact that they are simply not issued *before* panel meetings, the allegation that investors were caught unawares prior to the FDA making the panel package known made no sense at all. (Unless you were plaintiff's counsel or a judge, I guess.)

A lawyer explained to me the way the legal process works in this regard: the courts allow the plaintiffs to amend complaints for 21 days after serving it (or its responsive pleading). But Rule 15 of the Federal Rules of Civil Procedure also states, "The court should freely give leave [to amend a complaint] when justice so requires"—which gives plaintiffs an open-ended opportunity do so if they've got a compliant judge. As months passed, the progress we made in the MELA cause—the Progressive Policy Institute's white paper (positive independent party review), the Congressional Hearing, CE mark approval, extensive industry news about how dysfunctional the FDA truly was, the approvable letter, and finally the FDA approval—kept stripping away arguments they'd made in their original complaint. But the courts "freely gave leave" to the plaintiffs to continually amend it, including proposing entirely new bases for the lawsuit. And the plaintiffs did just that.

It is widely felt that plaintiffs' counsel in class action lawsuits are bloodsucking opportunists. This is a cottage industry that seems to just sit and wait for entry points like precipitous negative stock movements to justify filing a claim. The opportunity in our case was our blood that the FDA had drawn, principally in taking the position that the product put patients at risk. But even when that position was negated by the panel outcome, the courts just allowed the plaintiffs to amend their complaint, not simply for errors of fact but for otherwise entirely new issues. And don't even get me started about the drug/NDA point. There doesn't seem to be any other possible conclusion than that they had a shareholder solicitation template ready to go in their word processor and didn't remember to change some wording from the last one that they'd filed, which must have been a drug, and therefore an NDA. That such an error could even occur shows (to me, at least) how little they truly cared about our situation.

It is also common knowledge that shareholder lawsuits are routinely settled at the "inventory level" of plaintiff's counsel. This is to say at a slight premium to the amount of work (hours) that plaintiff's counsel has invested in the effort at a certain point (usually a week or two before the court appearance date). Typically, the shareholders then receive an inconsequential fraction, which on a per share basis is no more than a penny or two. We actually won the shareholder lawsuit. Meaning, we didn't settle it for a few hundred thousand dollars, which is all that plaintiff's counsel was looking to get (after starting with some astronomical number). Nope, we won; it was dismissed by the courts a couple of months following PMA approval.

Still, while the shareholder lawsuit was extant, investors asked about it, message boards mentioned it, and the pawns of the shorts and manipulators discussed it in their Internet research and commentary. The only people who wouldn't have cared about it were fundamental investors. They know that shareholder lawsuits are routinely filed in connection with significant stock price decreases, and they know that with companies like MELA that have relevant and appropriate risk factors outlined in their regulatory filings, shareholder lawsuits rarely have a significant monetary impact on a company because the likelihood of a huge settlement is *de minimis*. Our problem? We didn't have any fundamental investors in the stock.

It Was Truly All About Saving Lives

I AM TRULY blessed to be working in this industry. Knowing that something you have done can help others, and maybe even save lives, is indescribably rewarding. Whenever I give an interview to a reporter—trade press, financial press, TV or radio—I tell them to go home and tell their wife, boyfriend, children, or mother that they are heroes for simply mentioning melanoma and the importance of looking at your body. They're saving lives too. Because someone reading the piece on the train or hearing it on radio or seeing it on TV might very well look at their skin, or the skin of a loved one, see something "funny," and then go to a dermatologist who might find a melanoma that would otherwise have gone undetected.

The MelaFind marketing campaign was centered around increased awareness, and virtually every advertising piece showed images of lesions. We gave posters to dermatologists, and the patient website and brochures had visuals of melanomas and benign look-a-likes. We encouraged patients to show their dermatologists any lesions that resembled these. We also amassed quite a collection of stories from dermatologists using the product.

—A few weeks after launch, when we had placed MelaFind in the offices of only five dermatologists, I received a call from one of them who told me of a patient with a history of melanoma to whom he had given a whole body skin exam. He hadn't found anything he considered suspicious, but the patient asked him about a lesion near his eyebrow. The dermatologist told me that he'd felt it a little atypical, but not concerning at all. His procedure nurse felt similarly. But he used MelaFind on it anyway. MelaFind gave a high disorganization result, so they performed a biopsy and it came back as a melanoma. The dermatologist told me that he probably wouldn't have caught it until six months later (if the patient had returned), but also that he'd been letting lesions that looked like that one leave his office for years. In our last conversation before I left the company, he told me that he had found six melanomas that he wouldn't have detected without MelaFind.

—Another dermatologist told us about a 16-year-old fashion model, on whom she had used MelaFind to help determine whether a few atypical but equivocal lesions needed to be biopsied. MelaFind rendered low disorganization readings and so the dermatologist decided that the patient didn't require a biopsy. The dermatologist told me that with MelaFind, she was doing as many biopsies as before, but she was focusing on different lesions and catching more melanomas.

—At the American Academy of Dermatology meeting in Miami in March of 2013, two dermatologists came to our exhibit to tell us stories. Derm #1 (from the Boston area) told us that in the few weeks that he'd had MelaFind, he had already detected two melanomas that he would not have otherwise. Derm #2 (from Pennsylvania) told us that he had detected six melanomas that he would not have detected otherwise, and that he could not imagine making a decision about a clinically peculiar lesion without MelaFind anymore.

—Erin Gilbert, a dermatologist from New York who was not a MelaFind customer, told us of being on a flight from New York to Miami. A flight attendant had realized she was a dermatologist and wanted to tell Dr. Gilbert a story about a mole she'd been concerned about. She'd visited two dermatologists in Florida, both of whom had told her not to worry about it. Unconvinced, she went to a third dermatologist who used MelaFind, which indicated it was suspicious, and the biopsy came back as melanoma. The flight attendant told Dr. Gilbert that she would now only go to a "MelaFind" dermatologist.

—A thirty-four year old woman who was in the dermatologist's office for another procedure saw the promotion for the melanoma detection campaign, and she told the receptionist that she would like to participate. They used MelaFind on a suspicious lesion, and biopsy confirmed melanoma.

—A woman who had been trying to get her husband to have a skin exam for a couple of years was able to convince him to go the dermatologist because of our campaign. The dermatologist used MelaFind on two lesions and then biopsied one of them, which was a significantly invasive melanoma, but still considered "early."

—An elderly woman with a number of peculiar lesions that her dermatologist was following also had lymphedema, which made the healing process of biopsies on her legs quite difficult. She would frequently have negative biopsy results but her dermatologist felt he had no choice than to perform biopsies even on her more equivocal lesions, just to be sure. He used MelaFind on a few equivocal atypical lesions, all of which indicated low disorganization, and he did not biopsy the lesions. It was the first time that she'd had a visit with her dermatologist and he did not biopsy her. She started crying and hugged him.

—A woman saw the MelaFind poster in a dermatologist's waiting room and pointed to a lesion on her husband's body that looked like one of the nine lesions we'd shown. The dermatologist didn't even need MelaFind in that instance. On appearance alone, he felt that the lesion was sufficiently atypical to consider it suspicious and promptly biopsied it. The lesion was a melanoma. Our marketing efforts saved this life.

I kept a running tally of all of the stories that I heard from dermatologists or from the sales and service team. At last count, there were over 40 melanomas (that I knew about) that would not have been detected if not for MelaFind. That's pretty cool. Please encourage people that you know to look for the ABCDs—you may save a life. (If you do, please let me know.)

9

I Don't Want to Fight Anymore, Part II

See Rome and Live!

THERE'S AN OLD saying, "See Rome and die." Once you've seen the splendors of Rome, in other words, you've seen everything, so it's safe to die. (The actual saying is "See Naples and die," but the point remains the same.) I saw Rome (or Naples), figuratively speaking, in Munich on June 13, 2013. But I didn't die. I was meeting with two dermatologists who were MelaFind customers. We were discussing the second phase of the beta launch, which was predicated on patient awareness and mobilization. In the U.S., a large part of that plan involved a marketing effort on WebMD, but there is no WebMD in Germany, so they were advising me on how to best go about things in Germany.

At one point, one of the dermatologists said, "Joseph, I must tell you that I am finding melanomas with MelaFind that I was simply not finding previously." We were having lunch at a very casual outdoor Italian restaurant. There was a canopy of trees, the leaves on which were a rich and lustrous color. The sky was clear and vividly blue. In the background, I could see a three-story villa that had masonry walls painted yellow, clay-colored Spanish roof tile, and a black wrought iron railing on the widows walk atop the house. It was, in a word, bucolic.

I savored the moment. And I had a realization. For the first time in a tremendously long time, I was genuinely happy. After a prolonged period during which all sorts of bad actors had spread misinformation, MelaFind was finally speaking for itself. It was saving lives. It was helping dermatologists take better care of patients. It was doing what it was designed to do. Adoption was proceeding at its own pace, of course, but it was proceeding nonetheless.

On my flight home, I thought of many of the things that I had done and was doing to make MelaFind a success. I thought of the many "fights" chronicled in this book. And it occurred to me that all of the stories I told people about our struggle used the metaphor of fighting. In late 2012 and early 2013, for example, I had taken to challenging potential fundamental investors using the movie *Shane*, and how Shane (played by Alan Ladd) had single-handedly cleaned up the valley on behalf of the homesteaders against an evil cattle rancher and his hired gunfighter (Jack Palance) and then literally rode off into the sunset. I would then shift to the story of how Wyatt Earp had tamed the West, bringing law to a lawless land, but had needed the help of Doc Holliday (and a few others) to do so.

Up to that point, I told them, I had felt very much like Shane. Shane walked into that saloon, alone, one-against-three, and won. My foes were the FDA, the shorts, and the manipulators who had pushed the valuation of the company to less than $1 per share, for a total market value of just $50 million. But I had realized that I couldn't beat them single-handedly as Shane had done. No, this was more of an O.K. Corral kind of situation, and while Wyatt Earp did emerge victorious, he wasn't fighting alone. And I would ask them (the fundamental investors): "Will you walk into the O.K. Corral with me?"

No one volunteered. In fact, in one meeting, a potential investor asked me why our *last* financing—one he hadn't participated in— had been so significantly discounted. I told him that it was because he hadn't been there to help. He replied that he didn't consider it his job to save potential deals for MELA, even though he was already a large shareholder. I told him that I didn't think it was *my* job, either, but that I'd forfeited a million options in the heat of the moment to do so. His jaw dropped. But he still wouldn't walk into the corral with me. So there I was, alone, with bullets flying by my head. I had shown leadership, investing $85,000 in the December 2011 financing, $38,000 in May 2012, $26,700 in November 2012, $23,000 in March of 2013, and $27,000 in May 2013, totaling $200,000 of my own money. But they wouldn't follow my lead—Virgil, Morgan, and Doc Holliday were nowhere to be found. I wasn't Wyatt Earp. Nope, I was Shane. And I didn't think I could win.

Two weeks before, I had asked Adele what she wanted for our June 21 wedding anniversary. Her reply? "I want by boyfriend back!" When I got home, I told her that there was only one way that I could give her what she wanted. The way I saw it, the things that *only* I could have done for MelaFind were done. The recipe was set and the ingredients purchased. Someone else could surely make the donuts. It was time to hang up my six-shooter, lest I finally catch a bullet. I didn't want to fight anymore. She liked that idea. So did I.

On Saturday June 13, 2013, I let MELA's board know that after nine-and-a-half years of fighting, it was time for me to move on. MelaFind will be a very successful product, it will save many lives, and it will surely become the standard of care. The only question remaining is the precise length of the "runway" before takeoff—and whether MELA will go it alone, take a partner, or sell itself and become a subsidiary of another company. When I hung up from that phone call, I went to my weekly piano lesson. Four hours later, I played *Edelweiss, Someone to Watch Over Me, Satin Doll,* and *All I Ask of You* in a recital at Steinway Hall in New York City. I played well. And on Monday morning, I got serious about writing this book.

How Would You Score It?

BOXING MATCHES ARE scored round by round using a 10-point "must system." If a round is cleanly fought with no knockdowns or penalties, the winner by punches landed or "ring generalship" is awarded a score of 10 to 9. If the winner knocks the loser down, then it's scored 10 to 8. Penalties or knockdowns can further reduce either score. For example, if the winner knocks the loser down but is penalized for an illegal punch, then the score is 9 to 8—the winner gets a 1 point penalty for the illegal blow, and the loser is hit with 1 point for being beaten and another point for being knocked-down. At the end of the fight, the fighter with the most points wins. The following is my scorecard of the 10 major rounds in the near-decade fight to bring MelaFind to market. If it were a real match, there is usually a two-knockdown rule, and MELA would have lost it all by the fifth or sixth round. But we kept picking ourselves up off the mat. Not only that, we would have had only one opponent, who would have been as tired as we were. But our opponents kept changing, coming in with fresh energy against our increasing exhaustion. Anyway, it looks like we have a draw. And I don't want a rematch.

Round	MELA'S Opponent	Deductions & Rationale	Score
1—Obtaining Binding Protocol Agreement	FDA	1 point from FDA for not returning phone calls	W 10-8
2—Taking ownership of development and financing of company from founders and private investors	Founders/ Investors	1 point from both for not realizing the CEO must assume leadership immediately	L 9-8
3—Taking pre-revenue medtech company public	Bankers/ Funds	1 point from bankers for broken deal after first attempt	W 10-8
4—Amassing $45 million war chest with CEFF	Bankers	1 point deduction from bankers and funds trying to talk us out of using CEFF	W 10-8

Round	MELA'S Opponent	Deductions & Rationale	Score
5—FDA not approvable letter	FDA	3 points from FDA for unlawful not approvable letter; negotiating retraction of supervisory review without rescinding not approvable letter; setting, then moving panel date	L 7-1
6—Advisory Panel Meeting	FDA	4 points from FDA for making statements in panel package in an attempt to guide the panel vote; treachery/ set-up on indications for use; directing panel to violate binding agreement; incorrect definitions of safety and effectiveness	W 10-6
7—Citizen Petition, PPI White paper, trade and media coverage	FDA		W 10-9
8—Approvable Letter, PMA Approval, CE mark approval	FDA		W 10-9
9—Launch of product in US and Germany	Expectations	63% of US population within 75 miles of MelaFind; at least 40 potentially life-threatening melanomas discovered	W 10-9
10—Valuation decline of MELA from $300 million in Feb 2010 to $50 MM five quarters after launch	FDA, short sellers	3 points from FDA for forcing us to miss opportunity for big public follow-on, periapproval partnership/acquisition, and diminishing MelaFind in eyes of dermatologists	L 7-1

Natural Selection versus a Fair Fight

DARWIN, IT MIGHT be said, showed us that nature likes a good fight. Evolution, after all, is a series of fights between species—initially, it was the strongest and largest that survived. As the conditions changed, the species that could adapt best excelled and thrived—first, the ones that could fly, and then the ones that could swim, then those that could run and swim. When things stabilized a bit, the species that could sustain themselves efficiently had the upper hand. And then, the ones that could think and effectively communicate dominated.

Apart from the innate imperative to survive, there were no rules. Nomads did fine with no rules, but when groups formed, it was those groups that crafted the fairest rules, and rules that led to progress and advancement that flourished. Even with rules, it was competition (a euphemism for "fighting") that proved responsible for the advancement of the most successful societies. A more modern system of fair rules under which fighting occurs is capitalism, the single greatest force of societal and personal advancement in history.

Sporting events are actually just an organized—and planned—"fight." There are rules in sports that, by and large, are followed. Yes, there are mini-inequities everywhere you look—for example, the home basketball team seems to always have less fouls called on its players than the visitors—but the playing field is usually level enough. Setting home field advantage aside, both teams have to shoot at rims that are 10 feet high and from a foul line that's 15 feet away from the basket, or travel a 100-yard football field using only 11 players at a time, with exactly 10 yards required for first downs. (Well, not exactly—placement of the ball between downs is not exactly scientific!)

In sports, when the rules are seemingly not applied fairly and dispassionately, observers vocalize. During a December 2007 NFL game, the New England Patriots, who were having a tremendous, offensive record-breaking season en route to an undefeated regular season, were being outplayed by the Baltimore Ravens. There were a number of obvious miscalls that were ruled in favor of the Patriots, who wound up winning 27 to 24. The next morning, a radio talk show host commented that after the third official review of a call that definitely should have gone in favor of the Ravens and would have decided the game, "I got the feeling that the official was going to say, 'On further review, we are simply not going to let the Patriots lose this game.'" Whether or not he was right, the point was that people want rules applied fairly, with no partiality, no bias, and with no pre-determined outcome in mind.

So rules are important, especially in sports. Imagine what a game would be if the officials allowed the coach of basketball Team A to raise the height of the rim by five feet after a shot by a player on Team B who was still in mid-air! Or if the football coach of Team #1 was allowed to move the first down marker five yards further down field after a 12-yard run by the running back on Team #2.

Outside of sports, in the real world, the government is often tasked with being the arbiters and enforcers of fair play. Congress establishes written rules, called laws, to which all people, companies, organizations are expected to conform. Government agencies then craft guidelines that help them impose the laws fairly. Rules and guidelines are meant to maintain order, harmony, and confidence in the system, and a sense of fairness, all in the service of promoting overall prosperity. Some agencies are not only officials or enforcers, but also, arguably, participants in the game. The individuals in these agencies, and the agencies themselves, have an even greater responsibility to apply the rules fairly and without an agenda. The Food and Drug Administration is one such agency.

The implications of this are huge: the FDA regulates about 25% of the U.S. economy, including those sectors that provide the greatest engines of job creation and growth. What's more, the FDA is tasked with a sacred responsibility—to promote the health of the citizenry. As much as people—be they Democrats, Republicans, or otherwise—like to criticize our government, when it comes to issues that aren't as inflammatory as, say, taxes or Citi Bikes, most of us do want to believe what the government says. Because the FDA has the imprimatur of the U.S. government, then, it effectively has a seal of approval that gives it the benefit of the doubt. So there is a natural (and quite reasonable) acceptance on the part of the populace to accept as fact virtually whatever the FDA says. All the more reason that the FDA should be the leader among all government agencies in fair play. And by that I mean the leader not only in following the letter of the law (and of its guidelines), but also its spirit. In short, the FDA should be the leading agency when it comes to following the Rule of Law and Transparency.

The FDA is not comporting itself in this manner. And it needs to do so. Or else.

Or else what?

Or else health will not be promoted, sectors with great potential to drive job creation and prosperity will no longer do so, and medical innovation will be reduced to pure chance. This could not be happening at a more inopportune time.

Americans deserve better. We deserve fairness, intelligence, ethical conduct, leadership, and, when things go wrong—as all human endeavors sometimes do—rapid remediation, not cover-ups and agenda-driven outcomes from the likes of the FDA. And we are not getting it as a matter of course. The SEC isn't much better, by the way. The courts need to clean up their act as well, especially regarding frivolous investor lawsuits. (I have not given any mention, whatsoever, to the Centers for Medicare Services, or CMS, which is also broken and poses as fundamental an impediment to medical innovation as the FDA. But a man has to save something for his second book.)

For too long now, the FDA has not behaved in a consistent manner, in accordance with its own rules and guidelines. And we are already seeing the effects: inventors, entrepreneurs, and venture capital investors have begun to accept this as the new norm, the new *modus operandi*. Because of that, their investment of time, energy, and money in companies developing truly medically innovative products has diminished and they have shifted focus toward opportunities that do not rely on FDA approval. Jonathan Fleming, the managing general partner of venture capital firm Oxford Bioscience Partners, now tells companies seeking investment to present a compelling business opportunity that *doesn't* require FDA approval. He will accept a value-realizing event that is predicated on CE mark approval, or clearance in China or India, but not the FDA. Other venture capitalists have shifted from investing in healthcare product companies to healthcare service companies—the latter not requiring FDA approval. As a result, product-focused companies are increasingly focused on *incrementalism*—on new products that are merely slight twists on current products. And that won't significantly "promote" our collective health. Even if they dare pursue truly innovative ideas, they are increasingly doing so offshore. So much for American exceptionalism.

The Broken Funnel

IN FEBRUARY 2013, I was a member of a medical technology panel at the Harvard Business School Healthcare Conference. At one point, I suggested that the final "common pathway" of all medical innovation, the FDA, is broken. I explained that the development process for innovative products is often thought of as a funnel. Pour early stage products in the top, and those that get approved come out the bottom. The "pool" of products thins for a number of reasons, including the possibility that the products simply do not work or are shown to be too toxic. But it also thins due to many of the factors that I have described in this book, including the availability of financing or significant non-clinical setbacks that nevertheless derail the entire effort. Investors and entrepreneurs accept this. They know that not everything they invest money or time in will make it to the narrow channel at the bottom of the funnel. But here's the problem: as it stands, the funnel isn't even working anymore. Because that narrow channel is FDA review, and it's all clogged up—the FDA is basically closed for business when it comes to innovation. There's a stopper in the funnel.

There's an urgent need to fix it, because when it's obvious that a funnel doesn't work, only a fool would pour their valuable resources into it. In this case, those resources are time, money, and effort, which are effectively "poured" into the innovation funnel by inventors, entrepreneurs, and venture capital investors. If product approvals don't start coming out the bottom of the funnel again, people will not keep putting those resources into it. If nothing changes, the pool of innovation that the funnel is meant to empty into will dry up.

I am by no means alone in my opinion of the state of medical innovation in this country. Many people who do what I do, and have the know-how to get it done, are shying away from groundbreaking innovative ideas—the ones that have the potential to truly transform healthcare in a quantum manner. In pointing this out on the Harvard panel, I made the point that if things continue as they are, innovation will soon only progress at the pace that big companies want it to progress, which is both incremental and slow. (That's not an oversimplification. As readers of *The Innovator's Dilemma* surely know, huge and successful businesses are structurally opposed to rapid and wholesale innovation. It's too disruptive to their operations.) I joked that such a pace wouldn't provide "breakthrough" but rather "break wind" innovation. Everyone laughed.

For the last two products that I shepherded through to ultimate FDA approval—Valstar and MelaFind—the front end of the process proceeded more or less the way it always does. There were plenty of "fights" to win, but that is standard for a "hired gun" like me in this business. (I made the point in chapter three that what made MELA totally unique wasn't the nature of the battles, but simply the sheer number of them.) With both Valstar and MelaFind, we reached agreement with the FDA on the location of the goal line before we started playing, and then achieved all clinical endpoints—that is, made it into the end zone. And then the FDA decided to "review the play" and shifted the goal line.

In both circumstances, though, the wheels went flying off the train at the back end, once the process was squarely in the hands of the FDA. With Valstar, a mistake of panel constitution cost the company its ability to raise money via an IPO, money that could have been used to secure a steady and reliable manufacturing source, launch a sales and marketing effort, and acquire additional products to build a specialty urology business. With those opportunities lost, the product was off the market for years until a reliable manufacturing process was secured, depriving patients with refractory bladder cancer of a safe alternative to cystectomy.

With MelaFind, an agenda-directed FDA leadership rode roughshod over regulations and issued an unlawful not approvable letter. Even when that mistake came to light, that leadership did not reverse itself, but rather doubled-down in duplicity and cover-up to kill the product so as not to have to admit its failure. The outcome was a triple whammy:

1. The company was deprived of the ability to perform a large public follow-on financing that would have raised sufficient funds to sustain a multi-year commercial development effort;

2. The company was deprived of the ability to obtain a strong partner or to be acquired in one of the most important windows of opportunity for these things to happen, that is, in the peri-approval period;

3. The highly negative and misleading verbiage from the FDA, (which would never have been made if not to cover-up the unlawful not approvable letter, and which had no place in panel documents and panel slides), raised significant clinical questions in the minds of dermatologists even after the ultimate approval.

I did everything by the book on the front end—engaged the FDA, performed a large and robust positive clinical study, filed quality approval dossiers, and obtained Expedited Approval. And then, on the back end, I had to expend tremendous energy, take tremendous risk, and then engage in an "against all odds" effort to obtain product approval. But the FDA caused irreparable damage anyway.

In early 2012, before we'd even launched MelaFind, I was introduced at a conference as "the man who beat the FDA." People clapped. It was a nice moment, but the sad reality is that the fight wasn't really over. Just take a look at MELA's stock price. Even when you beat them, they win.

Breakthrough versus Break-Wind Innovation

AS AN EXAMPLE of breakthrough versus "break wind" innovation, let's consider the hearing aid. Hearing loss is a huge and growing problem—one in three Americans over the age of 65 has hearing loss, and the number of Americans suffering from it is projected to rise from 33.4 million in 2010 to 52.9 million in 2050. In other words, it's a major public health crisis—the third most common problem after arthritis and heart disease. In adults, the most common causes of hearing loss are noise and aging. And guess what? Noise pollution is on the rise and Americans are living longer.

In a single two-day period, I counted the number of insults that this 50 year-old's ears endured:

1. Fire engines and ambulances screaming by with shrill sirens and horns a-blarin';

2. City buses releasing hydraulics—either the brakes or lowering of the chassis;

3. Construction trucks on Second Avenue with empty cargo beds banging as they coursed over rough pavement;

4. Explosions detonating due to construction of subway stations on Second Avenue;

5. A pneumatic hose whistling as it was used to clean the street at a construction site;

6. Hand dryers that sounded like jet engines in the men's room at Grand Central Station;

7. Metro-North trains pulling in to Grand Central and applying their hydraulic parking brakes. The air pressure as well as the loud sound in an enclosed area is a double treat;

8. High pitch screeching of metal on metal in the subway, as well as thunderous clanking of train cars hitting switch rails.

Our eardrums were not built to take such abuse, certainly not for the 75-plus years that most of us can expect to live. So America is literally losing its ability to hear. Current hearing aids are pretty ugly, many require manual adjustment for ambient conditions, require batteries (lots of them), and are something enough people avoid getting that they drive their loved ones crazy for about five years until they do. It is also a problem that does not get a lot of attention, so much so that people don't even realize they are suffering from hearing loss at first, and can subsequently be embarrassed to admit it to themselves.

There has been some impressive innovation in hearing aids, but the way that hearing aids worked 20 years ago pretty much remains the way they work today—basically, delivering amplified sounds to the eardrum. There has been evolution of form that has helped cosmetically and with function (behind the ear open fit → behind the ear molded → in the ear → in the canal → completely in the canal), as well as technological advancement, including directional microphones, feedback suppression, and digitization. But it doesn't come cheap: In a recent Consumer Reports survey, the price for a pair ranged from $1800 to $6800.

I would love to develop—or, more likely, invest in—a profoundly different technology, an artificial eardrum overlay to replace the hearing aid. Mine would be nanotechnology-based to provide sound capture, conduction, and transmission that even exceeds that of a healthy set of ears. It would release tropic nerve growth factors to promote the repair and growth of nerves to receive the vibration impulses directly from the Nanodrum, in addition to the malleus and incus bones. It would be powered biologically, that is, cellularly, from glucose that the biocell would be fed from the body's extra-cellular fluid. It would be as thin, if not thinner, than the natural eardrum, and would be designed so as to be inserted on an out-patient basis within minutes by an ear, nose, and throat specialist. It would not be visible. Because I am a man of my time, it would be Bluetooth-enabled and contain a cell-based reprogrammable microprocessor that is both updatable and configurable via WiFi. It would not set off airport metal detectors, and would be safe to wear during MRIs. It would be completely bacteriostatic, thus presenting no increased risk of infection, and might even reduce the incidence of middle ear infections. It would be waterproof, for sure, although I wouldn't want to go scuba diving with it. (Technology does have its limits.) Target price for a pair + installation: $3,500. (Or $3,000 on Tuesdays, with a coupon).

Sounds cool, right? It *is* cool, and it would be amazing. And I have the experience to raise the money, assemble the right scientists and engineers, acquire or gain access to the technology, design the studies to get it approved, and then commercialize it. The only problem? Even though the fundamental technologies for everything I just described have been in laboratories for the past several years, the FDA has no clue what to do with them—more precisely, how to *regulate* them. Nanotechnology is the single most important platform technology today that promises to make drug delivery more targeted, or to make coatings more durable, less immunogenic, and more bacteriostatic. At the very least, it can dramatically improve the therapeutic index (the ratio of effectiveness and safety) of almost every product on the market today. Nanotechnology is a revolutionary platform, and I want to run a nanotechnology company.

And here's another issue—the FDA has done nothing substantive to promote the development of nanotechnology. While the FDA certainly recognizes its existence and has issued two related guidance documents (one on cosmetics products and the other on food additives and their production), it has not shown leadership in bringing the promise of nanotechnology into reality with respect to promoting the public health. This is a huge missed opportunity. If I were running the FDA, I would have announced a nanotechnology initiative on the day I arrived. I would have set goals for product approvals in various areas (drug delivery, implants, coatings, smart devices, whatever), and I would have established initiatives with both industry and academia to make that happen. I would not have spent my time on a Transparency Initiative and "interactive review" gobble-de-gook that did nothing to promote health and everything to stifle the approval process and medical innovation. If the FDA had grabbed the mantle on nanotechnology, it would have helped all form and manner of medical innovation. It would have spawned an incredible investment of money, time, and effort. Instead, we got a toothless and meaningless Innovation Initiative that was completely unnecessary because every element therein was already provided for in current laws.

It comes down to saying versus doing, walking the proverbial walk. It comes down to leadership. It comes down to courage. It comes down to passion and purpose. If the FDA had pursued a nanotechnology initiative, real innovation would have followed.

What Is the FDA Supposed to Do?

ACCORDING TO SECTION 1003 of the Federal Food, Drug, and Cosmetic Act, the FDA's mandate is as follows:

THE ADMINISTRATION SHALL—

1. promote the public health by promptly and efficiently reviewing clinical research and taking appropriate action on the marketing of regulated products in a timely manner;

2. with respect to such products, protect the public health by ensuring that—

   a. foods are safe, wholesome, sanitary, and properly labeled;

   b. human and veterinary drugs are safe and effective;

   c. there is reasonable assurance of the safety and effectiveness of devices intended for human use;

    d. cosmetics are safe and properly labeled; and

    e. public health and safety are protected from electronic product radiation;

2. participate through appropriate processes with representatives of other countries to reduce the burden of regulation, harmonize regulatory requirements, and achieve appropriate reciprocal arrangements; and

3. as determined to be appropriate by the Secretary, carry out paragraphs (1) through (3) in consultation with experts in science, medicine, and public health, and in cooperation with consumers, users, manufacturers, importers, packers, distributors, and retailers of regulated products.

The following is excerpted from the current FDA website:

WHAT WE DO

[The] FDA is responsible for protecting the public health by assuring the safety, efficacy and security of human and veterinary drugs, biological products, medical devices, our nation's food supply, cosmetics, and products that emit radiation.

[The] FDA is also responsible for advancing the public health by helping to speed innovations that make medicines more effective, safer, and more affordable and by helping the public get the accurate, science-based information they need to use medicines and foods to maintain and improve their health. [The] FDA also has responsibility for regulating the manufacturing, marketing and distribution of tobacco products to protect the public health and to reduce tobacco use by minors.

Finally, [the] FDA plays a significant role in the Nation's counterterrorism capability. [The] FDA fulfills this responsibility by ensuring

the security of the food supply and by fostering development of medical products to respond to deliberate and naturally emerging public health threats.

The first function of the FDA's mission as delineated in the FD&C Act pertains to timely (i.e., prompt and efficient) reviews and actions on the marketing of regulated products. That's the law. On the agency's website, however, that function has been subjugated to the second paragraph of "What We Do." Furthermore, the agency seems to have decided to unilaterally (i.e., without the support of actual law) alter one standard while also adding another: (1) the concept of *reasonable assurance* has been omitted from the language about devices; and (2) the notion of *relative/ comparative performance* (effectiveness, safety, and affordability) of regulated products has been added.

In the first case, the acceptance of reasonable assurance as opposed to definitive proof is critical. Why? Because definitive proof in the "art" of medicine is something that is quite elusive. Just think of how many articles have been written on the dangers . . . I mean the benefits . . . no, I mean the dangers . . . nope it's the benefits . . . of coffee or wine! Reasonable assurance means that we should seek the least burdensome proofs and enough data to make a conclusion that a product can be introduced into medicine and its exact usage will be refined and settle into use in those instances where it proves beneficial. "Reasonable assurance" was carefully selected wording in the law, and should not be replaced without debate.

Representing people like me in the debate would be Voltaire, who more than two and a half centuries ago said, "Doctors are men who prescribe medicines of which they know little, to cure diseases of which they know less, in human beings of whom they know nothing." While we know a lot more about diseases than we did then, we still don't know everything, and progress shouldn't be allowed to stop until we do.

In the second case, the law takes no position on the notion of relative performance. If a new device doesn't actually improve on the effectiveness or safety of current ones, does the FDA have the right to deny its approval? I don't think so, but according to its website, it seems to think it does. But I'd also be open to a debate as to why or why not that should be the case.

Another important point is that FDA seems to have decided it is not responsible for speeding all innovations, but only those innovations that they feel make things safer, more effective, and more affordable. Wrong again. Their mandate is to speed along safe and effective innovations. There is no use of the word "affordability" in the law. What's more, the FDA's presumption that it is even capable of judging improved affordability fails the laugh test. For one, the FDA staff has no expertise in health economics. Even more importantly, the law envisioned that competitive market forces would determine the relative value of safe and effective products. In this country, the market is— and always will be—the ultimate arbiter of price. If a product is too expensive, people (i.e., doctors or patients) won't buy it. Or a competitor will steal the business away. That's the way capitalism works. If people think the law needs to be changed, that's fine with me. But the way to do that is to go petition Congress to change it, not to simply change your stated mission because you feel like it.

Simply put, the FDA has not only reversed its priorities but perverted them, and without the authorization to do so. Their first priority as laid out in the law that empowers them has now become their second priority. More than that, though, they are abiding by standards not proscribed by law. Both of these subtle yet profound changes have added immeasurable amounts of time, development cost, and uncertainty to the innovation process. The FDA has gone beyond its legal limits and given itself a mandate that Congress did not. And the results are there for all to see—not just examples like MelaFind, but in stunted and underfunded innovation across-the-board.

The FDA needs to get back to its first principles, and they need to do it fast. It needs to stop being afraid to promote the public health. Many articles have been written about the FDA's aversion to risk, an aversion that is usually revealed when they roll out the term "patient safety," knowing full well that it will likely get them a pass from legislators, watchdog groups, and the public. But it's that aversion that is the reason for its complete dysfunction and the attendant regulatory uncertainty, long approval times, and escalating costs of new product development.

I have absolutely no problem with putting safety first, and making the whole argument about safety. None at all. But I should also make two points about the way the FDA views safety:

1. The inertia and trepidation when it comes to *promoting* health via timely, efficient, and consistent reviews of new products, especially breakthrough products, stems from a fundamentally flawed assumption—that current medical practice is safe. Because of this mindset, the FDA clearly views its number one mandate as *protecting* the public health. I hate to be the bearer of bad news, but in many circumstances, current medical practice is *not* safe! Consider the case of MelaFind. By effectively assuming that having one American die per hour of a disease that is visible on the skin is a "safe" state of affairs, the FDA tried to deny a product that they suggested could put the public at risk. I deconstructed this argument in previous chapters and shown it to be part of the cover-up of the original mistake that they refused to correct, but this is the simple explanation that the FDA has used to explain its actions with MelaFind and many other products.

   If there were a real understanding that in many instances medical practice is not safe—that's why it's called medical "practice" and not medical "science"—fewer products that might actually promote our health would be impeded. If you want to have a debate about safety, by all means, let's have it. But I will show you how the argument that the FDA is using in invoking the "first do no harm" credo of medicine has had the unintended effect of actually doing harm by slowing down innovation.

2. Fear is the enemy of change. It always has been, and always will be. Fear is also the enemy of breakthrough innovation. The FDA's leadership is afraid of making mistakes, and that

fear permeates the entire organization, especially among those people responsible for reviewing new products. The FDA's leadership is also afraid of being called out by the media or called to a Congressional Hearing to defend the approval of pacemaker leads that dislodge, drugs with severe (even fatal) adverse effects, implants that leach metals into the body, or X-ray machines that pump out more energy than they should.

They're also afraid of people like Sidney Wolfe, head of the Public Citizen's Health Research Group, a consumer and health "advocacy" group. They're afraid of Ralph Nader. And they shouldn't be. Once a product undergoes review by the FDA and by a properly constituted and executed panel, they should take pride in that approval. For every case of unfortunate and irreversible morbidity and mortality, there are thousands if not millions of examples of those same products delivering magnificent benefits. Perfection isn't possible. We've got to get back to reasonable assurance standards and look to improve, as opposed to being content with a philosophy of "do not hurt."

In short, unless the FDA gets back to its first principles, breakthrough medical innovation will neither deliver that which we have already seen it provide in the recent past, nor realize its true potential in the future.

What's Next?

IN APRIL 2013, I was invited to lecture to a class at Columbia University's Healthcare MBA program, providing insight on how to manage the major business risks inherent in medtech and biopharma companies that engage in breakthrough medical innovation. At the conclusion of the class, the course director, Cliff Cramer, asked me, "Surely you have two or three of these left in you?" Of course I did, I replied, but added that the definition of insanity is doing the same thing and expecting a different outcome, and I am not insane. If the system isn't changed, there's no way that I'd even consider participating in truly innovative medical innovation again in the role of a CEO. So I'm going to help change the system by building awareness and offering solutions.

This book is the first step toward that goal. I hope it emboldens others who've had similar experiences to speak up, unabashedly, about regulatory processes gone awry. And that their stories, along with that of MELA, can act as a clarion call to those people in a position to help fix a broken system. In the meantime, I hope that it will provide some much-needed optimism to those who find themselves in the kind of jam MELA found itself in *at this very moment*. And that they will come to me so that I might help them in ways that were not available to MELA, for the mutual benefit of patients, companies, and investors.

Even in a normal course of events, breakthrough innovation is extremely difficult and a very low likelihood endeavor. When the government acts capriciously and in bad faith, breaks its own laws, and then tries to make the problem go away not by correcting the mistake but by making a revolutionary product fail, then medical innovation is nearly impossible.

But not totally—MelaFind is on the market, after all. But the fight to get it there rendered an optimistic, high energy, savvy, and capable professional—a fighter by nature—unwilling to fight anymore.

The final chapter of this book offers a manifesto of solutions to get that fighter, and others like him, back in the ring, for the sake of medical innovation.

10

The Medical Innovation Manifesto

IN THE 1970's, a series of public service TV commercials ran in which people in their 40's discussed a number of topics *du jour* and one of them would say something like, "They need to do something about that," or "They should fix that," or "They shouldn't tolerate that." Then a faceless announcer would come on as the previous audio faded. "WE ARE THEY," the voice would say, then sound a call to action to get involved.

It is up to us, the people, to get involved, to speak out, to demand better, to start a serious conversation while showing the fortitude and staying power to make a real difference. In other words, to make change happen. I'm a pragmatic person, and have therefore focused the following manifesto on truly implementable ideas.

From my direct experience over the past 25 years, I believe there are several changes that can be made—most of which can be done immediately—which will help the cause of medical innovation. I urge policy-makers, industry advocates, industry leaders, patients, and citizens to help bring about these changes. I don't doubt that it will be an uphill fight. But I'm a fighter. That said, I also never fight battles that I don't think I can win. This is winnable, if we try.

THE MEDICAL INNOVATION MANIFESTO

1. *Encourage Leadership.* Let me be clear: there are many people at the FDA who want to do a good job, are earnest, smart, and honest. But they lack empowerment. They lack support. They lack leadership. And that has to change. We must identify leaders with a medical innovation compass; leaders who are unafraid, articulate, inspirational, smart, and savvy. They are out there.

   a. *Control.* The FDA Commissioner must meet with each Center Director on a weekly basis in order to be made abreast of any issues that arise so that these are promptly addressed with the help of the best and the brightest people that the Agency employs, and to make certain that the Center Directors are implementing FDA priorities appropriately. Direction from the top is critical.

   b. *Direction.* The FD&C is a very comprehensive and voluminous statute that is subject to interpretation by the people who implement it. That interpretation should be consistent with the intent of the law, as well as the policy direction of the Administration through the Commissioner. Without firm direction from the Commissioner, the 10,000+ permanent (and another 5,000 non-permanent) employees will not be capable of implementing it in a consistent, reliable, and productive manner thereby resulting in significant delays in drug, device, and biological product reviews and approvals. Inconsistent and inefficient review kills innovation because small companies, who do most of the innovating, cannot withstand the cost of unnecessary delay. Delays also increase the cost and time for development, which translates into higher prices.

2. *Clarify the Priorities of the FDA.* The FDA's number one priority should be "to promote health," consistent with its mission in the FD&C, and delete all references to comparative standards

in its mission, including affordability. It is not the FDA's job to engage in these analyses, and certainly not to make them "requirements" for approval. Rather, market forces should be left responsible for determining the winners between newer safe and effective products and older ones.

a. All FDA leadership (Commissioners and Center Directors and Division Directors) must be committed to medical innovation and the approval of safe and effective new products. How these products perform relative to others is not their concern, unless the manufacturers are seeking comparative performance claims.

b. In addition, the cost and payment of new products is NOT the purview of the FDA, and should not factor into determinations of approvability.

   i. Interaction between the FDA and any payers (private payers and Centers for Medicare/Medicaid Services—CMS) must not be initiated by the FDA or by CMS. If a sponsor seeks to engage both groups in the design of a study that could satisfy the requirements of FDA approval, as well as CMS (reasonable & necessary standards) or private payers (cost-effectiveness) end-points, that is a business decision that must be left to the sponsor.

   ii. If joint FDA/payer (CMS or private) review is imposed by regulators, the risk of payment considerations permeating the approval decision has too great an abrogating effect on medical innovation. This represents a much greater threat than the opportunity of more rapid reimbursement of new products.

3. *Define the FDA Review Guidelines Once and For All.* To do this, we must impose an immediate moratorium on all new FDA review guidelines, and conduct an independent review of all new guidelines introduced over the past three years. This is a must

because FDA over the past several years has sought to impose a new and often inconsistent interpretation of the FD&C Act by issuing guidance documents that too often tread well beyond the letter and intent of the Act.

a. Score all recent new and amended guidelines, as well as future guidelines, through the creation of an "Innovation Impact Index." This needs to have teeth—for example, if there were a scale of 1-10 with 10 being the most favorable for medical innovation, no new guideline could be implemented with a score less than 7.5 without Congressional approval. [A comment period that involves multiple stakeholders would be required prior to final scoring.]

b. Establish Hearing Officers under the Commissioner—this will allow industry and the public to challenge any new or existing guidelines relative to the FD&C Act itself. We cannot tolerate FDA leadership changing the law via guidelines.

4. *Have The Ombudsman Report to the Commissioner.* This is the way things were previously organized, but today, each Center of the FDA has a separate ombudsman. Grievance resolution is not effective when the arbiter is part of the team. Further, the Commissioner must be made aware of potential problems.

a. Ombudsman should issue quarterly reports to Congress regarding ongoing cases that are submitted for review.

b. This will provide independent oversight of the Centers.

5. *Reform the Advisory Panel Process.* The best, brightest, and most appropriate medical and scientific experts are not participating on FDA panels. Too often, individuals on panels seek to give the agency what it "wants to hear," rather than behave truly independently. In other cases, panel members are in pursuit of personal agendas outside the review of the product, which undermines the purpose of the panel.

a. Establish a voir dire process for panel selection—industry must be able to disqualify panel participants

    i. Industry must be able to appoint at least one-third of the panel members, subject to FDA voir dire.

b. Financial interest rules must be reconsidered—the reason industry seeks consultation from certain physicians is because they are experts in the disease state. The FDA's strict conflict of interest policy is depriving the process of some of the best minds.

c. Panel members should be vetted by the appropriate medical societies. For instance, when a product for insomnia is to be reviewed by an advisory panel, the American Academy of Sleep Medicine, American Psychiatric Association, American Neurological Association, and the American Academy of Neurology should be asked whether the members of the panel are the most appropriate (i.e., the best qualified) to participate.

    i. Of course, physicians who treat the disease under study must constitute at least 50% of the medical experts on the panel.

d. All advisory panels MUST vote on the approvability (consistent with the FD&C Act, but countermanded by Guidance Document fiat) of the product under consideration for the indications for use under consideration, as well as for alternative indications for use.

e. Panel members must sign a declaration that they thoroughly read the panel briefing packages. The FDA literally banks on them not doing so, and relies on the accumulated effect of the weight of the FDA portion of the panel briefing as well as its imprimatur to influence the panel. Ensuring that panel members review the sponsor's submission is one way to counter this effect.

6. *Expand and Enforce the Binding Protocol Agreement Process.* This should extend to all products requiring Phase III studies. The goal posts should be set in concrete, immutable and not subject to trend or the whim of new reviewers and new management.

   a. (The protocol agreement provisions do allow reconsideration if a scientifically valid reason emerges since the agreement was entered; the law requires that they first meet with the sponsor to explain their rationale.)

7. *Hold the FDA Accountable When It Fails to Meet Review Deadlines.* When the FDA does not meet its target MDUFA and PDUFA review deadlines for applications that are ultimately approved:

   a. Extend the life of the entire patent estate, not just one patent, when the FDA delays product approvals beyond statutory review times.

   b. Reimburse companies with revenues < $100 MM for money spent during the delay period, either in the form of cash or a fully transferrable tax credit. (In a merger/acquisition, the tax credits would apply to the acquiring business; these would be assets to the company.)

   c. Extend the marketing exclusivity period for an equal amount of time beyond the target review period.

8. *End the Prospective Designation of Applications as Having "Major" or "Minor" Deficiencies "In the Moment."* These should be designated in retrospect, *at the end of a review,* not at the beginning. It is too easy for the FDA to declare an application to have a Major Deficiency under the auspices of merely asking questions, thereby "stopping the clock" unilaterally and extending the statutory review period. This has become nothing more than a tactic to buy time. While convenient for the FDA, these terms are also pejorative and represent a stigma that is not understood by the public.

a. "Major Deficiencies" should be items that the sponsor required more than 90 days to address;

b. "Minor Deficiencies" should be items that the sponsor required 45-90 days to address;

c. "Questions" should be items that the sponsor required < 45 days to address;

d. End the prospective review clock stoppage mechanisms. Review performance will be judged in arrears (days in the hands of FDA versus sponsor). Status of all reviews must be counted in calendar days—sponsors have market incentives to act expeditiously.

   ii. Review clock stops and starts are responsible for a great amount of unnecessary work, which, if spent on the actual review, would result in speedier actions.

9. *End the Transparency Initiative.* Our agencies should be honest and open. Our government is for the people, NOT for the government—transparency is an expectation.

10. *End the "Interactive Review" Initiative.* Truly effective review includes open communication between applicant and reviewer, therefore labeling something as "interactive," which is limited and often unproductive, does not advance product reviews and ultimately the public health.

11. *End the Innovation Pathway.* This is a distraction, propaganda, and complete waste of time and resources. Expedited Review and binding protocol agreements provide for all that is needed. Similarly, end the *Breakthrough Therapy, Fast Track, Priority Review, and Accelerated Approval Pathways* as these are not working, merely serve as propaganda to mollify criticism of the performance of the FDA, and actually have the perverse effect of dictating the direction in which new innovative products are developed, rather than allowing for the science and medicine to

direct these critical, time consuming, and costly pursuits. These programs also grant tacit permission for the FDA to allow products that do not fall under these banners to languish in regulatory limbo. The FDA does not need any of these programs; their mandate to promote health provides them with the necessary broad flexibility to streamline the review of new innovative products that promise to, indeed, promote health.

a. As discussed earlier, because FDA reviewers do not feel supported, they are wary of blazing new trails, and so they are reticent to approve new and innovative products for which the therapeutic index (benefit/risk ratio) is not overwhelmingly obvious for fear of negative repercussions. [No one ever gets reprimanded or fired or lateralized for rejecting applications.] The pathways designed to expedite the review process, typically do not, ironically. Rather, they channel product development to areas for which the therapeutic index cannot be questioned, for example, in end stage cancer, and diseases for which good therapeutic alternatives are not available.

b. I was recently at a large biotech conference; over half of the 45 cancer companies whose presentations I attended were developing their initial products for AML (acute myelogenous leukemia) or pancreatic cancer. Sure, new and better products are needed for AML and pancreatic cancer. But why aren't the most cutting edge approaches that are being pursued by the most innovative and entrepreneurial companies undergoing testing to extend survival in earlier stages (or in remission) of breast cancer, lung cancer, colon cancer, and prostate cancer, the most common cancer types? Or, why aren't companies aiming the latest discoveries in science to stop the steps in the process of tumorigenesis, before overt aggressive cancer is established? Because, there will be much more FDA scrutiny for these claims, and qualifying for one of the above pathways is much more difficult. But, these are where we really have an incredible opportunity for obtaining breakthrough innovation.

12. *Remove Excessive and Burdensome Regulatory Requirements For Growth Companies at Securities Exchange Commission and FINRA.* For companies with revenues < $100 million, market capitalization < $750 million, or with stock trading under $5.00 per share:

   a. Eliminate dark pool trading (this one should be for all companies)

   b. Eliminate shorting

   c. Eliminate options and derivatives trading that has the effect of "shorting"

   d. Require financial message board participants and financial newsletter providers and bloggers to disclose financial relationships with entities that own securities in companies about which they are commenting

   e. Eliminate Sarbanes Oxley requirements of:

      i. Independent Auditors' inability to provide accounting services

      ii. Three-year review of financials by preceding Independent Auditors

   f. Eliminate 13-D filing/reporting requirement for funds owning > 5% stake (require listing of holdings in reports to fund participants, only)

   g. For funds owning a > 5% stake of a company, have long-term capital gains kick-in immediately

   h. Enforce existing laws regarding manipulative and predatory trading

13. *Eliminate Unnecessary Shareholder Lawsuits.* When it pertains to FDA regulated products for periods during FDA review (prior to final FDA action):

a. Loser pays expenses of winner

b. Amend Rule 15 of the Federal Rules of Civil Procedure such that part of the definition of "when justice so requires" with respect to amending complaints includes what is fair to the defendant in a securities class action. Justice should NOT be construed to require giving plaintiffs in securities class action lawsuits repeated opportunities to amend complaints when amendments are NOT based on new facts in evidence or other specific factors.

14. *Eliminate Programs and Policies That Demand Evidence-Based-Medicine and Comparative Effectiveness Analyses Prior to Payment / Reimbursement of New Medical Innovations and Products.* These are seen in Obamacare, Accountable Care Organizations, and capitated systems. Breakthrough medical innovations require many years—up to 10 or more—to be fully and properly inculcated into practice. The manner in which they are used in years 1 to 5 can be quite different than in year 10. Requiring evidence-based-medicine and comparative effectiveness studies prior to payment means improper evaluation, which will kill innovation. As always, clinical performance and market performance are the best ways to determine the viability—the best interventions survive this natural selection without arbitrarily limiting choice, possibility, and innovation.

Two new groups pose a great threat to medical innovation along these lines:

a. PCORI's (Patient Centered Outcome Research) mission is "producing and promoting high integrity, evidence-based information that comes from research guided by patients, caregivers, and the broader health care community." Obtaining data on these sorts of measures is quite difficult (validated endpoints) and takes time, as discussed above. Withholding payment until the data are available poses a great risk to medical innovation;

b. AHRQ (Agency for Healthcare Research & Quality) is focused on developing comparative effectiveness data and evidence-based medicine for outcomes associated with the use of drugs, devices, medical tests, and surgeries. Their mission: "[to] improve health care quality by providing patients and physicians with state-of-the-science information on which medical treatments work best for a given condition."

i. Two points here—the apparent belief that medicine is a SCIENCE and not an "art" dramatizes the fundamental bias and fallacy in this group's mandate. It is simply impossible to prospectively study many things in medicine, especially breakthrough products that have yet to find their niche;

ii. If AHRQ ratings and assessments are used to decide which products and interventions are to be reimbursed, innovative medical products will suffer because of the difficulties in executing these sorts of studies (selection and validation of appropriate endpoints), as well as the time, cost, and duration required for truly breakthrough products to be adopted and used most effectively in order to undergo proper study.

15. *Expand Patients' Ability to "Pay Up" for New Products.* For example, CMS pays for lens replacement in cataract surgery. It does not pay for accommodating lenses. But CMS does allow patients undergoing cataract surgery to self-pay for accommodating lenses the amount above which it reimburses for non-accommodating lens replacement. The same is true for basic wheelchairs and those with more advanced features.

a. Congressional action will be required to expand this into other appropriate areas;

b. This program could provide a template for the partial payment of new breakthrough products in the early phases of adoption until market determinations of relative performance can be performed to satisfy payers;

   c. This could also be helpful with respect to initiatives by PCORI and AHRQ.

16. *Establish an Innovation Impact Index for CMS.* A great example of the need for such a thing: On July 19, 2013, CMS proposed a new rule that would impose new standards on IDE (Investigational Device Exemption studies) that are approved by the FDA for breakthrough medical products under investigational study and review. Presently, CMS pays for the normal course of care that a patient would typically undergo for a particular condition/intervention, except for the cost of the experimental product under IDE study. This encourages Medicare patients to participate in clinical studies, which all parties (FDA, CMS, and sponsors) want to see happen. It is a system that has worked well for years. Under the new proposed rule, CMS would pay for the normal care of the condition under study ONLY if the IDE studies met a list of 15 criteria that CMS devised, independent of the FDA having approved the IDE study. This will have a significant negative impact on medical innovation and should not be permitted.

   a. Similar to 3.a., proposed rules with scores below a threshold value would require Congressional approval, and stakeholder comment prior to final scoring would be required.

17. *Replace Redundant Initiatives with a Continuous Improvement Program.* Given that all organizations should seek to constantly improve and that the medical device and biopharma industries pay for product reviews in the form of the PDUFA and MDUFA provisions, the FDA should implement a continuous improvement program that will replace the Transparency Initiative, Innovation Pathway, Interactive Review, and Breakthrough Therapy Designation by simply ensuring *effective reviews.* All of these "programs" are simply propaganda—mere words, as it were—being thrown at a problem, rather than true attempts to address the problem itself. Leadership and communication

are steps 1 and 2 to having effective reviews. Step 3 is feed-back—the FDA should solicit feedback from sponsors relative to the performance of the review team and management. The ratings should include areas such as scientific knowledge, medical knowledge, problem-solving, responsiveness, leadership, and job knowledge. These surveys should be placed in the file of the managers and reviewers, just as 360 reviews are used in human resource management in industry.

18. *Encourage Feedback.* In addition to conducting high quality clinical studies, submitting quality dossiers containing all relevant data, and following the laws and guidelines, sponsors must be encouraged to be vocal about problems they encounter with the regulatory process. Many sponsors, particularly the larger companies with the most credibility and trust, simply do not want to risk retaliation in the form of longer delays of current and future submissions, as well as FDA audits.

   a. Medical innovation means better products for patients—a new product that could be available three-to six months or one year sooner with appropriate challenging from sponsors could mean a tremendous amount to the lives of patients.

Acknowledgements

There are many people who made significant contributions to the preparation of this book, many who co-lived the stories and experiences about which I have written, and many who made me the person that I am today. I will try to thank them now.

Adele.

My brother, Vincent, who taught me, well, everything, most importantly, what it means to be a leader. He was there at the lowest point, and without Adele and him, I would not have made it through. And, his girls—Mary, Katie, Laura, and Michelle . . . the thought of watching *The Lion King* with them still makes me smile.

My parents (Betty and Vincent), and sisters (Mary and Liz, and their children John Michael, Christopher, Emily, and Natalie), and Godparents (Joseph and Marie Clementi), and cousin (Michael Clementi). Adele's family, who provided great support to Adele, and encouraged me—Felix, Adelaide, Tom, Lisa, Donna, Elaine, Michael, Rob, John, Devon, Robby, and JenJen; for a guy who hates sand, some of my happiest moments are at the Jersey Shore with them.

Duff McDonald, experienced business journalist (*Last Man Standing* and *The Firm*), and collaborator. Gene Timmons, creative and graphics consultant. Melissa Hurley and Tess Woods, PR and marketing. And Debra Englander, advisor and publishing coach.

Professional colleagues and friends from whom I learned a great deal and whose approach I modeled—Bob Maguire, Aileen Ryan, Bob McCormack, George Ebright (deceased), John Simon, Michael

Walker, and Kirk Maslin (deceased). Professional colleagues with whom I worked shoulder to shoulder and without whom the achievements discussed herein would not have been possible— Dina Gutkowicz-Krusin, Nyq Kabalev, Michael Greenebaum, Jeff Wallace, Claudia Beqaj, Mrinalini Roy, Gabe Cruz, Jenna Glauda, Vivian Yost, Diana Garcia-Redruello, Denise Webber, Al Maroli, Mervyn Israel, Bob Humphries, Al Thunberg, Tazewell Wilson, Jack McGrann, and Janice Pruch.

Venture Capital and public investors who either invested in me, or encouraged me—Dan Lufkin, Ken Langone, Steve Dow, Allan Ferguson, Jonathan Fleming, Lew Pell, Dennis Purcell, Adam Gurney, Paul Weiss, Rob S, Rob J, Angus M, and Matt C. Bankers and analysts who cared—Rudy Balseiro, Rob Sine, John Prior, Dalton Chandler, Jonathan Burklund, Josh Jennings, Larry Smith, and Caroline Corner.

Lawyers whose counsel was invaluable—Jim Snipes, Beth Roberts, Glenn Burlingame, Mark Heller, Stephanie Philbin, Arlene Bender, and Peter Hutt.

Media and policy professionals whose stories had significant impact on the outcome—Michael Mandel, Holman Jenkins, Pimm Roberts, Tom Burton, Jonathan Rockoff, Tory Newmyer, Michael McKee, Mark McCarty, Amanda Pedersen, and Jim Stommen.

Doctors who were instrumental in the development and commercialization of the breakthrough products that I had the privilege and opportunity to advance—Brian Leyland-Jones, Mark Ratain, Al Sunshine, Bart Grossman, Dick Williams, Gerry Chodak, Charles Neal, Howard Scher, Dan Petrylak, Paul Lange, Mark Soloway, Al Kopf, Darrell Rigel, Robert Friedman, Armand Cognetta, Arthur Sober, Laura Ferris, Liz Tanzi, Marty Mihm, Clay Cockerell, Dan Siegel, Mark Lebwohl, Marcella Kollman-Hemmerich, Christian Mensing, Gary Peck, Doris Day, Gary Goldenberg, Harold Rabinovitz, Gary Monheit, Ken Gross, and Mary Martini, Peter Soyer.

FDA staff and reviewers with whom I worked who are professional, data driven, and fair. You are a service to your country.

Teachers with great patience, ability, and passion—Al Klainer, Norman Lasker, Charles Shioleno, Glen Mogan, Dennis Quinlan, Gary Weine, Gary Gerstein, Saad Habba, Carroll Rawn, Pete Stamer, Roberta Moldow, Bill Smith, Paul Ward, and Br. Michael Dwyer (deceased).

Priests who inspired me in The Way—Robert Sheeran, Ed Cuiba, Anthony Randazzo, Bob Stagg, Joseph Nealon (deceased), and Ed Duffy (deceased).

A few critical contributors asked me not to mention their names—you know who you are, and I know who you are.

Friends I made along the way—Jim Quinn, Cliff Cramer, Dean Siegal, Bob Lippert, Mark Fabiani, and Anne Egger.

My piano teacher, Frances Kramer, and her dog, Freddie.

For More Information

THANK YOU FOR reading my book. Please visit the book's website—www.innovationbreakdownbook.net—for more information about *Innovation Breakdown*, as well as my blog about news topics and developments relative to the book.

As I said at the end of the introduction, I hope that you enjoyed reading it more than I enjoyed living it. If you are aware of, or the victim of, a related biopharma / medtech nightmare, or if you are aware of other examples, I would love to hear from you—you can contact me through the website.

Please follow me on Twitter—@josephgulfo. I look forward to hearing from you.

Joseph V. Gulfo, MD, MBA

About The Author

JOSEPH V. GULFO, MD, MBA is the author of *Innovation Breakdown: How the FDA and Wall Street Cripple Medical Advances* and *The Care Quotient: Transforming Business Through People*. He has more than 25 years of experience in the biopharmaceutical and medical device industries. In 2012, he received the American Business Awards' Maverick of the Year Award and was an Ernst & Young Entrepreneur of the Year Finalist. Dr. Gulfo also teaches graduate Cancer Biology and business classes in entrepreneurship.

He is currently CEO of Breakthrough Medical Innovations, a team of industry experts specializing in Biopharma/Medtech product and commercial development, sales and marketing, regulatory (FDA and CE), quality, and policy advocacy. Prior to this, he served as President & CEO at MELA Sciences from 2004 - June 2013, and was Chairman of the Board from November 2011 through June 2013. While at MELA Sciences, he was responsible for (1) effecting an IPO in 2005 and consummating 11 public financings totaling ~$160 MM: (2) obtaining FDA approval of MelaFind, a breakthrough PMA smart diagnostic device for early melanoma detection through which he gained national attention for the process that included the issuing an illegal not approvable letter by FDA, a Citizen Petition filing requesting that the FDA enforce the company's Binding Protocol Agreement, and a Congressional Hearing at which the FDA admitted the error; and (3) launching MelaFind in US and Europe, and placing MelaFind systems within 75 miles of 63% of the US population in the first 12 months on the market.

He was responsible for the 1998 NDA approval of Valstar (as President & COO of Anthra Pharmaceuticals and Chairman of its

UK Subsidiary), a drug for superficial bladder cancer, which had sales of $27 MM in 2012, 14 years after its approval. He was also responsible for the development of ProstaScint (Cytogen Corporation), a BLA-approved monoclonal antibody for prostate cancer. He is currently on the board of directors and audit committee of Procertus Biopharma, a company developing palliative care products for radiation dermatitis and oral mucositis. Dr. Gulfo was CEO and Chairman of Antigen Express, an immunotherapy company in the field of vaccines for cancer therapy, antiviral therapy, and asthma, responsible for its merger.

He received his MD from University of Medicine and Dentistry of New Jersey, and his MBA from Seton Hall University. Dr. Gulfo is a leader in medtech / biopharma innovation, a skilled entrepreneur, manager, and product/market development executive. He lives in New York with his wife, Adele.

THE CARE QUOTIENT

TRANSFORMING BUSINESS
THROUGH PEOPLE

JOSEPH V. GULFO, MD, MBA

Praise for *The Care Quotient*

"The key to any successful organization is it's people—their skills, loyalty, their character and dedication to the company. If it's a small business, the people are all—it's make or break. Joseph Gulfo gives the key to caring for and listening to your people in this magnificent book. Skip it at your risk."

—Dan W. Lufkin, Co-Founder, Donaldson Lufkin & Jenrette

"Take the Care Quotient survey to see how much you care about creating the best environment for your employees so that they can flourish and bring your business to new heights."

—Kay Koplovitz, Founder and Former CEO of
USA Network and the *Syfy Channel,* and author of
Bold Woman, Big Ideas and Been There Run That

"Nothing that I have read on management... becomes more real world than *The Care Quotient* when it comes to smaller companies which represent 99.7% of employers in the U.S. Building the passion and excitement of a small company is a differentiating advantage. Thousands of people around the world will benefit from this book."

—Fred Hassan, Managing Director, Warburg Pincus and
author of *Reinvent: A Leader's Playbook for Serial Success*

"Small businesses account for 54% of all U.S. sales and 66% of all net new jobs since the 1970's, however, they face a multitude of special challenges often neglected in management and leadership books. *The Care Quotient* provides unique and powerful management techniques for this critical segment of the economy—the engine of innovation and job growth in the U.S."

—Jeffrey B. Kindler, CEO of Centrexion,
Chairman of the GLG Institute, and former CEO of Pfizer

What Does Caring in Business Mean?

I was having pizza on August 15, 2015 with my 16-year-old niece, Jennifer, who was trying out for her high school volleyball team. We had just gotten off the beach where I was simulating spikes for her to save by using her arms, shoulders, and pectoral muscles to block the fast-moving ball and keep it alive. She did very well.

I asked how try-outs were proceeding and whether she thought that she would make the team. She told me that her chances were very good and that many of her peers don't quite have the knack. She said that she would like to help some of them by providing tips that were useful to her, but she doesn't want to do so because if they get really good at it, they may become better than she and possibly replace her.

I told her that she should help her potential teammates without worrying about the outcome because sharing knowledge and helping others is always the right thing to do—this is what our faith teaches us, and what Jesus practiced, and so should we. Her father chimed in by saying that the coach will notice and see that you are a leader and a team player and will want you even more. While I agreed whole-heartedly with his point, it bothered me. I did not want Jennifer to care for personal gain; the moral satisfaction that she would feel deep within should provide sufficient reward.

I then thought about the situation more and made the point that, throughout my career, I actually couldn't think of a single instance in which selflessly caring about a fellow employee, or customer, or investor, or patients did not enhance the business, project, them, or myself, in the long run. And so I realized that selflessly caring not only enhances my chances of being counted among the sheep, as opposed to the goats, but it also is really good for business.

Actually, it is great for business. Selfless caring blinds and numbs you to pain and personal risk; it emboldens you to keep trying—to come up with new solutions, work harder, work smarter, work differently, sacrifice your pride, accept a good idea from wherever it emanates, invite input, and deliver—come what may. Once you behave in a manner in which your personal immediate gain is not your highest priority, the potential for extraordinary results is boundless.

This is the spirit in which this book is written. Selfless caring is not only a great way of life; it also provides for tremendous business success. It is my secret to becoming a manager of very successful companies and projects, and a leader whom many employees I've had the pleasure and privilege of managing would like to work with again.

Selflessly caring in business is my "secular theology."

How did I develop it? I was an altar boy and lector since the age of ten; to this day, when I see a priest celebrating Mass alone, I walk up on the altar and help out in any capacity. To me, Jesus is the greatest manager and leader the world has ever known. I think that the Bible, *The Seven Habits of Highly Effective People* (Steven Covey), and *Crazy Times Call For Crazy Organizations* (Tom Peters) are the best leadership and management books ever written.

The reason that this tome is not in the Religious Studies section of your bookstore is because I don't like turning the other cheek! Not really. Seriously, a business is not church, but it is life—messy, complicated, ugly, and beautiful, all at the same time, and replete with people who are simultaneously damaged in some ways and wonderful in others.

I truly hope that you read this book and elect to selflessly care because in your heart you know it to be the right thing to do, as your mother told you so many times. I also hope that this book will show you how selfless caring is a mission statement, code of conduct, and business policy that will bring great success to those who practice it.

Being a Good Manager and Leader Takes Just One Thing: Selfless Caring

I have worked in start-ups and large corporations for more than twenty-five years and I pride myself on being a manager who truly cares about colleagues. I did not include anecdotes from people talking about their experiences working with me to stroke my ego, but rather to demonstrate the enormous impact that this approach provides. I know that "selfless caring" is a far more effective management style than what many leaders use. I include a lot of details about my experiences—positive and negative—because I know they will be instructive. Some of you may think that I'm patting myself on the back. That's not the point of this book.

Whether you're just starting out in your career or you're an experienced manager, I believe you'll find this book helpful as you focus on "selfless caring." The examples and anecdotes from people working in a variety of fields will show you how relatively small changes in your management style will make a huge difference.

Being an all-star manager is not about dedicating five or ten minutes per day, or following three to ten steps. It is more than platitudes, goals, and aspirations. If you care enough to be the best leader and manager you can be, you will do what I'm discussing in this book naturally, with no checklist required. If you truly care, your customers, company or department, and employees will be on your mind twenty-four hours per day, seven days per week. If they aren't, you don't care enough to be the best, and you will not be.

Managing is a moral responsibility. You literally are responsible for the lives and well-being of those who report to you and those, in turn, who depend on them. The way you make them feel about themselves and the value that you add to their lives will be what they project outwardly to the people with whom they have influence. This multiplier effect is a daunting responsibility. You truly can change the world, one corner at a time, if you care.

Care about what?

Good question. Many business leaders care deeply about themselves—their income, lifestyle, standing in the community, pride, cars, home, and many other externals. Often, these people amass significant wealth; however, they are poor managers and have non-existent leadership skills. But, they care.

However, it is **selfless caring** that is the key to doing the right things at the right time and becoming a highly effective and respected leader. If you selflessly care you will faithfully practice the two most important behaviors that lead to success:

1. Tirelessly prepare by searching high and low for the answer in textbooks, papers, the Internet, and in the heads of experts; and if there is no answer to your exact problem, then

2. Relentlessly trying until something works.

The keys to the latter are having: (a) no pride in objectively determining something you have tried has failed; (b) back-up plans, assuming that the course of action you are attempting will likely need tweaking or may fail; and (c) no fear in reinventing yourself to come up with novel approaches that may work.

Selflessly caring leaders don't hold back; rather they find a way to deliver business results, have their messages resonate, reach employees (even the difficult ones), satisfy customers, and advance their companies.

Selfless caring is a character trait that is grounded in a moral belief system whose basic tenets include:

1. Holding principles and truth as your highest order goals
2. Taking personal responsibility for outcomes and results
3. Leaving people and circumstances better than you found them
4. Applying all of the gifts that God, your genotype, and your phenotype have bestowed upon you, even for the most menial of tasks
5. Taking responsibility for the overall well-being of those whom you manage.

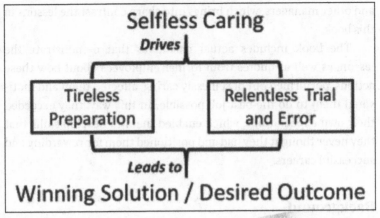

Selfless caring drives tireless preparation and relentless trial and error, which leads to the discovery of the winning solution and desired outcome.

Organization of the Book

The book is a collection of anecdotes from my experiences managing numerous people and projects, and running several companies in the biomedical field—biotechnology, pharmaceutical, and medical device. The stories are cataloged under six chapters that represent major themes that flow from selfless caring. The first six chapters answer the questions, "Selflessly care enough to do what?" Along with caring about the right things, they constitute the elements of the "Care Quotient," a tool to evaluate leadership potential and to identify areas of improvement for leaders. Chapter 7 contains specific insights that have been amassed on various topics based on the principles contained in the first six chapters in the form of articles and editorials that I have published. The Conclusion contains a summary of the important lessons of the book, as well as the specifics of the Care Quotient instrument, a management and leadership tool to help identify areas for leadership development.

As part of the research and vetting of the concepts in the book, I contacted several former employees who worked on projects that I managed and in companies that I previously ran. I had not worked directly with any of these individuals for some time, from two to twenty years. Many of them went on to work for other companies and other managers, which brings into sharp contrast the lessons in this book.

The book includes actual narratives that demonstrate the lesson, as well as quotes from former employees about how these actions, performed out of selflessly caring, affected them and motivated them to do the best job possible. In this way, they exceeded their own expectations, which enabled them to develop skills that they never thought they had and positioned them for rewarding and successful careers.

Background

The specifics about many events that are discussed in *The Care Quotient* are analyzed and presented in dramatic living color in my first book, *Innovation Breakdown: How the FDA and Wall Street Cripple Medical Advances.* (See innovationbreakdownbook.com for more information.)

CHAPTER 1

Management is a Gift
and a Profound Responsibility

Having a position of authority relative to others is an honor; it also comes with an implicit promise to enhance the lives of those whom you've been appointed to oversee. Make no mistake, done correctly, it is very hard work; in fact, how often have you heard managers say that the hardest thing to do is to get their work done through other people? The challenging side of managing often obscures the gift and responsibility it represents. The person who selflessly cares enough thinks about this every day, and it often frightens him. The opportunities that a manager has to enhance or diminish employees' lives, and the lives of their dependents, is enormous. A simple smile or compliment on a job well done or a "thank you" can change the mood of an employee, who in turn may treat his or her loved ones in a manner that inspires or encourages them to do something wonderful, and so truly great things can happen for so many because of you.

If you selflessly care enough, you will take this responsibility seriously and tremendous results will follow.

Backdoor Escape

A former colleague, Penny Humphries, who supported me as an administrative assistant at MELA Sciences while she was completing her Speech Pathology degree, told me that she was most taken by how I always gave employees an "out," a gracious way to move on or back down from a circumstance in which they had not performed as required for the good of the project and company. The agreement we had with Penny, who was over-qualified to be working with me as an administrative assistant, was that she would do the work if I made a special effort to include her in business analyses and decisions because she ultimately wanted to run a department or company in her field. It was a two-way street—Penny's insights were very valuable and greatly factored into many decisions that I made.

The fact that she singled-out this behavior speaks volumes to me, because we had many conversations about business, and I included her in virtually everything I was doing; so she saw quite a lot. I firmly believe that when delivering negative feedback to an employee, it is necessary, right up until the moment that the person is no longer an employee, to do so in a manner that preserves his dignity. I think that when pointing-out shortcomings in performance, a manager not only has the opportunity to challenge employees to do better, but also to inspire them to want to be an even greater contributor than is expected. It is more likely that the employee listens, accepts, and changes his behavior for the good of the company if this is done compassionately, and in a manner that not only leaves the dignity of the person intact, but also gives him an opportunity to build upon his self-worth quickly. It is necessary to do this for the psycho-emotional health of the employees; it keeps them motivated and teaches them compassion and empathy, which they will pass on, while, at the same time serving the critical business need. It is an approach that requires knowledge of the person and great touch. You need to deliver the message so that the action is corrected for the moment and doesn't happen again in the future, but you need to leave the person with his pride.

This is difficult to do, especially when you are busy and acting in the heat of the moment, which as CEO of a medical device start-up under great duress from many external forces, was a routine occurrence. Penny had a front row seat to situations like these. Giving a gracious "out" requires a deep knowledge of the person to whom you are delivering the negative feedback, and a focus on the behavior, not the person—hate the sin and love the sinner, so to speak. It also requires empathy and a long view. If you selflessly care, you will take the time to get to know the employees well enough to know how to play moments like these and develop a customized formula for every employee who reports to you.

Perched on a Train

I was once traveling by train with an employee and I was explaining a trick that I use in meetings and presentations. I actually pretend there are two of me—one in the thick of the action (meeting, presentation, debate, or conflict) and a two-inch size me perched with a view of the whole situation. Mini-me is constantly giving feedback about how I am being received, while I then adjust my approach to have maximal impact, or at least to cease doing anything offensive. This discussion took place at the end of the day as we were traveling back to New York from Washington, DC. I made the point that I have been doing this so long that it has become second-nature to me, and that I am doing it right now. This surprised her. I explained that I realize I am the boss and that she is captive and that the last thing I want is to be overbearing and detract from her personal time and invade her personal space. So I said, I am perched right over there (I pointed to the overhead luggage rack across the aisle), looking at whether you are leaning in or pulling back, turning away or anticipating my next word, whether there are any reactions that might suggest I have bad breath, and whether you are feeling good about this or would rather be sleeping. She looked at me quite shocked, as if to say, "Why would you be doing this during a friendly exchange?" and then she said aloud, "Wow, it must be very difficult being you."

Indeed, it is difficult. But, I realized that we are not "friends." Rather as her manager and leader, I had the responsibility to enhance her career. I was doing my job. Selflessly caring managers don't allow themselves to be delusional, that is, to think that employees are their friends. No, every interaction with an employee must be viewed from the perspective of a work relationship and responsibility. This also makes the job very lonely, but, so it is if you want to be an effective leader.

Lending a Helping Hand

In my sophomore high school English class, the American Literature teacher, Br. Anthony Lamb asked us one day, "What is the difference between being kind and being considerate?" No one raised a hand as Br. Anthony searched the room for someone to step-up. Finally, I spoke up making the point that if I were kind, I would give Greg money for lunch if he asked to borrow some; if I were considerate, upon overhearing him earlier telling John that he left his wallet home, I would offer money to him before he even had to ask. "Right," said Br. Lamb, surprised that anyone got the right answer.

Fast forward twenty-five years—an employee got into an accident on the way to work; she was in the middle of a divorce and was living in a small apartment with her two children. She was asking our lawyer whether the company would pay the deductible because she had no money, and she was returning to the office from a work-associated function. The answer was no. Later in the day, I gave her a personal check for more than the deductible. Two years later, I overheard her telling a colleague that her apartment was robbed and her son's school computer was stolen. She was distraught—he absolutely needed the computer for school and couldn't graduate without it. I asked how much a new computer would cost and I gave her a check to pay for it. She was a very proud, independent woman who emigrated to the U.S. from Eastern Europe, and kept her emotions to herself.

I cannot tell you how rewarding it was to see the look of appreciation on her face. I believe that this contributed to her ongoing love of the company. It also established a bond between us, and she felt comfortable giving me honest, and critical feedback on various things like my message(s) at the company meetings or new policies that we implemented. I got back many fold what I gave her, but I didn't do it for that reason, and it is probably why I received such dividends. Employees can detect the intent behind a manager's actions.

Even the Interns

Having summer interns is a great idea for a company, especially a small company, because they are eager, typically high academic achievers, and if you treat them well and they like your company and the staff, you will be successful in recruiting them to the company when they graduate. That wasn't the intent when one of the software engineers asked whether he could have a summer intern to do some routine programming. Then others heard the news and also asked if they could have a summer intern after justifying the need. Poof. We went from a small company of thirty-five employees not really looking to establish a talent-cultivation and acquisition program, to a company with an excellent summer internship program.

I didn't know what was happening until I was told by our HR Director, Vivian, that five interns would be starting the following week, basically one for each department in the company, and one would function as my administrative assistant. I worried that the experience would not be rich enough, that we couldn't provide exposure to a wide enough range of things to make it worthwhile for them. I felt that we shouldn't be doing it because we could not live up to our end of the bargain, and it bothered me, a lot.

So I came up with a plan. The interns would meet as a group for two hours every week with a different department head. The department heads would spend the first hour teaching all of them about the area of discipline in general, as it would be in many different companies, then for the second hour, how that discipline was applied at our company. This would expose them to several different managers and teach them about many different aspects of the company. Also it was an opportunity for our managers, who were young and lacking a great deal of experience, to teach—to organize their thoughts and intelligently and cogently present their departments and their work. This went on for seven weeks. I met with them on the first day for one hour to kick it off and get to know them and explain how the summer would proceed. I also met with them for two hours at the end to explain financing and corporate considerations as the "capstone" session for their summer experience.

It was a resounding success; our HR director presented our program to many universities from which we were able to pick the best and brightest interns for subsequent summers. We kept doing it year after year and wound up hiring some outstanding talent that came to us through the intern program; we attracted superlative performers who would never have come our way had it not been for the summer intern program. In fact, Maceij, one such talent who joined us full time, devised the final algorithm that was selected for use in our FDA-approved melanoma detection device, MelaFind.

This is an excellent example of a small company instituting a phenomenal policy that made tremendous business sense and paid huge dividends. However, it was not borne from explicit research on the topic, best practices sharing, or perceived need; rather it arose from a belief that management is a gift, as well as a profound responsibility because we selflessly cared.